*Every Hour, Every Atom*

THE IOWA WHITMAN SERIES

Ed Folsom, series editor

# *Every Hour, Every Atom*

A Collection of
*Walt Whitman's*
Early Notebooks
& Fragments

EDITED BY
Zachary Turpin and Matt Miller

UNIVERSITY OF IOWA PRESS, IOWA CITY

University of Iowa Press, Iowa City 52242

uipress.uiowa.edu
Printed in the United States of America
Design by Sara T. Sauers

ISBN 978-1-60938-703-7 (pbk)
ISBN 978-1-60938-704-4 (ebk)



Printed on acid-free paper
Cataloging-in-Publication data is on file
with the Library of Congress.

THIS BOOK IS

for the many enthusiastic collectors, archivists, and scholars who dedicate their time—and often, their lives—to Whitman

for Markie McBrayer and Sue Miller, our true fancies, as Whitman would say: "If we go anywhere we'll go together to meet what happens"

and for Charles Feinberg (1899–1988), who delighted in sharing

Every hour, every atom, every where is chock with ~~beautiful~~ miracles
—WALT WHITMAN, manuscript fragment

## *Contents*

*Fragments*

## *Acknowledgments*

THIS BOOK WOULD not have been possible without the ongoing generosity of the institutions that house Whitman's manuscripts today. In particular, we're grateful for the New York Public Library's Berg and Oscar Lion Collections, the Duke University Trent Collection of Walt Whitman Manuscripts, Yale University's Beinecke Rare Book and Manuscript Library, the University of Virginia's Valentine-Barrett Collection, the Boston Public Library's Whitman Collection, Rutgers University's Special Collections and University Archives, the University of Pennsylvania's Annenberg Rare Book and Manuscript Library, the University of Tulsa's Whitman manuscripts collection, and above all the Library of Congress's Charles E. Feinberg and Thomas Harned Collections. Together, their Whitman holdings help keep the poet's memory and influence alive today. So do the many dedicated contributors to and editors of the online *Walt Whitman Archive*, a vast digital playground of nearly all the poet's writings and manuscripts; may this book be an affirmation of everything they do. We would also like to thank the University of Iowa for leading the way in Whitman studies worldwide, and our own institutions, the University of Idaho and Yeshiva University, for enthusiastically supporting our work. Finally, the craft and beauty of this book are no accident. They are the result of the tireless attentions (and infinite patience) of the University of Iowa Press's editors and staffers, all of whom deserve our deepest gratitude: Meredith Stabel, Carolyn Brown, Karen Copp, Susan Hill Newton, Allison T. Means, Suzanne Glemot, Sara Hales-Brittain, Angie Dickey, Sara T. Sauers, and James McCoy, who foolishly gave us carte blanche.

# *Foreword by Matt Miller*

DURING THE SUMMER of 2003, I was invited to accompany two senior scholars to the Library of Congress to assist in taking digital photographs of Walt Whitman's notebooks and manuscripts. Because of their fragility and importance, we had been told we would probably be among the last people to handle these precious documents, the actual notebooks and manuscript fragments Whitman used to compose many of his greatest poems. At the time, I was one of the earliest staff members of the then nascent *Walt Whitman Archive*, a new PhD student and as green as the leaves of grass in the Capitol lawn outside the library. As a longtime fan of Whitman considering a dissertation on his work, I was thrilled at the opportunity to actually see and touch these notebooks I had been studying by way of transcriptions contained in the Whitman edition of the *Major Authors on CD-ROM* series, a medium that even then seemed obsolete.

I arrived at the Library of Congress directly from the flight, jetlagged and a little late, and after passing through security (my third time that day), I found Whitman scholars Ed Folsom and Ken Price with a surprisingly small digital camera, hunched over what looked like an even smaller ledger book. The first thing I noticed about notebooks like this one was their size: they are *tiny*; I could easily slip one in a shirt pocket, and I did (just to test the theory, of course). Anyone who has only seen the online images will surely come away with a mistaken impression of the size of both the notebooks and Whitman's handwriting. The available online images can give the impression that the notebooks are the size of a typical paperback and that Whitman's script is as sprawling and expansive as his lines. In reality, these notebooks are about the size of your palm, and the economy of his handwriting is meticulous, at times even fussy.

Studying transcriptions from the CD-ROM, I had become particularly obsessed with a document named "The Talbot Wilson Notebook," a title that refers not to someone named "Talbot Wilson" but rather to Jesse Talbot, a landscape painter and close companion of Whitman's who lived on Wilson Street in Brooklyn. While working that weekend, I had the opportunity to actually read the "Talbot Wilson Notebook" cover to cover and to study it closely. Holding this notebook that Whitman himself once held and into which he first wrote such lines as "I am the poet of the body / And I am the poet of the soul," I was inspired. My hands were holding the very pages Whitman's hands touched as he committed to history some of the greatest lines ever composed. My research assistantship was, I decided, the greatest job ever.

After I returned home and finished my own transcription of this notebook for the *Walt Whitman Archive*, I found myself wanting to share it with as many of Whitman's readers as possible. I felt that it held not only scholarly and historical interest but also contemporary literary worth, presenting a deliciously jagged and immediate record of poetic thought, full of "diamonds-in-the-rough" fragments and at least one complete prose poem, titled "Dilation" in the manuscript, that could ostensibly be presented as a "previously unpublished poem by Walt Whitman." I also felt that in these notebooks, more than in any of Whitman's poems, no matter how personal, we come closest to the heart and mind of the poet himself. What reader and lover of Whitman's poetry wouldn't relish this experience?

For readers considering this book who haven't already spent a lot of time with Whitman's notebooks, some guidance might prove useful. What exactly are we seeing when we look at these transcriptions? How might we best approach reading them, and just as important, what can we expect to get out of our reading? It is helpful to keep in mind that this book is a collection of fragments. Overall, each notebook is a fragment of the larger record of thought they collectively record. None of these notebooks coheres around a single poem or idea. Within a particular notebook, readers will discover notes, trial lines, and revisions for a variety of poems, though where one poem stops and another starts is not always clear in their inchoate forms. A single page (or "leaf," as scholars like to call them) may contain lines later used in several poems, and these lines are often assembled into trial poems that never saw print. In their rough presentation, such drafts read as strange medleys of moments from various finished poems woven together in fascinating formations.

Because the book is a collection of fragments, I suspect many readers will prefer to read it nonlinearly, skipping around and following where their fancies lead them. If a section seems trivial or boring, skip ahead, but do consider returning to such sections again, because these notebooks can give the illusion of having changed while readers are away from them. What once seemed uninteresting may reveal hidden layers of significance when read in a different mood or with different experiences in one's immediate memory. If, while reading, you experience a kind of whiplash from Whitman's abrupt fits and starts, know you are not the first. If one page of a notebook is so radically different in tone or texture from the next that it seems as if one part were written months or years after the other, that very well may be the case. Whitman often returned to notebooks he had abandoned for years—sometimes drawn back to language still seeking a poetic home, other times just trying to save paper.

There can be a tremendous reward in coming to understand the imaginative, psychological, and historical contexts that led to Whitman's greatest poems. One of my most thrilling experiences reading Whitman was when I first encountered the notebook given the title "No doubt the efflux." This might be a good notebook to start with, because it is concise, richly textured, and contains passages that led to some of the most mesmerizing moments in poems such as "Song of Myself" and "The Sleepers." More than anything else I had previously read, this notebook made me feel a sense of intimacy with Whitman and his writing process.

It opens with prose passages recording Whitman's experience of the "efflux" of his own soul as he encounters individuals on his regular walk through Brooklyn. Just glancing at a fisherman in what is today Brooklyn's Navy Yards area leads an ecstatic Whitman to declare that "the subtle chloroform of our spirits is affecting each other." Although they do not seem to speak, Whitman feels that by merely exchanging looks they have "exchanged the ∧right ~~mysterious~~ ~~unspoken~~ password ∧~~of the night,~~ and ~~have~~ are thence free ~~entrance~~ comers to ~~each~~ the guarded tents of each other's ~~love~~

most interior love." Whitman's many revisions convey the impression he was either struggling with his own feelings for what appear to be mere strangers or acquaintances or struggling with how to convey an experience so overwhelming that it defies language. If you have ever hoped to read Whitman directly describing a mystical reverie, this may be as close as you will come, for this passage records extreme experiences of love and compassion that might seem either absurd or inspiring. Some of his descriptions are so extreme as to seem foreign in their simultaneous intensity and precision—foreign, that is, if he was not also revising them into lines later used in some of the greatest poems ever written.

As is often the case with Whitman in his best pre–Civil War poetry, elevated experiences of spiritual grandeur evolve into and merge with passages of frank and intense eroticism. In the "No doubt the efflux" notebook, the spiritual comradery just described leads to descriptions of Whitman's bringing a stranger "naked to his bed," and, fascinatingly, in this notebook Whitman's erotic feelings appear to be directed to both men and women, if we trust his pronouns (which may not always be wise). Something about these erotic feelings left the ever-garrulous Whitman without adequate language: "he shall see the naked breast and the most private            ~~of Delight~~.—" Such blank spaces represent some of the most charged moments in these notebooks. Perhaps the most resonant silence in all of Whitman's writing is in the "Talbot Wilson" notebook, when he finds himself unable to complete this sequence:

> I am the poet of slaves,<br>
>         and of ‸the masters of slaves<br>
> I am the poet of the body<br>
> And I am

The finished version of these lines is so powerfully chiseled into the minds many of Whitman's readers that it can be thrilling to experience him struggling for the right word. When he finds it on the next page, it feels like a cause for celebration—both for Whitman and for us, even as he proceeds into some of the most challenging and conflicted claims in all of his work:

I am the poet of the body
And I am the poet of the soul
~~The~~ I go with the slaves ∧of the earth ∧equally with the ~~are mine, and~~
~~the~~ masters ~~are equally~~ ~~mine.~~
And I will stand between
the masters and the slaves,
~~And I~~ Entering into both, ~~and~~
so that both shall understand
me alike.

Not all of this collection's pleasures are directly related to Whitman's poetry. One notebook that may seem rather prosaic (but which I find endurinngly fascinating) is the notebook that our naming conventions require us to call "Dick Hunt." Lewd humor aside, this notebook appears to have mainly been a combination address book and list used to help Whitman recall the names of dozens upon dozens of Brooklyn and Manhattan acquaintances. The notebook confirms Whitman's intense sociability and genuine respect for working people. It also expresses Whitman's obsessive attention to the sensuous physical details of men—men he found both handsome and ugly—and I do mean *men*. While it contains well over a hundred listings of men along with their appearance and comments about Whitman's appreciation for them, he seems to mention only a single woman's name in the address section of the book, one "Martha, ([15])(in Burroughs." In a fascinating entry, Whitman records the name, "Bob," followed by what appears to be the word "hermaphrodite," though whether he meant that literally is unclear. Later, Whitman returned to his book of names and used it for drafts of poems, and he also used it for games of "twenty questions," which he played with friends and acquaintances, likely while sharing rides on ferries or dining in eating houses. Several of these games are recorded in the "Dick Hunt" notebook. While at first it may appear that this notebook is starkly divided between poetry and biographical ephemera, perhaps even the "twenty questions" and address sections of this book are conceptually linked to his poems—alternate prose versions of the catalogues that have caused Whitman's readers so much pleasure and consternation over the years.

I believe the most important purpose of this collection is to help readers to intimately experience Whitman's mind at work, from its greatest heights to its most revealing ordinary moments. While we may no longer be able to actually hold and touch the notebooks, we can approximate the experience in a couple of different ways: through accurate and complete transcriptions that are visually faithful to the originals and through digital images of the originals. Many such transcriptions and images are available online, but the process of scholarly transcription, editing, proofreading, digital encoding, and publication can be painfully slow; it is only recently that readers have been able to access complete transcriptions of some of these notebooks through the digital *Walt Whitman Archive,* which the present volume is meant to complement. This book also supplements, for the time being at least, the contents of the *Archive,* as there are many notebooks and fragments in this book that haven't yet been transcribed and made widely available to the public. And then there is the value of having an inexpensive reader's edition that we can actually hold in our hands, as Whitman imagined us doing with his poems.

Perhaps the most difficult part of the otherwise pleasant job of editing and transcribing Whitman's notebooks is deciding what to leave out. While some notebooks, such as "Talbot Wilson," were obvious and essential choices, the ultimate value of some others was more ambiguous. To make matters more manageable, we first decided to limit our transcriptions to pre–Civil War notebooks. Aside from leaving open the possibility of a second volume, we feel this decision has the advantage of providing a more consistent tone and focus for the present volume, as well as an intuitive separation point for limiting our selections. Even so, many more omissions were needed, and after extensive conversations, we decided on the following criteria for inclusion: relevance to Whitman's poetry, relevance to scholarship, quality of writing, and insight offered into Whitman's mind, especially his poetic imagination. We decided to include many short fragments of uncertain origin—snippets of text that Whitman or one of his literary executors cut away from their original homes, often gluing them together or pasting them onto pages for display. We included these in part because they involve some of Whitman's most important and fascinating remarks, but also because it is likely that many of these fragments were originally a part of notebooks that have been cut up and disassembled.

Returning to these notebooks and fragments has reminded me of the profound joy I experienced "holding Whitman in hand," to paraphrase one of his lines, and it is with similar joy and excitement that we offer these transcriptions to readers. Like Whitman, we expect great things to follow.

## *Introduction by Zachary Turpin*

CHARLES FEINBERG, to whom this book is dedicated, almost single-handedly made it possible. Born in 1899 in England and raised in Canada, he became a collector of manuscripts while still a teenager. Having just encountered Walt Whitman for the first time in a dime anthology of American verse, he had the good fortune to secure—for the princely sum of $7.50—a handwritten letter from the poet himself. Thus began a lifelong devotion to all things Whitman. Truly, *all* things: Feinberg collected poetry manuscripts, letters, diaries, first printings, address books, photos, memorabilia, personal effects—even the poet's receipts. Perhaps most fortunately of all, Feinberg tracked down many of Whitman's personal notebooks and manuscript fragments, in which the poet had written down anything and everything that crossed his mind—a collector's quest that became substantially easier when Feinberg ended up making a small fortune as a fuel oil executive. After years spent securing countless manuscripts and memorabilia, Feinberg retired early and dedicated the rest of his long life to sharing with the world his vast trove of Whitmaniana, first by lending it and later by donating much of it to the Library of Congress. Today, Whitman's many notebooks and fragments survive thanks to passionate collectors and archivists like Feinberg, who seems to have believed, with Whitman, that "without one thing all will be useless," and whose generosity has informed Whitman scholarship ever since. Thus, we offer this book in the spirit of Charlie Feinberg, who would be the first to tell you that it is clear from Whitman's notebooks and fragments that *Leaves of Grass* came about like no other book before it.

Unlike many nineteenth-century volumes of poetry, *Leaves of Grass* didn't emerge on a writing desk, neatly penned into some clean, leatherbound journals. Instead, it began on scrap paper. Nearly all his life,

Whitman wrote prose and poetry alike on thousands of loose bits of paper, often swiped from newspaper offices. Perhaps realizing the need for some order, Whitman began in the 1840s to paste or sew together stacks of loose paper into small handmade notebooks. These now priceless objects are, as Matt Miller notes in his foreword, tiny things, "well loved" in the way that a favorite teddy bear is. Many of their pages are smudged with pencil lead or creased with wear, pasted together or torn out, dog-eared from being leafed through or jammed into pockets. Whitman's notebooks have none of the neat fastidiousness of Nathaniel Hawthorne's or Thomas Hardy's, to say nothing of their linear orderliness. Instead, they are crammed to the edges with a hodgepodge of journalistic notes, housebuilder's calculations, lists of men's names, doodles, shopping lists, and trial verses for *Leaves of Grass*. That this compendiousness began seeping into his poetry, Whitman was likely aware. His notebooks and fragments were something like private treasures; Whitman kept them his entire life. (By contrast, he left the handwritten fair-copy manuscript of the first edition of *Leaves of Grass* at the printer's, where, he later claimed in a letter to his friend and amanuensis Horace Traubel, it was "used to kindle the fire or to feed the rag man.") In recognition of their value, we present, for the first time in an affordable and reader-friendly edition, a substantial collection of Whitman's early notebooks and fragments.

The manuscript scholar Clifton Furness called the early notebooks Whitman's "workshop," though that image is probably too orderly and professional. While there is an insatiable omnivorousness for things, facts, people, and the pulse of life in these manuscripts, orderliness of thought does not seem to have mattered much to Whitman. His notebooks are all mixture. If anything, the hodgepodge is more than half the point. Like his beloved "promenade" of Broadway pedestrians, in his notebooks the various modes and genres and shapes of his writings begin to blur together, become one. Many of the pages that follow trace almost no discernable rhyme or reason at all—are they prose-poetry? quotes from books Whitman had read? cryptic receipts? notes to self? Whatever they are, you will nevertheless find their every word and stanza joined with the utmost care—"plumb in the uprights," as Whitman the housebuilder would say—with a pile of strikethroughs and overwrites testifying to just how painstaking the construction was.

Given the sheer volume of Whitman's notebooks and fragments, we have limited this volume to those he wrote before the Civil War, for their common tone of joy and discovery. Before war takes him to Washington, DC, Whitman's notebooks are exuberance itself, foaming over with boyish self-centeredness and a zest for daily life. You might imagine that manuscripts with such gusto would have been published many times before, but you'd be wrong. Whitman's early notebooks and fragments have hardly seen print compared to his wartime manuscripts, which were actually published during the poet's lifetime. A decade after Appomattox, Whitman gathered together a number of his Civil War notebooks and, with relatively little revision, released them as a chapbook titled *Memoranda during the War* (1875–76), around which he would later construct his episodic autobiography *Specimen Days* (1882). The early notebooks presented in this volume were, by contrast, private. Whitman drew from them often for his writings but never collected or printed them, bound between covers. Yet he seems to have anticipated that someday, somewhere, you would be reading them anyway. In his later years, Whitman lightly edited his early notebooks here and there, possibly thinking of his legacy. For many of these manuscripts, then, the fulfillment of that legacy has been a long time coming, as has this book. It is the first affordable reader's edition of Whitman's notebooks ever published—and with luck, the first of many.

The journey of these early notebooks begins in newspaper offices and on printer's floors, where Whitman, a young, not too handsomely paid journalist, would regularly swipe scrap paper to take home and jot on. Because he returned to those jottings, sometimes years later, for poetry ideas and journalism notes, Whitman developed the habit of taking his notes and scraps—*all* of them—with him each time he moved to a new house. In his final years, Whitman's piles of personal papers had grown to dizzying heights, as can be seen in several of his late-life portraits. The piles inevitably toppled and were tracked out into the hallway by visitors and well-wishers. Sometimes important items were lost for years, only to turn up under someone's shoe. Most infamously, Whitman managed to lose track of the letter Emerson had sent him in 1855, "greet[ing] him at the dawn of a great career"—a line the poet had jubilantly embossed on the spine of *Leaves of Grass*, to Emerson's consternation. A year before

Whitman surrounded by paper in his upstairs bedroom, Camden, New Jersey. Photograph by Dr. William Reeder, 1891.

Whitman died, when asked if he'd found it, he responded: "No, but I shall," adding, "I know *about* where it is." It was later located under his papers, in an envelope hand-addressed by Emerson to "Walter Whitman, Esq."

After his death in the spring of 1892, Whitman's literary executors divvied up all these papers, thousands upon thousands of them, and crammed them into barrels. Three days after the poet's death, Horace Traubel wrote in his journal, "we filled them. Many manuscripts and letters on the floor. Turned up in different places letters from Symonds, Tennyson, Mrs. Gilchrist. Four or five old scrapbooks (containing manuscript beginnings from notebooks, etc.). We packed things together, pell-mell, intending to send them to my house for me to sort." Such "scrapbooks" constitute the core of this book. Since Traubel's time, and for nearly 130 years, dedicated men and women have stewarded these notebooks and fragments "for thee in the future," as Whitman would say—preserving them, transcribing them, and even, on occasion, stealing them.

In 1942, concerned about a possible Japanese bombardment of Washington, DC, the Library of Congress sent a train full of valuable collections, including ten of Whitman's early notebooks, to a remote site for storage. There they stayed, or so it seemed, until war's end. But when the collections were eventually shipped back to the library, it was discovered that all ten notebooks had vanished, along with a cardboard butterfly that Whitman had held on a finger for one of his most famous portraits. They would stay missing for more than fifty years. It was only in 1995 that a Sotheby's representative contacted Whitman scholar Alice Birney (and the FBI) to say that four of the notebooks had reappeared, along with the butterfly. Told of their recovery, Librarian of Congress James Billington called it nothing less than "an event of national importance."

The other six notebooks are still missing, though photographs of them still exist; the text preserved in those photos is represented in these pages. Indeed, with exceptions, most of Whitman's early notebooks and fragments appear in this volume. Many have seen print before, some of them the better part of a century ago. Because of the manuscripts' value and fragility, early scholars (some of whom knew the poet personally) labored to publish transcriptions as soon as possible, in now rare editions that include Richard Maurice Bucke's *Notebooks and Fragments* (1902), Emory Holloway's *Uncollected Poetry and Prose* (1921), Clifton Furness's *Walt Whitman's Workshop* (1928), and Clarence Gohdes and Rollo Silver's *Faint Clues and Indirections* (1949). These volumes may have given readers a preliminary glimpse into Whitman's writing process, but it would decades more before any careful concerted effort was made to transcribe and collect all, or nearly all, Whitman's notebooks and fragments. The final results, edited by scholars William White and Edward F. Grier, are NYU Press's three-volume *Daybooks and Notebooks* (1978) and its six-volume *Notebooks and Unpublished Prose Manuscripts* (1984), both still the standard scholarly resource for students of Whitman. But what about general readers, who perhaps can't afford—and certainly don't want to lug around—three thousand pages of scholarship, with footnotes? For them, we've made this book.

Whether well-known notebooks or items that have only recently been recovered, the manuscripts collected in this volume are represented in as close to their original appearance as possible. This is in contrast to Grier's editorial philosophy, and to a lesser extent, White's, who generally tried to "clean up" the notebooks they had access to, often editing and reordering them toward an imagined final version. It was not until Joel Myerson's *The Walt Whitman Archive: A Facsimile of the Poet's Manuscripts* (1993) that any attempt was made to present the poet's notebooks as they are, not as they "should" be. Myerson's facsimile edition represented a major leap forward, and in more than one way. Its organizing principles would go on to inform a similarly titled but even more ambitious project, the *Walt Whitman Archive* (https://whitmanarchive.org), a vast digitized collection of Whitmaniana that has become the ultimate repository of all things related to the Good Gray Poet. Interested readers will find digital images and transcriptions of all Whitman's known books, novellas, tales, and uncollected poems, as well as many of his letters, manuscripts, notebooks, journalistic series, scribal documents produced while working in the Office of the US Attorney General, interviews, photographs, and more. This book would not exist without the substantial efforts of the many dedicated contributors to the Walt Whitman Archive.

As some of those contributors will tell you, from a certain point of view editing Whitman's notebooks—or, as he sometimes called them, "daybooks"—may seem like a straightforward task. After all, Whitman wrote in a (mercifully) neat hand. His notebooks often have a clear page order, and more often than not Whitman crossed words out rather than erasing. Making these pages into a book should be as simple as transcribing each notebook carefully, taking note of lines, strikethroughs, and symbols, and then typesetting them for print. Yet it is almost never this straightforward, for the simple reason that notebooks do not follow the rules that books do.

Notebooks have few rules at all, which suited a rebellious young Whitman perfectly. In these pages, you will find passages that were originally written upside down or sideways (in one of our few interventions, we have rotated upside-down text for readability), as well as words overwritten two or three times, lines annotated or erased later on, conflicting arrows or directions for printing, entire pages canceled, and half or whole pages torn out here and there. Whitman even pulled some of the bindings apart. In some cases, loose leaves were clearly once part of a larger bound item, with other extant leaves sharing the same paper and a similar script size and style. Such leaves may have once been bound together, though in many cases putting them back together may not be possible. In such Humpty-Dumptyish instances, we chose to classify these items as "fragments" rather than "notebook fragments" or "loose leaves" in recognition of their irreconcilability. Like Whitman's poetry, the notebooks and fragments presented in this collection are a record of flux, so translating them into rigid text and symbols will always be an approximate business at best.

Still, for whatever fidelity this book has, we are indebted to four or five generations of dedicated Whitman manuscript scholars, men and women who spent months or years at a stretch scrutinizing and transcribing, often under magnification, every last mark of Whitman's hand, even the most ambiguous or obscured. In that regard, this new volume follows their lead: each transcription has been created anew from—and checked against—images of the originals. Only when a notebook is no longer extant *and* no images of it are known to exist have we had to rely on early, unreliable transcriptions. Whitman's "Autobiographical Data" notebook, which we have included, is a prime example. Stolen circa 1942, the notebook is one of the six still missing today, and photographs of its pages are incomplete, making the original page order unknown. From the page images that remain, it is clear that Emory Holloway, a pioneering Whitman scholar and the last person to transcribe them from the manuscript, made silent editorial changes that he did not fully explain. (Later, and more infamously, Holloway would fail to record erasures in other manuscripts that indicated Whitman's strong sexual yearning for men.) Until the original "Autobiographical Data" notebook resurfaces, Holloway's transcriptions, cross-referenced against a few remaining photos of its pages, are the best that we have. Other than that, however, virtually every page in this volume has been checked against digital images of original manuscripts.

Throughout this volume, we have endeavored to be as faithful as possible to the originals. The images of individual pages interspersed throughout this volume should make the difficulty of transcribing readily apparent. If you note a discrepancy, some letter or mark that you calculate reads another way, we ask you to remember the words of Johannes Kepler who, when publishing his work on planetary orbits, begged those who would double-check his math to "take pity on me, for I have repeated these calculations seventy times."

Why, in the end, are Whitman's early notebooks worth all this effort? They are not, after all, a finished artistic product, nor necessarily anything Whitman would have wanted us to see unedited. To put it another way, they are not *Leaves of Grass*, no matter how much early scholars may have wanted them to be—and that, as we see it, is precisely the point. Whitman's poetry conveys the sense of someone baring all (not to say "oversharing"), because this is a persona Whitman cultivated deliberately, knowing as he did the value of being seen as a breaker of norms. When it came to the compositional origins of *Leaves of Grass*, however, Whitman tended to keep his cards close to the vest. Asked in late-life interviews how his great book first came to be, he shared virtually no real information at all: "I got a bee in my bonnet," Whitman told one interviewer, "and took to the pen. I soon published 'Leaves of Grass.'" He was rarely more forthcoming than this. Of the prime period of 1852–54, for example, to which much of the draft poetry in this volume may be dated, he says only this in his memoir *Specimen Days*: "Occupied in house-building in Brooklyn." As we now know, houses were not all he was building. Thus, to read Whitman's early notebooks is to see the construction of his very own genre in all its beautiful messiness. For that reason, these notebooks also help demythologize Whitman, who did all he could in life to present himself as a poet who'd entered the world of poetry fully formed. This was not remotely true, of course—and in any case, Whitman no longer needs the assistance of myth. He is formed and complete, even if his body of work, like his country, is still growing.

We present these notebooks in print, a few of them for the first time, for the reason that we do not know what they may lead to. In the past few years, more than one unknown, book-length Whitman publication has been rediscovered thanks to information contained in the poet's manuscripts. More may be waiting for us. As scholar Betsy Erkkila writes of Whitman's early notebooks, "items that appear to be mere noise in our current readings of Whitman might turn out to be sites of meaning and significance in future analyses of his life and work."

These pages offer untold treasures for the future—and to you, whoever you are, we entrust them.

# *A Key for Readers*

PAGE NUMBERS OF WHITMAN'S MANUSCRIPTS

Whitman almost never numbers his manuscript pages, but for the reader's convenience editorial page numbers have been provided, in bolded brackets. For example:

**[1]**
**[2]**
**[3]**

In the case of a brief editorial note or description of Whitman's holograph page, our note will appear italicized within the brackets, after the number. For example:

**[1, *front cover*]**

or

**[22, *bottom half of page is torn out*]**

Page numbers with no ensuing text are blank in Whitman's original.

JUSTIFICATION

All right, left, and center justification of Whitman's writing approximates his text as it appears on the manuscript page.

LINE BREAKS

We maintain line breaks for all passages that appear to be trial poetry. For example:

~~And that~~

And the ~~[knotty?]~~ tree-toad is a chef'
douvre for the highest,

And the running-blackberry
~~mocks the ornaments of~~
~~would adorn the house~~ parlors
of Heaven

And the cow crunching with
depressed neck surpasses
~~all statues~~ every statue,

However, for sentences or paragraphs that seem to be prose (from their content or context), we ignore Whitman's line breaks (except when a new paragraph begins).

### ILLEGIBLE WRITING

In cases of illegible or erased writing, we indicate as much with the bracketed, italicized editorial note [*illegible*].

### SEMILEGIBLE WRITING

When Whitman's handwriting is partially obscured but nearly legible, we fill in the likely reading in brackets, with a question mark. This is true even for text Whitman has struck through, as in

tha[t?]

or

[~~human?~~]

### MISSPELLINGS AND VARIANT SPELLINGS

All of Whitman's misspellings are maintained. Any misspelled or variously spelled word appears as such in the original manuscript, though we do not use [*sic*] to indicate it.

### VERTICAL STRIKE-THROUGHS

Whitman often vertically cancels, or strikes out, paragraphs or even whole pages. Struck-through text is a key feature of Whitman's notebooks; it can be found throughout this volume.

### HAND-DRAWN BRACKETS AND INSERTION LINES

Whitman often uses insertion lines, carats, or large brackets (curly or square) to indicate words or passages that belong together or that need reordering. Whenever possible, we reproduce these elements as they appear in Whitman's manuscripts. When their reproduction is not feasible (brackets being particularly difficult to maintain at times), we represent them with simple typographical substitutes, inserted below their originating line or word: [ and {.

### EM DASHES

Whitman frequently uses long dashes to variously connect or separate thoughts. In this book, they are represented with em dashes, their closest typographical approximation.

### MANICULES

As a longtime newspaper editor, Whitman was exceedingly fond of the manicule, a small pointing hand icon that was widely used in nineteenth-century newspapers: ☞. We reproduce all of Whitman's hand-drawn manicules typographically.

### PASTE-INS

Whitman occasionally pastes clipped newspaper columns, business cards, and other paper items into his notebooks. Though we reproduce them visually in a few instances, in most case we merely acknowledge their presence in a bracketed editorial note.

### DRAWINGS

Some of Whitman's manuscripts contain pencil drawings, as in the heavily illustrated notebook *81 Clerman*. While we reproduce a few of these images, most are visually described in bracketed editorial notes.

*Notebooks*

## *Poem incarnating the mind*[1]
## [pre-1855]

**[1]**

Poem incarnating the mind of an old man, whose life has been magnificently developed — the wildest and most exuberant joy — the utterance of hope and floods of anticipation — faith in whatever happens — but all enfolded in Joy Joy Joy, which underlies and overtops the whole effusion

---

Why are you cautious ~~and~~ of the ? and of your eyes?— I guess it is because they incarnate to me the

**[2]**

^Crossing the Fulton ferry to-day, I met an old acquaintance, ~~to-day~~ whom I had missed from the city these three years.— He told me his experience that time.— He had been ~~reporting and lobbying~~ at Albany and Washington ^employed as reporter and lobbyer.— .— He corresponded with newspapers and received pay.— ~~He~~ When dull legislators made dull speeches, he licked them into sleekness, and so had synopses of them put in print, and received pay.— He took hold of some scheme or claim ~~before~~ upon the legislature, and lobbied for it;— he helped men who were office seeking; he put

*

**[3]**

with merchants ~~and tradesmen~~ and factors the point of honor is to pay notes punctually,— to pay off the men every Saturday night,— to ~~have~~ ^~~receive~~ permit no demands which they cannot satisfy at an appointed day.—

---

~~We are~~ Concerned in the make of ~~th~~ a grand steam ship We cannot sleep nights for thinking on the pennant halyards, ~~of the steamer~~ ^and the ~~little~~ gaskets, but ~~we~~ feel no speck of anxiety about the style and strength of the engines.—

**[4]**

~~from a score of~~
~~His blood~~ My gore presently ~~oozes from~~ ^trickles ~~down~~
~~and~~ [*illegible*] ~~and~~ thinned with ~~the~~
~~plentiful sweat~~ ~~salt~~ ooze of my skin,
~~And~~ ^~~See how it~~ ^as ~~trickles down the black sk~~
I ~~He~~ ~~slowly~~ falls on the ^reddened grass and stones,
And the hunters haul up close
with their unwilling horses,
~~And~~ Till ~~the~~ taunt and ~~curse~~ oath ~~sink~~ swim
^away from my dim and dizzy ~~^away from my~~ ~~in his~~ ears
tr *
~~What Lucifer felt,~~ ~~^cursed when~~ ~~tumbling from~~
~~Heaven~~
What the rebel, ~~when he~~ felt gaily
adjusting his neck to the
rope noose,
*
What the ~~red~~ ^~~brown~~ savage, lashed to
the stump, ~~but~~ ^spirting ~~launching~~ ~~yelling still~~
~~his~~ yells and laughter ~~to~~ at every foe
What rage of hell ~~of~~ ~~spirted~~
urged

**[5]**

* greenhorns through their noviciate; he manufactured public opinion at a distance, and so forth, and so forth.— For all these he duly received pay.—
~~from~~ the lips and ~~fingers~~ hands
of the ~~vict~~ ~~captors~~ victors.—
How fared
The young captain ~~that lay~~ ^[*illegible*] ~~dying~~ ~~pale~~ ^pale and ~~ebbing~~

∧ flat on his ∧ own bloody deck
The pangs of defeat ~~more~~ sharper than
~~death to his hearts breast~~ the green edged wounds ~~of~~ of his side,
What choked the throat of
the general when he sur-
rendered ~~with all~~ his army,

(over leaf ☞

**[6]**

But the spirits, effusing mind, character,

No man and no woman can ~~with bruise~~ gash or starve or overburden ~~or pollute~~ or imbibe ~~bad~~ rotten stuff in ~~the~~ that superior nature of his or her's, any more than one can poison or starve his body.—

~~What minutes of damnation~~
What heightless dread, ∧ falls in the
click of a moment

**[7]**

story of Julia Scudder whose husband left her

Is not the faculty of sight better than the ? of the eye?— Is not the human voice more than the rings of the windpipe?
No man ~~and no woman will~~ means to ~~stab~~ deform or sicken the body.— ~~Of~~ For that wonderful and beautiful vessel, we ~~are pro~~ make

**[8]**

Lotos — the water lily of the Nile
honey-lotus — honey-clover

Amelioration is the blood that runs through the body of the universe.— ~~I grow~~ I do not lag — I do not hasten — ∧ ~~— it appears to say —~~ I bide my ~~time~~ day hours over billions ∧ of billions of years — I exist in the ~~formless~~ void that

~~through~~ asks for takes uncounted ~~ages forms~~ time and coheres to a nebula ?, and in further ~~ages~~ time coheresing to an orb, ~~and~~ marches, ~~like~~ gladly round, a ∧beautiful tangible creature, in ~~its~~her place in the ~~newer~~ processions of God, ~~whither~~ where ~~the troops are hastening for~~ ∧new accessions comers have been falling in the ranks for

**[9]**

ever, and ~~now~~ will be so always — I could be balked no how, not if all ~~the~~ worlds and living beings ~~in~~ were ∧this hour minute reduced ~~turned~~ back into the ~~fog~~ ∧impalpable film of chaos — I should surely bring up again where we now stand, and go ~~on~~ as much further and ~~still~~ thence on and on — ~~I think a few n~~ my right hand is time, and my left hand is space — both are ample — a few quintillions of cycles, a few sextillions of cubic leagues, are not of ∧~~special~~ importance to me — ~~I~~ what I ~~attain~~ shall attain to I ~~do not know~~ can never tell, for there is something that

**[10]**

underlies ~~and overtops~~ me, of whom I am ~~an effusion~~ a part ~~an attribute~~ and instrument.=

such is the
Tongue of a million voices,
~~And will you~~ ∧tell us ~~no~~ more,. ~~of tongue of a million voices~~?— Come, ~~we listen O mouth of mystery~~ we listen, we listen with ~~dreaming stretched pangs~~ itchings of desire, ~~for~~ to hear your tale of the soul.—
~~We~~ Throb and wait, and lay ~~your~~ our ears to the wall ~~as y~~ as we may, we throb

**[11]**

and wait ∧for the god in vain.— I am vast — he seems to console us with, ∧a whispering undertone in lack ~~instead~~ of an answer — and my works ~~are what~~ is wherever the universe is — but ~~we are only the morning wakers to the soul of man.—~~ the Soul of man! the Soul of man! — To that, we do the office of the servants who wakes their master at the dawn.

**[12]**

Of all the plenty ~~in nature~~ there is, no plenty is comparable to the plenty of time and space.— Of these there is ample store,— there is no limit

**[13]**

All truths lie ~~hidde~~ waiting in all things.— They neither urge the opening of themselves nor resist it (The heart of man alone is the one unbalanced and restless thing in the world)

~~And the~~ For their birth you need not the obstetric forceps of the surgeon. ~~Approach them with love~~ They ~~∧~~perhaps unfold to you and emit them∧selves, more fragrant than roses from ~~their~~ living buds, ~~if~~ whenever you fetch ~~in yourself~~ the spring sunshine ~~and~~ ∧moistened with summer rain.— But it must be in yourself.— It shall come

**[14]**

from your soul.— It shall be love.—

---

We hear of miracles.— But what is there that is not a miracle? ~~What Of~~ What ~~can~~ may you conceive of or ~~propound~~ name to me in the future, that ~~were a greater miracle than~~ ~~stranger or subtler~~ shall be beyond ~~me any~~ ~~∧~~ ~~all or~~ ∧the least thing around us?— I am looking in your eyes;— tell me ~~O~~ then, if you can, what is there in the immortality of the soul more ~~incomprehensible~~ than this ~~curious~~ spiritual and beautiful miracle of sight?— ∧By the equally subtle one of Volition, ~~is an~~ I open ~~to almond-sized~~ two pairs of lids, only as big as ~~a~~ peach-pits, when lo! the unnamable variety and whelming splendor *

**[15]**

We know that sympathy or love is the law ~~of~~ over all laws, because in nothing else but love ~~does~~ is the soul conscious of pure happiness, which ~~is~~ appears to be the ultimate resting place ~~of~~ and point of all things.—

---

* of the whole world ~~to~~ come to me.— with silence and with swiftness.— In an instant ~~I ma Then~~ make I fluid and draw to myself, ~~however dense~~ ∧keeping each to its

distinct isolation, and no hubbub or ~~jam or~~ confusion, or jam, the whole of physical nature, though rocks are dense and hills are ponderous, and the stars are ~~far~~ away off sextillions of miles.— All the years of all the beings that have ever ~~life~~ lived on the earth,

*

**[16]**

If the light of a half day dawn were arrested, and held so for a thousand years

~~How~~

---

And ~~wrote~~ chalked on a ~~great~~
board, Be of good cheer, we
will not desert you,
and held it up ~~as they~~
~~to against the~~ and did it;

---

The thin swift passing clouds like lace, blown overhead during a storm are called the flying scud

---

~~If~~ Let us suppose ~~for fo~~ that all the most rational people of the world had gone no further than children of twelve years old — or, as this seems forced, suppose the utmost advance yet made was the advance of the Camanches and kindred peoples of

**[17]**

The Poet
All the ~~greatness and beau~~ large hearts of heroes,
All the courage of olden time and new
~~What~~ How spied the the captain and sailors ^ the [*illegible*] great wreck with its helpless drifting hundreds,
~~did when they~~ ^ How they waited, their craft shooting ~~madly~~ like an arrow up and
down ~~in~~ the storm.
~~And in that deadly sea waited five~~ ^ How they gripped close with Death ^ there on the

sea, and gave him not one inch, but held on

days and nights ~~near the helpless~~ ∧ ~~fogged great~~ ~~wreck,~~

* over leaf

How the ∧ lank white faced women looked

~~as they~~ when ferried ~~them~~ safely at last

as from ∧ the sides their ~~waiting~~ prepared graves

How the children, and the ∧ lifted sick, and

the sharp-lipped, unshaved men;

All this ~~he~~ I ~~drinks~~ swallows in ~~his~~ my

soul, and it becomes ~~his~~ mine,

and ~~he~~ I likes it well,

~~He is~~ I am the man; [*illegible*] ~~he~~ I suffered, ~~he~~ I was

there:

~~And more:~~

~~He is the brave boy that saved them too:~~

All the beautiful disdain and

calmness of martyrs

**[18]**

The old woman that was

chained and burnt with dry

wood, and her children looking on,

The great queens that walked

serenely to the block,

The ∧ hunted slave ~~that~~ who ~~stood could~~

~~run no longer,~~ ∧ flags in the race at last and

~~then stood by~~ leans ~~leaned~~ up by the fence,

blowing ~~pants~~ and covered with sweat,

~~And his eye that shoot~~ burns ~~defiance~~

and desperation hatred

~~And the buck shot,~~ were

And ~~the how~~ the twinges that

sting like needles his

breast and neck

The murderous buck-shot

~~planted like terrible~~ and the bullets.
~~This~~ All [*illegible*] this ~~he~~ I not only feels and sees ~~feels~~ am but
~~He is~~ I am the hunted slave,
Damnation and despair are close upon ~~him~~ me
~~He~~ I clutches the rail of
the fence.
* (back

**[19]**

All around me I hear how great is Adam or Eve — how ~~illustrious~~ significant ~~are~~ the illustrious Greeks, or later Italians and Germans, and modern ~~En-~~ celebrities of England and France.— Yes Christ was ~~great~~ large and ~~so was~~ Homer was great; and so Columbus and Washington and Fulton. But ∧ greatness is the other word for developement, and in my soul ~~to me~~ I know that I am ~~great~~ large and strong as any of them, probably ~~greater.—~~ larger.—

Because all that they did I feel that I too could do, and more ∧ and that multiplied; ~~; and~~ ∧ and ~~with~~ after none of them or their achievements

**[20]**

does my stomach ∧ say ~~fully~~ ∧ enough and satis ~~fully satisfies me.~~— Except Christ; he alone ~~is the~~ brings the perfumed bread ~~for~~ of ~~to~~ ~~my soul~~, ∧ ever vivifying and clean, to me, — ever fresh and plenty, ever welcome and ~~sufficient~~ to spare.—

Not even God, ~~that dread ?~~ is so great to me as Myself is great to me.— Who knows but I too shall in time be a God as pure and prodigious as any of them.— ∧ Now I stand here, ~~an existence~~ a personality in the Universe, ∧ ~~isolated,~~ perfect and sound, ~~is isolated~~; ~~all~~ ~~to~~ all things and all other beings ∧ as an audience at the play-house perpetually and perpetually calling me out from ~~my recesses~~ behind ~~the~~ ∧ my curtain.—

**[21]**

shall we sky-lark with God
The poet seems to say to
the rest of the world

Come, God and I are now here
What will you have of us.

---

* with all the science and genius, ~~for implements,~~ ~~were~~ were nobly occupied in the ~~single~~ employment of investigating this ~~one~~ single ~~abstract one minute~~ minute of my life

**[22]**

Blacksmithing

when they have a great heat in the fire.—

Five or six blacksmiths swing their sledges ~~in~~ overhand overhand overhand —

It would be as though some publisher should reject the best ~~and~~ poems ever written in the world because he who brings them to be printed has a ~~worn~~ shabby umbrella, or mud on the shank of his boot.

**[23]**

---

The creek on Long Island when the boating party were returning and capsized, and the young man saved his sweetheart and lost his sister

---

~~I~~ One grand faculty [*illegible*] we want,— and that is the power to pierce ~~all~~ fine clothing and ^thick coated shams, and settle for sure what the reality of the thing clothed and disguised is, and what it weighs stark naked; the power of ~~eluding and~~ slipping like an eel ~~from~~ through all blandishments and graspings

~~* back~~

**[24]**

of convention~~.~~; the power

## *a schoolmaster*[2]
## [Before or early 1852]

**[1, *cover*]**

**[2]**

**[3]**

a schoolmaster ^while intoxicated, was married to a woman, by certain persons to cover their own guilt.

———

Money (bills) taken from a person who was down (died) of the smallpox, carried the contagion; and those who took it died of the same dis. -

———

horrible effects of the taking of mercury — the swelled tongue

———

**[4]**

Introduce a character (pick-pocket — bad) who goes to California in haste, to escape detection and punishment for crime — After a short while they receive a letter — or read in a newspaper — an account of his being hung

———

? make the pickpocket the husband of a worthy woman who has been inveigled into marriage with him.—

**[5]**

***[Pasted-in newspaper clipping, an account of a Boston man saving a mother and two children from a fire in Cambridge, MA] X***

[*Pasted-in newspaper clipping describing the sale, by a "free negro" in North Carolina, of his own wife (whom he had purchased before marrying) and children to pay his debts.*]

Tribune
March, 12
1852

**[6]**

**[7]**

**[8]**

Introduce Jack's friends — two or three —

---

An elderly ~~man~~ woman comes to the office to secure Covert's services ~~fo~~ in behalf of h~~is~~er son, who is arrested for

**[9]**

**[10]**

Martha, is the ward of Covert, inheriting property, so situated as to require the services of a limb-of-the-law.— (Her ~~mother,~~ aunt, the Old Quaker lady)

Jack, on going to Covert's house, ^one evening recognizes the ~~like~~ portrait of the Old Lady — it affects him to tears

is dead — and Martha lives in Covert's house, in the situation of half servant —

**[11]**

Make Wigglesworth

Some remarks about the villainy of lawyers — tell the story of Covert's ^father's swindling, about the house in Johnson st — damn him

---

Make Wigglesworth tell Jack a good long account of Covert and his character and villainies

(Covert ~~has licentious feelings toward Martha and wishes to effect~~ a marriage with her — also for the sake of her property

**[12]**

— He is divided in his libidinous feelings between Martha, and Miss Seligny

**[13]**

— The main hinge of the story will be Covert's determination to embezzle Martha's property — by means of withholding deeds, wills documents, &c &c — and Jack Engle, who early discovers that intention — being pervaded by a determination ~~th~~ to foil him —

With this view, he applies himself with zeal to study law, and watches with great sharpness —

**[14]**

The story of Martha shall be is that her ~~father~~ Uncle, wealthy ∧who had adopted her a fine hearted man, (but possessed of a frightfully passionate temper,) — under the influence of his passion, commits homicide — (the victim is Jack's father) — He is arrested the shock is too much for him — while in prison, — he ~~divides his~~ makes a will,

**[15]**

dividing his property equally between Martha and the offspring of his victim — or the latter failing, it was all to go to Martha.—

The widow left Philadelphia, (where these sad events happened,) and came on to New York.— In consequence of the nature of the affair, she gradually withdrew from all her ∧relations and former friends, (she was extra

**[16]**

sensitive) and lived with Martha, shut out from the world and

---

Introduce some scene in a religious revival meeting —

———

Make a character of a ranting religious exhorter — sincere, but a great fool.

Make Wigglesworth "get religion," through Calvin Peterson

**[17]**

Dont forget Seligny

(describe Tom
    Peterson
    fine young fellow

Smytthe
Pepperich Ferris

**[18]**

**[19]**

"The cup goes round,
And none so artful as to put it by."

O, earth how coulds't thou rudely push him back when he had but just crossed thy threshold?

**[20]**

**[21]**

**[22]**

Hildreth vol 1
page 42,

## *No doubt the efflux* [3]
## [pre-1855]

**[1]**

No doubt the efflux of the soul ~~is~~ comes through beautiful ∧gates of laws that ~~we may~~ at some future period ∧perhaps a few score millions of years, we may understand better.— At present, its ∧tide is what ~~we~~ folks call capricious, and cannot well be traced * ( ).— Why as I just ~~catch a~~ look ∧in the railroad car at some ~~workman's~~ half turned face, do I love that ~~being,~~ woman? Though~~tless that~~ she is neither young nor ~~beautiful?~~ fair ~~featured~~ complexioned, — — ~~she~~ remains in my memory afterward for a year, and I calm myself to sleep at night by thinking of her.— Why ~~are~~ be there men I meet, and ~~many~~ others I know, that ~~when~~ while they are with me, the sunlight of Paradise

**[2]**

~~warms~~ expands my blood — that ∧when ~~if~~ I walk with an arm of theirs around my neck, my soul ~~leaps and laughs like a new-waked child —~~ scoots and courses like ~~a caressed~~ an unleashed dog ~~caressed~~ — that when they leave me the pennants of my joy sink flat ~~from the~~ and lank in the deadest calm?—

Why, ~~do I as I sit at my table in~~ do flocks of ~~thoughts,~~ ideas, some twittering as wrens ∧or chirping or ~~robins~~ pee [tweets?]?some soft as pigeons, some screaming as ~~eagles~~ sea-hawks, some shy and afar off as the wild brant, some ∧invariably why do these ~~swarms~~ beat their ∧countless wings and clutch

**[3]**

their feet upon me, as I sit ~~in the adjoining room~~ near by, ~~to~~ where my brother is practising at the piano?— There is a certain block between my house and the South ferry, not especially different from other blocks ∧[*illegible*] bordered by trees;: Why ~~then~~ do I never pass ~~it~~ there, without new and large and ~~beautiful~~ melodious ~~thoughts~~ thoughts descending upon me?— ~~I think~~ ∧I guess ∧they hang there, winter and summer, [ply?] the limbs of those trees and continually drop the [fruit?] ~~upon~~ if I travel that [~~block~~?] way. Some fisherman that ~~always — stop to pass the time-O-day with~~ give good morning to, and pass ∧ten or twenty minutes as he draws his seine by the shore — ∧some carpenter working his rip saw through a plank — some driver, as I ride on top of the stage, — men rough, ~~rough,~~ not handsome, not accomplished — why do I know that the subtle chlo-

**[4]**

roform of our spirits is affecting each other, and though we may ~~never meet~~ encounter not again, we ~~know feel that we two~~ have ~~pass~~ exchanged the ∧right ~~mysterious~~ ~~unspoken~~ password ∧~~of the night,~~ and ~~have~~ are thence free ~~entrance~~ comers to ~~each~~ the guarded tents of each other's ~~love~~ most interior love? *(What is the ~~cause~~ meaning, any how, of my ~~love~~ ∧~~attachment~~ adhesiveness ~~for~~ toward others?— What is the cause of theirs ~~love~~ toward ~~for~~ ~~for~~ me?) — (Am I loved by them boundlessly because my love for them is more boundless?—)

**[5]**

∧While the curtain is down at the opera ∧while I swim in the bath while I wait for my friend at the corner, while I [*illegible*] ~~swim in the bath,~~ I behold ∧and am beheld by people ~~men and women~~; I speak little or nothing; I ~~offer~~ make no gifts to them; I do not ∧so much as turn my neck or pat my ~~boot in their behalf~~ ∧instep to gain [any?] [~~thing~~?] ~~from them;~~ of their [favor?]; we never met ~~nor~~ before, — never heard ~~of or~~ shall ∧hear ~~eachs other before~~ ~~each's~~ names.— nor dates nor employments.— With all this, some god ∧walks in noiseless and resistless, ~~takes~~ and takes their hearts out of their breasts, and gives them to me for ever.— Often I ~~see it, and get~~ catch the ~~hint~~ sign; and oftener, no doubt, it ~~goes~~ ∧flies ~~over~~ by me ~~over~~ as unknown as my neighbor's dreams.—

**[6]**

and bring her naked to his bed, that ~~he~~ they ~~together~~ may sleep~~,~~ ∧together ~~with her~~; and she shall come again whenever he will, and the taste shall ~~always~~ be sweeter and sweeter always)

President ~~Lo~~ ∧Their ~~Their Ruler~~ and their Pet! I see them lead him ~~onward~~ now.— I see ~~the~~ his large slow gait, his face ∧illuminated ~~and gay~~ like the face of a ~~happy~~ young child.— ~~I see him shooting the light of his soul~~

---

Onward ∧he moves ∧with the gay procession, ~~to the music of laughter~~ ~~and the~~ [~~swing?~~] ~~band~~ of laughing pioneers and the ∧wild trilling bugles of joy.—

---

Onward he moves with the gay procession, and the laughing pioneers, and the wild-trilling bugles of joy

**[7]**

<u>The Poet</u>

~~I think~~ His sight is the sight of the ? (bird and his scent the instinct of the ? dog

---

I think ten million supple-∧fingered gods are perpetually employed hiding beauty in the world — ~~hiding~~ burying its every-where in every-thing — ~~but~~ and most of all ~~where~~ in spots that men and women do not think of ~~it~~, and never look — as ~~in~~death, and ~~misery~~ poverty and wickedness.— Cache ∧~~after~~ and cache — ~~it is —~~ ~~again they~~ all over the earth, and in the heavens ~~above~~ ∧that swathe the earth and in the ~~dept~~ waters of the sea.— ~~Thei~~ They do their ~~work~~ jobs well; those ~~supple-fingered gods.~~ journeymen divine.

**[8]**

~~But~~ Only ~~to~~ from the poet ~~do~~ ~~can~~ they ∧can hide nothing; ∧and would not if they could.— ~~hide.~~—

---

Him they ~~attend~~ wait on night and day and ~~show where they take~~ uncover all, that he shall see the naked breast and the most private
~~of Delight.~~—

---

I ~~think~~ reckon he is ~~the really the god~~ Boss of those gods; ~~for they~~ and the work they do is done for him, and all that they have concealed they have concealed for his ~~sake~~ sake — ~~Ahead~~ ∧~~For~~ Him they attend outdoors or indoors; ~~to his perceptions they open all.~~— They ~~ru~~ run ~~nimbly~~ ahead ~~as~~ when he walks, ~~and~~ and ~~to~~ lift their cunning covers, and ~~poi~~ signify ~~to~~ him with ~~pointed~~ pointed stretched arms.— ~~The~~ ~~The~~ (They undress Delight

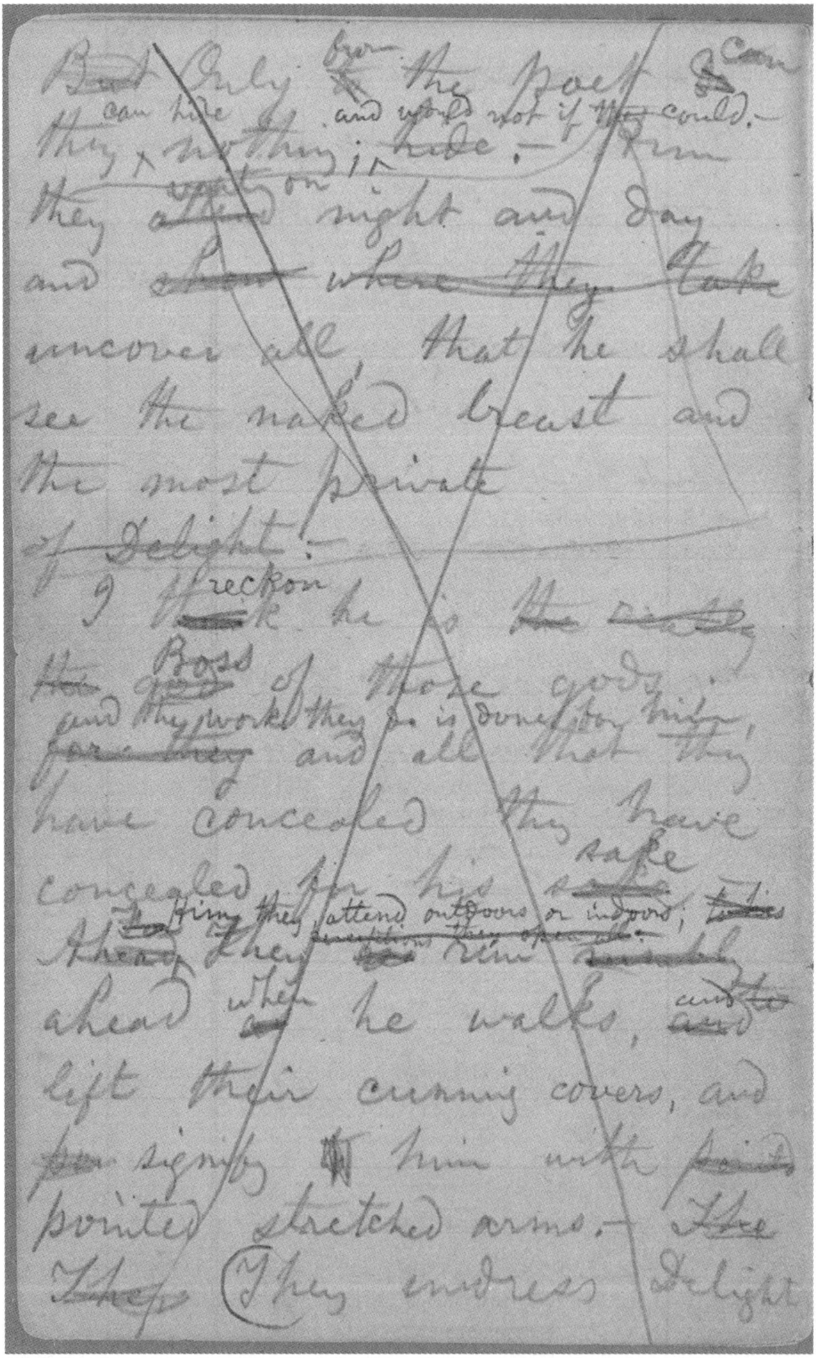
Only from the Poet can they hide nothing, and would not if they could.— Him
they wait on night and day
and uncover all, that he shall
see the naked breast and
the most private
I reckon he is
the Boss of those gods
and the work they do is done for him,
and all that they
have concealed they have
concealed for his sake
Him they attend outdoors or indoors,
ahead when he walks, and
lift their cunning covers, and
signify him with
pointed stretched arms.—
They undress Delight

Leaf from *No doubt the efflux* notebook (pre-1855).

**[9]**

What variety what richness in life:
But ~~grea~~ richer than life ~~is~~ spreads out what we call Death
How supple is youth,
How muscular, how full of
love and grace and unspeak-
able fascination,
But old age may wear ~~more~~
~~love and~~ graces and fascinations
a thousand fold.
How large and splendid is
the sunlit day
Till the night comes with
~~its mystery and darkness~~ ^transparent darkness and mystery
and the stars,~~And those~~ Touching the soul
closer than the grandest
day.
How magnificent ~~are riches~~ is wealth
~~that spread over one~~ affording
gifts ~~without stint~~ from the

**[10]**

ample hand, and superb
clothes and hospitality
But ~~all riches are~~ wealth is nothing to the
soul's, which ~~are~~ is candor
~~and life~~ and ~~all~~ enfolding love,
Did not Jesus show that
what we call poverty
is ~~great~~ the greatest ~~riches~~ wealth?

**[11]**

Why what is this curious little ~~thing~~ ^~~creature~~ thing ~~you pr~~ you ~~out~~ hold before
~~us?— We read in the advertisements of your new and edition of our~~ the ~~race,~~
~~enlarged and improved.~~ Do you call ~~this~~ ~~such as this~~ such an ~~abject~~ wretched ~~thing~~

creature as you have pictured here a man?— ~~A~~ Man is the President of the earth. ~~Why~~ This is no man ^ ~~Man is~~ [a?] ~~master of~~ the President of the ^ ~~whole~~ earth..— This is ~~some~~ ^ the abject louse — ~~some~~ the milk-faced maggot

**[12]**

What an abject
creature ~~would~~ make a ~~human being~~ man.— Notice! what louse is this — ~~you~~ what ~~crawling snivelling~~ milk faced maggot,

---

that ~~falls lays~~ ^ flattens itself upon the ground, and asks leave to live, ~~as of no~~ not as of right of its own, but by special favor; ~~snufflin~~ snivelling how it ~~is~~ were righteously condemned, being of the vermin race, and ~~is~~ will ~~crawl~~ be only too thankful if it ~~be let~~ can, ~~creep crawl escape~~ ~~to go to its hole under the dung, and escape~~ dodge the stick or booted heel~~!~~ and escape to its hole under the dung!

**[13]**

I should think poorly of myself if I ~~could~~ should be even a few days with any community ^ either of sane or insane people, and not make them convinced, whether they acknowledged it or not, ~~with~~ ^ of my truth, my sympathy, and my dignity.— I should be ~~assured~~ certain enough that those attributes were not in me.— ~~The~~ Although it may balk and tremble a few moments on its balance? it ~~is~~ will surely signify

**[14]**

No piety that macerates and flogs itself, and refuses women and laughter and a ~~rich florid~~ long, strong florid life, ~~is equal~~ begins to be piety in comparison with that which

---

If your souls do not

The most accomplished lapidary cannot ~~tell~~ separate the real opal an ? and from their counterfeits in glass, ~~as~~ so unerringly as the soul can tell what is its truth and what is sham.— Yet in the ~~superb~~ ordinations, this clarifying and separating power ∧in any thing like perfection is not arrived at ~~in any thing like perfection,~~ hastily.— Nature is not a young fellow *

**[15]**

In the city when the streets have been long neglected, they heap up banks of mud in the shape of graves, and put boards at the head and feet, with very significant inscriptions.—

---

Comparison between a sincere devotee of any time, and a fashionable preacher.—

---

O yes the Fugitive Slave Law is obeyed northerly every day in the year — except three hundred and sixty-five

**[16]**

All this Religion of the world -          - as it is let us not be too stern with it — it is the meagre grass thin and pale and yellow which shows the life of the soil~~; and~~

A bell-ringer went out ∧at night to sound his alarm for a fire.— After two or three rings, the notes ceased, and when they went to see, the bell ringer was dead.—

**[17]**

~~are~~ ∧be ready.—

amplitude of her means, [*illegible*] time is inconceivably ample.— ~~Therefore~~ It is for She does not rush, ~~and~~ nor get in any tight spot that needs hard scratching

---

Give ∧me the commander who carries a thousand regiments in his breast ∧both horses foot; and ∧in his head whole packs of artillery, the swiftest and best disciplined in the world

**[18]**

---

Comes some one to a man saying, your mother is famished, your brother is blue and dead with cold, and the man answers, I have [~~his?~~] meat, but it is inconvenient to go for it ∧just now; and I have cloth but it is out of reach on a ~~high~~ shelf

**[19]**

Inexplicably curious is ~~the con~~ what we call happiness.— I have felt the ~~strange~~ sweet mystery more for forty minutes cleaning ∧and gresing my boots, than

---

Has what I have said an

seized upon your soul

and set its sign there

If not then I know there is no elementary vigor ~~the~~ in my words

If ~~it have~~ not, then I throw my words ~~with~~ among the ∧other parings and crusts of the swill tub, and go home and bathe myself, and listen to music, and touch my lips to the flesh of sleeping children, and ∧come and try again.

**[20]**

The Poet

What you call your Religion, ~~however warm it may~~ paint ~~it as~~ with as much red as you can stick on — wrench the biggest words [*illegible*] to describe it — and then multiply many fold; ~~yet~~ it is ∧yet too ~~feeble~~ feeble and ~~cold~~ babyish for the Poet.— He ~~must~~ will have something ∧infinitely more alive and ample and strong and fiery and comprehensive.—

There is an ugliness undone and unspoken, worse than ~~the~~ any sins of ignorance or ~~bad temper~~ uncouth ways..— A man shall maliciously tell of ~~some~~ the chap ∧at the table picking his teeth with the dinner fork, and show

**[21]**

~~This hat~~ ∧This being a little hood and ~~coat~~ tunic ~~you have~~ tailored ∧~~too small~~ for ~~the soul is~~ for some ~~wilted sickly~~ poor consumptive ~~wasted~~ child, and gaudy with spangles of tin.— ~~you [bring?] your clothier's tapes and~~
For thy soul, ~~that is so large that~~ ∧whose far spreading ~~the breasts~~ shoulders burst the overcoat of the universe, as ∧~~too~~ insupportably ~~inconceivably cramping~~ pinching and scant and of ~~no~~ small account.— ~~that~~ who t takes the suns for its ~~toys~~ toys, and soon wants ~~something~~ better — ~~they will~~ you ~~bring a~~ ~~piece~~ tailor up the little hood and tunic ~~tailored for~~ ∧sizable to some poor consumptive child, and ~~made~~ horribly gaudy with spangles of tin?

---

an ill bred ~~soul~~ heart far ~~worse than~~ more dismal than any want of etiquette.

**[22]**

Looking to the ~~outer~~ scrofulous politics ~~whose~~ of Europe, and what comes thence, ~~Men~~ folks think it a dismal ~~thing when the kings~~ that some king or kings daughter, ~~un~~ unseated from their thrones and exiled, should pine and linger, and be starved of the grand ~~pre-sustenance which~~ honors and prerogatives of

But all

---

Greatness is simply development

**[23]**

~~Shall~~ ~~Does~~ The clothier comes supercilious ∧and swallow tailed ~~and swallow-tailed~~, ~~wh with~~ ∧and flirts his measuring tape, ~~and shears~~ for ~~the~~ ∧my Soul ~~whose~~ — my Soul ~~that~~, with far-~~stretching~~ bulging shoulders bursting the overcoat of the ~~universe~~ heavens as insupportably pinching and scant — ~~who takes fiery suns for toys, and soon wants some thing brighter;—~~ and ~~can~~ will the ~~swallow tailed gentlemen~~ loud promising gentlemen duly send home to me nothing better than this ∧little tunic for some poor consumptive child — this baby hood, with spangles of tin?

**[24]**

I think ten million supple-~~fingered~~ wristed gods are ~~perpetually employed~~ always hiding beauty in the world — burying it every where ~~in~~ every thing — and most of all in spots that men and women do not think of and never look — as Death and Poverty and Wickedness.— Cache! and Cache again! all over the earth, and in the heavens that swathe the earth, and in the waters of the sea.— They do their jobs well; those journeymen divine. Only from the Poet they can hide nothing and would not if they could.— I reckon he is Boss of those gods; and the work they do is done for him; and all they have concealed, they have concealed for his sake.— Him they attend indoors and outdoors.— They run ahead when he walks, and lift their cunning covers and signify him with pointed stretched arms.

Their President and their Pet! I see them lead him now.— I see his large, slow gait — his face illuminated like the face of an arm-bound child. Onward he moves with the gay procession, and the laughing pioneers, and the wild trilling bugles of joy.—

## *Talbot Wilson*[4]
## [ca. 1854]

**[1, *front cover*]**

**[2]**

Talbot Wilson st.
go to corner Division av. & 7th st.

~~Walter Whitman~~
466½
~~71 Prince street and 30 Fulton st.~~
~~Brooklyn~~
~~106 Myrtle~~
avenue
Brooklyn

---

Mr. Stebbins
110 Broadway Room 8
over the Metropolitan Bank

**[3]**

Jeff's [*illegible*] 46
Joseph Pemberton
maker Liverpool
No. 41,303
Lever
cover R.S.

---

W. [~~Watch?~~]
Quartier Au Loete
Swisse
No. 51,575

---

**[4–18 *are cut away, leaving solitary letters and numbers visible on the slender strips that remain. These pages may have been used as business ledgers.*]**

**[19]**

Be simple and clear.— Be not occult.

True noble expanded American character is raised on a far more lasting and universal basis than that of any of the characters of ~~of~~ the "gentlemen" of aristocratic life, or of novels, or in the European or Asiatic forms of society or government.— It is to be illimitably proud, independent, self-possessed ~~and~~ generous and gentle.— It is to accept nothing except what is equally free and eligible to every body else.— It is to be poor, rather than rich — but to prefer

**[20]**

death sooner than any mean dependence.— Prudence is part of it, because prudence is the right arm of independence.

Every American young man should carry himself with the finished and haughty bearing of the greatest ruler and proprietor — for he is ~~the~~ a great ruler and proprietor — ~~th~~ the greatest.

Great latitude must be allowed to others

~~Bring~~ Play your muscle, and it will be lithe as ~~willow and gutta~~[?]

**[21]**

caoutchouc and strong as iron — I wish to see American [young?] men the workingmen, carry themselves with ~~a~~ high horse

---

**[22]**

Where is the being of whom I am the inferior?— It is the          of ∧the sly or shallow to divide men like the metals, into those more precious and others less precious, intrinsically

I never yet knew ~~what it was to feel~~ how it felt to ∧think I stood in the presence of my superior.— ~~I could now abase myself if God~~ If the presence of

~~Jah were~~ God were made visible immediately before ^me, I could not abase myself.— How do I know but I shall myself

**[23]**

I will not ~~have~~ be the cart, nor the load on the cart, nor the horses that draw the cart; but I will be the little ~~pair of little~~ hands that guide the cart.—

**[24]**

Ask Mr. Dwight about the highest numeral term known

**[25]**

**[26]**

Different objects which decay, and by the chemistry of nature, their bodies are           into spears of grass —

---

American ~~under takes~~ receives with calmness the spirit of the past

---

**[27]**

Bring all the art and science of the world, and baffle and humble it with one spear of grass

---

Liberty is not the ~~end~~ fruition but the dawn of the morning of a nation.— The night has passed and the day appears when people walk abroad — to do evil or to do good

**[28]**

The soul or spirit transmutes itself into all matter — into rocks, and cand live the life of a rock — into the sea, and can feel itself the sea — into the oak, or other tree — into an animal, and feel itself a horse, a fish, or a bird — into the earth — into the motions of the suns and stars —

A man only is interested in any thing when he identifies himself with it — he must himself be whirling and speeding through space like the planet

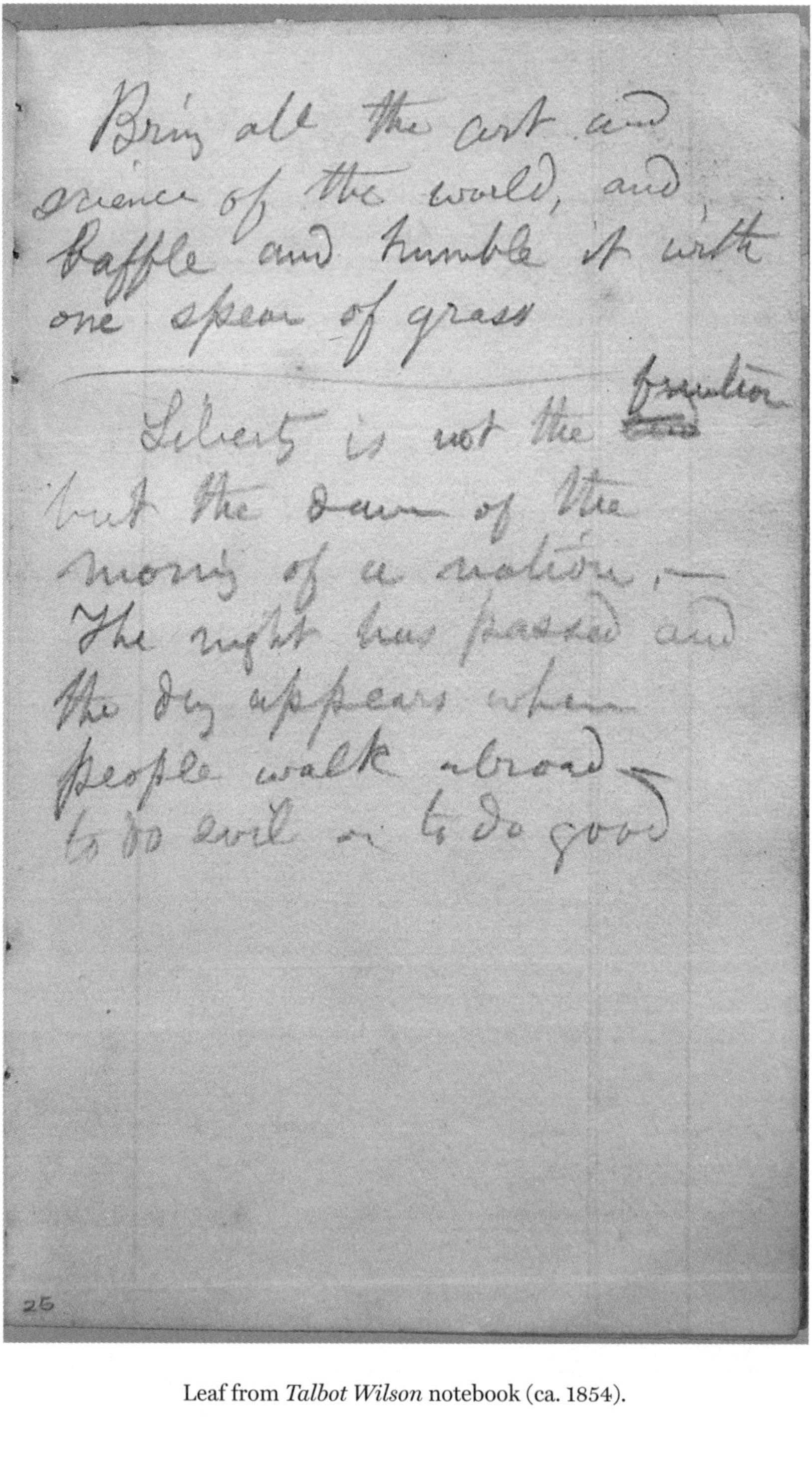

Bring all the art and science of the world, and baffle and humble it with one spear of grass

Liberty is not the fruition but the dawn of the morning of a nation,— The night has passed and the day appears when people walk abroad to do evil or to do good

25

Leaf from *Talbot Wilson* notebook (ca. 1854).

[29]

Mercury — he must be driving like a cloud — he must shine like the sun — he must be orbic and balanced in the air, like this earth — he must crawl like the pismire — he must

— he would be growing fragrantly in the air, like ~~a~~ the locust blossoms — he would rumble and crash like the thunder in the sky — he would spring like a cat on his prey — he would splash like a whale in the

[30]

The mean and bandaged ~~soul~~ spirit is perpetually dissatisfied with itself — It is too wicked, or too poor, or too feeble

[31]

Never speak of the soul as any thing but intrinsically great.— The adjective affixed to it must always testify greatness and immortaliy and purity.—

[32]

The ∧effusion or corporation of the soul is always under the beautiful laws of physiology — I guess the soul itself can never be any thing but great and pure and immortal; but it ~~is~~ [~~*illegible*~~] makes itself visible only through matter — a perfect head, and [~~bot?~~] bowels ∧and bones to match ~~will~~ is the easy gate through which it comes from its ~~wonderful~~ embowered garden, and pleasantly appears to the sight

[33]

of the world.— A twisted skull, and blood ~~made~~ ~~becom~~ ~~thin~~ watery or rotten by ∧ancestry or gluttony, or rum or bad disorders, — they are the darkness toward which the plant will not grow, although its seed lies waiting for ages.—

[34]

**[35]**

Wickedness is most likely the absence of freedom and health in the soul.— If a man ∧babe or woman ∧babe of decent progenitors should grow up without restraint or starvation or

**[36]**

Every soul has its own language, The reason why any truth ~~is~~ which I tell is not apparent to you, is mostly because I fail of translating it from my language into

**[37]**

Every soul has its own individual language, often unspoken, or lamely feebly haltingly spoken; but a ~~perfect~~ true fit for that ~~a and~~ man, and perfectly adapted ~~for~~ to his use.— The truths I tell ∧to you or any other, may not be ~~apparent~~ plain to you, ~~or that other,~~ because I do not translate them ~~well~~ right fully from my idiom into yours.— If I could do so, and do it well, they would be as apparent to you as they are to me; for they are ~~eternal~~ truths.— No two have exactly the same language, but and the great translator

**[38]**

and joiner of ~~all~~ ∧the whole is the poet, ~~because~~ He ~~enters into th~~ has the divine grammar of all tongues, and ~~what~~ says ∧indifferently and alike, How are you friend? to the President in the midst of his cabinet, and Good day my brother, to Sambo, among the ~~black slaves~~ ~~rowed~~ hoes of the sugar field, and both ∧understand him and know that ~~his~~ his speech is ∧right, ~~well,~~ ~~right.—~~ ~~for his hi~~

**[39]**

The universal and fluid soul impounds within itself not only all the good characters and heros, but the distorted characters, murderers, thieves

**[40]**

~~and~~ I said to my soul When we become the ~~god~~ enfolders of all these ∧orbs, and open to the life and delight and knowledge of every thing in them, or of

them, shall we be filled and satisfied?
and the answer was
No, when we fetch that height, we shall not be filled and satisfied, but shall look as high beyond.

**[41]**

Dilation

I think the soul will never stop, or attain to any ~~its~~ growth beyond which it shall not go. ~~no further.~~— ∧When I ~~have sometimes when I~~ walk~~ed~~ at night by the sea shore and look~~ed~~ up ~~to~~ at the ~~stars~~ countless stars, ~~and~~ ∧I ~~have~~ ask~~ed~~ of my soul whether it would be filled and satisfied when it ~~was~~ ∧should become ~~the~~ a god enfolding ~~an~~ all these, and open to the life and delight and knowledge of every thing in them or of them; and the answer was plain[~~er?~~] to ~~my ear~~ me

**[42]**

th~~an~~ at the [~~sa?~~] breaking water on the sands at my feet; and ~~it~~ ∧the answer was, No, when I reach there, I shall want ~~more~~ to go further still.—

**[43]**

**[44]**

The run of poets and the learned have

When ~~you show me how~~ I ~~inquire~~ see where the east is greater than the west, — ~~how~~ where the ∧sound man's part of the ∧~~new born~~ child is greater than the ∧sound woman's part — ~~how~~ or where ~~the~~ a father [~~than?~~] is more needful than a mother to produce me — then I ~~know~~ guess I shall see how spirit is greater than matter.— ~~On~~ Here The run of poets and the learned ~~invariably~~ always ~~stub their toes here, and generally fall and sh~~ *

**[45]**

You have been told that ~~intellect~~ mind is greater than matter

* [~~run?~~] always strike ~~here,~~ and here [~~it?~~] shoots the ballast of many a

grand head.— My life is a miracle and my body which lives is a miracle; but of what I can nibble at the edges of the limitless and delicious wonder I know that I cannot separate ~~the~~ them, and call one superior and the other inferior, any more than I can say my sight is greater than my eyes.— *

**[46]**

I cannot understand the mystery, but I ∧am always ~~think~~ ∧conscious of myself as two — as my soul and I; and I ~~gu~~ reckon it is the same with all ~~oth~~ men and women.—

**[47]**

I know that my body will ~~decay~~

**[48]**

whose sides are crowded ~~with~~ the rich cities of all living philosophy, and oval gates [~~hop?~~] that ~~let~~ pass you in to ~~immortal gardens landscapes of hill sides and~~ fields of clover ~~and sass~~ and landscapes ~~of~~ clumped with sassafras, and orchards of good apples, and ~~if you~~ every breath ∧through your mouth shall be of a new perfumed, ~~immortal~~ and elastic ~~air~~, which is love.—

But I will take ~~every~~ each ~~man~~ ~~on~~ ~~or~~ ~~and~~ ~~woman~~ ∧man and woman of you to the window and open the shutters and the sash, and my left arm shall hook ~~him~~ you round the waist, and my right shall point shall point you to the ~~road~~ endless and beginningless road along

(up ∧

**[49]**

I will not be a great philosopher, and found any school, and [~~bring?~~] build it ~~on~~ with iron pillars, and gather the young me around me, and make them my disciples, ~~and found a~~ that ~~a~~ new ∧superior churches and politics. ∧shall come.— — But I will

☞

~~show every man, unhook the sh~~ open the shutters and the ~~window~~ sash, and ~~you shall stand at my side, and I will show~~ hook my left~~ing~~ arm around your waist till I point you ∧to the road ∧along which ~~leads to all the learning~~ ~~knowledge~~ ~~and truth~~

~~and pleasure~~ are the cities of all living philosophy and ~~all~~ pleasure.— Not I ~~or any~~ — not God — can travel

**[50]**

~~it~~ this road for you.— It is not far, it is within ~~reach~~ the stretch of your ~~arm~~ thumb; perhaps you shall find you are on it already, and did not know.— Perhaps you shall find it every where ~~on~~ over the ocean and ∧over the land, when you once have the vision to behold it.—

**[51]**

**[52]**

~~If~~ I am hungry and with my ~~money~~ last dime ~~buy a loaf of~~ get me some meat and bread, and ~~would~~ have appetite enough to ~~eat~~ relish it all.— But ∧then like a phantom at my side ∧suddenly appears a starved face, either human or brute, uttering not a word;. ~~but with — Am I a~~ ~~Have I then~~ ~~the passionless squid or clam-shell, not to feel in my heart that now I am it were my~~
Now do I talk of mine and his?— ~~Is~~ ∧Has my heart no more passion than ~~the~~ a squid or clam shell has?

**[53]**

1847
April ~~20~~ 19th mason commenc'd
work on the base-
ment rooms

paid mason in full

---

I know the bread is ~~mine, I have not a [fip?] dime more~~ my bread, and ∧that on it must I dine and sup. ~~for the dime that bought it was my last.—~~ I know ~~tha~~ I may munch, ~~and munch~~ and not grit my teeth against the laws of church or state. What is this then that balances itself upon my lips and wrestles ~~like~~ as with the knuckles of God, for

(3

**[54]**

The ~~world~~ ∧ignorant man is demented with the madness of owning things — of having ~~title~~ by warranty deeds and ~~lawful possession~~ court clerks' records, ~~and with perfect~~ the right to mortgage, sell, ~~dispose of~~ give away or raise money on certain possessions.— But the wisest soul knows that ~~nothing~~ ∧no ~~not one~~ object ~~in the vast universe~~ can really be owned by one man or woman any more than another.— The ~~measureless fool~~ orthodox ~~who fancies that who~~ proprietor says [~~t?~~]This is mine. I earned or received or paid for it, — and ∧by [~~an?~~] positive right of [my own I?] I will put ~~this~~ a fence around it, and keep ~~the~~ it exclusively to myself — . . . . . . Yet — yet — what ∧cold drop is

**[55]**

~~that it~~ that ∧which slowly patters, patters ~~like water~~ ~~fine points cold~~ with sharp and ~~specks of water down~~ poisoned points, on the skull of his greediness, and go whichever way he ~~will~~ may, it still hits him, ~~as~~ though he see not whence it ~~comes~~ drips nor what it is?— ~~How can I be so~~ that dismal and measureless fool not to ~~understand~~ see the hourly lessons of ~~an~~ the ∧one eternal law, ~~which~~ that he who would grab blessings to himself, ~~and~~ as by right, and deny others their equal chance — and will not share with them every thing that he has

**[56]**

He cannot share ~~with them~~ his friend or his wife because ~~no man owns these~~ of them he is no owner, ~~except of He~~ except ~~of~~ by their love, and if any one gets that away from him, ~~he had should~~ lets ~~wife and friend the whole~~ wife and friend go, the tail with the hide.

**[57]**

~~may as well be~~ it is best not to curse, but quietly call the offal cart to his door and let ∧physical wife or friend go, the tail with the hide.—

**[58]**

The dismal and measureless fool called a rich man, or a thriver, ~~What folks call a thriving or rich man is more likely~~ some dismal and measureless fool, who ~~leaves the fields~~ leaves ~~untasted~~ untouched ~~all the million~~ ~~the [immortal?] tables spread~~

[~~every?] part of~~ those countless and [every?] spread tables thick ~~with~~ in ~~the~~ immortal dishes, ~~every one~~ heaped with the meats and drinks of God, and ~~thinks hi~~ fancies himself smart because he tugs and sweats ~~in the slush after~~ among cinders, and parings, and slush

**[59]**

~~While the~~

The ignorant think that to the entertainment of life, ~~you are~~ they will be admitted by a ticket or check, and the ~~air of~~ dream of their existence is to get the money that they may buy this ~~env~~ wonderful card.— But the wise soul

**[60]**

the sidewalks of eternity ∧they are the freckles of Jupiter

(3 every bite, I put between them, and if ~~I my~~ my belly is ~~the~~ victor, ~~it~~ that ~~will not~~ cannot ~~then so~~ ∧even then be foiled, but follows the ~~crust~~ innocent food down ~~my throat~~ my throat and ~~is like~~ ∧~~makes it~~ ∧turns it to fire and lead within me?— What ∧angry [~~man?~~] snake ~~that hisses whistles softly~~ hisses at my ear, ~~as saying, deny your greed and this night your soul shall~~ O fool will you stuff your greed and starve your soul?

**[61]**

(And what is ∧it but my [*illegible*] soul that hisses like an angry snake, ~~O~~ Fool! will you stuff your greed and starve me?

**[62]**

The being I want to see you ~~develope~~ become

If ~~God himself~~ ∧If I walk with Jah in ∧Heaven and he assume to be intrinsically greater than I, it offends me, and I ~~will~~ ∧shall certainly withdraw ~~myself~~ from Heaven, — for the ~~great~~ soul ~~will~~ prefers freedom in the ~~lonesomest~~ prairie ~~to to~~ or the ~~woo~~ untrodden woods — and there can be no freedom where

**[63]**

~~Shall we never see a being~~ Why can we not see beings who by the ~~majesty~~ manliness and transparence of their natures, disarms ~~all criticism and~~ the ~~rest of the~~ entire world, and brings ~~them~~ one and all to his side, as friends and believers?— ~~W Are we never to~~ Can no father ~~and~~ [*illegible*] beget or mother conceive ~~I would see that~~ ∧a man ∧child so entire and so elastic ~~tha and so free from all discords~~, that whatever action he do or whatever syllable he ~~utt~~ speak, it shall be melodious to all ~~men~~ creatures, and none shall

**[64]**

be an exception to the universal ∧and affectionate Yes of the earth.

The first ~~effusions~~ inspiration of ∧real wisdom in [*illegible*] our souls lets us know that ~~all human beings~~ the ~~selfishness and malignity that appeared~~ self will and wickedness we thought so ~~vast~~ unsightly in our race ~~are~~ [~~makes?~~] are ~~but~~ as the freckles ∧and bristly beard of Jupiter — [*illegible*] ~~in to~~ to be removed by washes and razors, ~~from the~~ ~~if~~ under the judgment of genteel squirts, ~~and~~ but ∧in the sight of the great master, proportionate and essential and sublime.— ~~in the sight of the master — grand great master~~

**[65]**

~~not~~ ∧by no means what we were told, but something far different, ~~and better~~, — ~~These are~~ and ~~an essential part of the universe.— a p which cannot and must~~ not ~~ungrateful to~~ amiss to ~~the keen accomplished d any~~ t es ~~but~~ except to ∧the spirits of the feeble and ~~the shaved.—~~ the shorn.— ~~spirits taste. spirits.—~~

**[66]**

**[67]**

I will not descend among professors and capitalists ~~and good society —~~ I will turn ~~up~~ the ends of my trowsers ~~up~~ around my boots, and my cuffs back from my wrists and go ~~among~~ with ~~the rough~~ drivers and boatmen and men ~~who~~ that catch fish or ~~hoe corn,~~ work in the field, I know ~~that~~ they are sublime

**[68]**

**[69]**

**[70]**

I am the poet of slaves,
and of ^the masters of slaves
I am the poet of the body
And I am

I am the poet of the body
And I am the poet of the soul
~~The~~ I go with the slaves ^of the earth ^ equally with the ~~are mine, and~~
~~the~~ masters ~~are equally mine.~~
And I will stand between
the masters and the slaves,
~~And I~~ Entering into both, ~~and~~
so that both shall understand
me alike.

**[71]**

I am the poet of Strength
and Hope
~~Swiftly pass I~~
Where is the house of
any one dying?
Thither I speed and ~~raise~~
turn the knob of the door,
Let ~~Let~~ ~~And~~ The physician and the
priest ~~stand aside,~~ ^timidly withdraw,
^That I seize on the ~~despairer~~ ghastly man
and raise him with
resistless will;
O ~~ghastly man~~ despairer! ~~you~~
~~shall~~ I ~~say~~ ^tell you, you
shall not ~~die~~ go down,

Here is my ~~hand~~ arm, ~~sink~~
press your whole
weight upon me,

**[72]**

~~In my~~ ~~O Lo! with~~ With tremendous ~~will~~ breath,
I force him to dilate,
~~I will not~~
~~Doubt and fear~~
~~With Treading~~
~~Baffling doubt and~~
~~I will~~
~~Doubt shall not~~
Sleep! for I and they
stand guard
this night,
And when you rise
in the morning you
find ~~that I told the~~ what I told you is so.
<u>take [in?] X</u>
Not doubt not fear not
death ~~itself~~ shall ~~lay~~
~~fingers on [*illegible*] man~~ ~~him~~ I lay finger [on?] you ~~whomsoever~~ I
~~For I have [*illegible*] said the word and~~
~~And you are mine~~
And I [*illegible*] have him all
to myself
tr up X
Every room of ~~the~~ your house ~~will~~ do
I fill with armed men
Lovers of me, [*illegible*] bafflers of
hell,
~~Keeping back~~
~~And while~~
~~Th~~

**[73]**

I am the poet of reality
~~The~~ ∧~~know~~ I say the earth is [*illegible*] not ∧an echo;
~~Man is not~~ Nor man an apparition;
~~What we see is real;~~ But that all ~~I see~~ ∧[the things seen?] [all?] is real
~~And~~ It ~~is~~ The witness and
    albic dawn of ∧things equally real ~~wh[*illegible*]th~~
    ~~we~~ ∧ [*illegible*] ~~do~~ [*illegible*] not ∧yet seen
~~But which is~~ ~~I know to be~~ ~~equally~~
    real~~, I know.~~
~~I know you too, solid~~
    ~~earth~~ ~~hills~~ ground ~~and~~ and rocks,
~~I have been~~
¶ I ~~believe in~~ have split the earth
    and the hard coal and rocks
    and the solid bed of the sea
And ~~have sent my soul~~ And went down to
    to ~~take board~~ reconnoitre there
    a long time,
And [~~I?~~] ~~may~~ [*illegible*] bring ~~me~~ back
~~its~~ a report,

**[74]**

And ~~now~~ I ~~know~~ ∧understand that
~~it is what the~~
~~it is all~~ ∧those are positive and dense ∧every one
And that what ~~it~~ they seems to
the child ~~it is~~ they are
~~And that~~
~~For G God~~ [*illegible*] ~~does not joke~~
~~Nor is any thing~~ ~~man~~ ~~there~~ any
~~sham in the universe.~~
~~And the world is no joke,~~
~~Nor any th part of it a sham,~~

---

I am ~~the~~ for sinners and the
    unlearned

**[75]**

~~I am~~
I am the poet of little
things and of babes
~~I am I The~~ Of ~~the~~ each [~~ab?~~] gnats in the air,
and ~~the~~ ~~every~~ of beetles rolling ∧~~his~~ balls ∧of dung,
~~I built a nest in the~~ Afar in the sky ~~here~~
was a ~~sky~~ nest
And my soul ~~staid there~~ flew thither
~~to~~ [st?] ~~reconnoitre~~
and squat, and looked
~~long upon the universe~~ out,
And saw ~~millions~~ ∧the journeywork of of
suns and systems of
suns,
~~And has known since that~~
And ~~now I know~~ that
~~each~~ a leaf of grass
is not less than
they

**[76]**

And that the pismire
is ∧equally perfect, and all ~~the~~ ~~every~~
grains of sand, and
every egg of the wren.
~~And that~~
And the [~~knotty?~~] tree-toad is a chef'
douvre for the highest,
And the running-blackberry
~~mocks the ornaments of~~
would adorn the ~~house~~ parlors
of Heaven
And the cow crunching with
depressed neck surpasses

~~all statues~~ every statue,
* And ^ ~~a thousand~~ pictures [*illegible*] great

and small crowd the ~~the~~ [*illegible*] rail-fence, ~~with~~ and [*illegible*] hang on its
~~loose~~ heaped stones and ~~some~~
elder and poke-weed.
~~Is picture enough~~ *

**[77–84 *are cut away, again leaving slender strips of paper on which solitary letters and numbers are visible.*]**

**[85]**

Amount rec'd from Mr. V. A.

1847

I am the poet of Equality.

* And a mouse is miracle
enough to stagger ~~an infidel,~~
trillions of infidels.
And I cannot put my toe
anywhe to the ground,
But it ~~shall~~ must touch numberless
and curious books
Each one ~~above~~ scorning all that
~~science of~~ schools and
science ~~of the world~~
can do fully to ~~read~~ translate them.
on ☞ x

**[86]**

~~Buoyed with tremendous breath~~
~~shall you be, and dilated~~
I dilate you with tremendous
breath[;]

I buoy you up,
Every room of your house do
    I fill with armed men
Lovers of me, bafflers of hell,
Sleep! for I and they stand
    guard ~~all~~ this night
Not doubt, not fear, not
    Death shall lay finger
    upon you
~~God and~~ I have ‸embraced you, and
    henceforth possess you
    all to ~~our~~myselves,
And when you rise in the
    morning you shall find it
    is so.—

**[87]**

**[88]**
☞ X ~~And the odor~~ of the
    ~~salt marsh is~~ ‸delicious ~~perfume,~~
    ~~enough~~
And the salt marsh ‸and creek have
    ~~a~~ delicious odors,
And a potato and ears of
    maize make a fat
    breakfast, ~~when need~~
And ~~a handfull of~~ huckleberrys from the woods
    distill ~~an a a~~ joyous
    deliriums

---

God and I are [now here?]
Speak?! what would you
    have of us?

**[89]**

**[90]**

I am the Poet

**[91]**

~~Do~~ Have you supposed it beautiful
to be born?
I tell you ∧I know ~~it~~ it is ~~more~~ just as
beautiful to die;
For I take my death with the dying
And my birth with the new-born babes

**[92]**

I am the poet of sin,
For I do not believe in sin
¶ In the silence ~~of~~ and darkness
Among murderers and cannibals
        and traders in slaves
Stepped my ~~soul~~ spirit with
        light feet, and pried among
        ~~them~~ their heads and [~~drew in?~~] made fissures
        ~~in their breasts,~~ to look through
And there ~~like~~ [saw?] folded fœtuses of twins
~~And not in a single one~~
        there in every brain
        of the earth
~~saw truth and sympathy~~
        ~~lay folded,~~ like ∧the fœtus of twins in the womb,
Mute with bent necks, ∧ Waiting to be born.—
And one was sympathy and one was truth.

**[93]**

**[94]**

I am the poet of women as well
as men.
The woman is not ~~the same~~ less than the man as
But she is ~~not~~ never ~~less~~ the same,
I remember I stood one Sunday
forenoon,
(the Peasemaker)

**[95]**

Strength

Where is one abortive, mangy,
cold?
Starved of his masculine lustiness?
~~Weakened,~~ Without core
Loose in the knees, ~~without core?~~ and [*illegible*] ~~grit and~~
~~and grit~~?

Clutch fast to me, ~~my~~ my
ungrown brother,
~~And~~ That I ~~will~~ infuse you
with ^ grit and jets of ~~new~~ ~~grit~~ life
I ~~will~~ am not to be denied — I compel;

* I have stores plenty and
to spare —
And ^ of whatsoever I have I ~~share~~ bestow
~~fully with~~ upon you.
And first I bestow of my love,
* It ~~is~~ quite indifferent to me
who you ~~are~~ are.

**[96]**

It were easy to be rich
owning a dozen banks
But to be rich

---

It were easy to grant
offices and favors being
President
But to grand largess and
[favor?]

---

It were easy to be
beautiful with a fine
complexion and regular
featurs
But to beautiful

---

It were easy to ~~be~~
shine and attract attention
in grand clothes
But to outshine ?
in sixpenny muslin

**[97]**

One touch of a tug of
me has ~~made~~ unhaltered all
my ~~other~~ senses [~~run?~~]
but feeling
That pleases the rest so,
they have given up to it f ~~themselves~~
in submission
They are all emulous
to swap themselves
off for what it can do, to them,
¶ Every one ~~wants to~~ must be ~~feeling~~ a touch.—
Or ~~if that cannot be~~ else,
~~they~~ she will abdicate
and nibble only at
the edges of ~~a touch.~~ feeling.

They ~~bring gifts to the~~
~~come~~ move caressingly ~~all~~
~~over~~ ^up and down my body

**[98]**

~~They stand on [my?] each finger~~
~~end and promontory,~~
They ~~have left~~ leave themselves
and ~~brought all their~~ come with bribes
^~~their store~~ ~~to whatever~~ ^[their?] to whatever part of
me touches.—
~~Sometimes~~ To my lips, ~~and~~
~~and~~ to the palms of
my hands, and whatever
my hands hold.

Each brings the best she
has,
For each is ~~now~~ in love
with touch.
~~Each would be touc~~

**[99]**

~~Now~~ I do not wonder
~~a touch~~ ~~now why~~ that ^one feeling now, ~~or~~ does so
much for me, ~~now,~~
He is ~~recruited from~~ free of all
the rest.— and ~~improves~~
swiftly begets offspring of
them, better than the
dams.

A touch now ~~shows me~~
~~how~~ ^reads me a library of knowledge ~~delight~~
~~can be read~~ in an
instant.

~~It shows me how~~
It smells for me the
 fragrance of ~~roses~~ wine and lemon-blows,
It tastes for me ripe
 strawberries and
 melons.—

**[100]**
It talks for me with
 a tongue of its own,
It finds an ear wherever
 it ~~taps or~~ rests or taps,
It brings ~~all~~ the rest around it,
 and ~~to~~ enjoy [them?] ~~and them~~ awhile and [then?] ~~and~~ they ^[all?] stand on a
headland and
 mock me
~~I am all given up by~~
 ~~traitors,~~
~~An I am myself the greatest~~
 ~~traitor.~~
~~All~~ ^The sentries have deserted ~~and the~~ every
 other part of [*illegible*] [home?] ~~but one,~~

---

I roam about drunk, and
 stagger

---

They have left me to touch ^and ~~gone~~ taken to be
 their place on a headland
 ~~the better to witness~~
They have left me helpless
 to the torrent of touch
They have all come to the

**[101]**

I am given up by traitors,
I talk wildly I am surely out of my head,
I am myself the greatest
traitor.
~~For~~ I went myself first
to the headland

Unloose me touch ~~I can~~
~~stand it no longer~~ you are taking the breath from my throat
Unbar your gates — I
~~can hold~~ ~~would keep~~ you ~~no~~
~~longer, for if I do~~ you are too much for me.—
~~you will kill me~~
~~Pass out of me~~
~~Pass as you will~~
Gods! will
headland to witness and
assist against me.—

**[102]**

Fierce Wrestler! do you keep
your heaviest ~~strokes~~ grip for
the last?
~~Gods!~~ Wrestler! Will you sting
me most even at
parting?
Will you struggle even
at the threshold with
~~gigantic~~ ~~delicious~~ spasms
more delicious than all before?
~~Will you renew th~~[*illegible*]
~~and~~
Does it make you ache
so to leave me?

~~W. Even as you fade~~
~~and withdraw~~

Do you wish to show me
that even what you
did before was nothing
to what you can do?
Or have you and all the
rest combined to see
how much I can
undergo

**[103]**

Pass as you will;
take drops of my
life, ~~only go.~~
~~or is~~ if that is
what you are
after
Only pass to some one
else, for I can
contain you no longer.

I held more than I thought
I did not think I was big
enough for so much exstasy
Or that a touch could
take it all out of me.

**[104]**

I am a Curse:
Sharper than ~~wind~~ serpent's
eyes or wind of the
ice-fields!

O topple down ~~like~~ Curse!
topple more heavy than
death!
I am lurid with rage!

I invoke Revenge to assist
me.—
I

**[105]**
A ~~divine fa~~

Let fate pursue them
I do not know any horror
that is dreadful enough
for them —
What is the worst whip
you have

May the ~~genitals~~ — — that
begat them rot
May the womb that begat

**[106]**
I will not listen
I will not spare

They shall ‸not hide themselves
in their graves
I will pursue them thither
Out with them [~~from?~~] coffins —
Out with them from their
shrouds!
The lappets of God shall
not protect them

This shall be placed in the
library of the laws,
And they shall be placed in
the childs — doctors
— song-writers

**[107]**

~~The sepulcher~~
The sepulchre and the white
+ ~~Observing the shroud~~
linen have yielded me
up
Observing the summer grass

---

In vain ^were ~~the~~ nails driven through my
hands, ~~and my head my~~
~~head mocked with a~~
~~prickly~~
~~I am here after~~ I remember my
crucifixion and ~~my~~
bloody coronation
+/ ~~The~~ I remember the mockers and the buffeting insults
I am ~~just as~~ alive in
New York and San
Francisco, ~~after two thousand~~
~~years.~~
Again I tread the streets after
two thousand years.

**[108]**

~~Nothing~~
Not all the traditions can
put vitality in ~~ch~~
~~built~~ churches

They are not alive, they are
cold mortar and brick,
I can easily ~~can~~ build as good, and so can
you.—
~~The~~ Books are not men —
all the
~~they but~~

---

In other authors of the
first class
there have been celebraters
of ? low life and characters
— holding it up as curious
observers — but here is
one who enters in it
with love

**[109]**
I follow (animals and birds.)

Literature is full of perfumes

(criticism on Myself)
the ~~tow trowsers thee~~
~~lodge hut in the woods~~
~~the stillhunt~~

---

[*cut away*]

**[110]**
The highway
The road

---

It seems to say
sternly, ~~Back~~

Do not leave me
— Loss — — is [an?]
O road I am
not [*cut away*]

**[111]**

These are the thoughts of all
men in all ages and
lands —
They are not original with
me — they are mine
— they are yours just
the same
If these thoughts are not
for all they are
nothing
If they do not enclose
everything they are
nothing
If they are not the
school of all [the?]
physical moral
and mental they are
nothing

**[112]**

Test of a poem
How far it can elevate, enlarge, ^purify deepen, and make happy the ^attributes of the body and soul of a man

---

* the people of this state ~~shal~~ instead of being ruled by the old complex laws, and the involved machinery of all governments hitherto, shall be ruled mainly by individual character and conviction.— The recognized character of the citizen shall be so pervaded by the best qualities of law and power that law and power shall be superseded from the government and transferred to the citizen

[113]

Justice ~~does not depend upon~~ is not varied or tempered in the passage of ~~an~~ laws by legislatures.— ~~The~~ legislatures cannot ~~settle~~ alter it any more than they can ~~settle~~ love or pride.— or the attraction of gravity. The quality of justice is in the soul.— It is immutable .... it remains through all times and nations and administrations .... it does not depend on majorities ~~and~~ and minorities .... Whoever violates it ~~may shall fall~~ pays the penalty just as certainly as he who violates the attraction

[114]

of gravity .... whether a nation ^violates it or an individual, it makes no difference.

~~The test of justice is~~ The consciousness of ~~any~~ individuals is the test of justice.— What is mean or cruel for an individual is so for a nation.

---

I am not so anxious to give you the truth,

But I am very anxious to ~~see~~ have you understand that ^all truth and power are feeble to you except your own.— ~~You~~ Can I beget a child for you?

[115]

This is the common air ....
it is for the heroes
and sages .... it is for
the workingmen and
farmers .... it is for the
wicked just the same
as the righteous.
I will not have a single
person left out .... I
will ^have the prostitute and
the thief invited .... I
will make no difference
between them and the rest.

---

Let every thing be as free as possible.— There is always danger in constipation.— There is never danger in no constipation.— Let the schools and hospitals for the sick and idiots and the aged be perfectly free

**[116]**

No matter what stage of excellence and ~~pr~~ grandeur a nation has arrived to, it shall be but the start to further excellence and grandeur.— It shall enlarge the doors.— If it once settle down, placidly, content with what is, or with the past, it begins then to decay

---

There are many pleasant

Man has not art enough to make the truth ~~of~~ repulsive — [~~a~~?] nor of all the beautiful things of the universe is there any more beautiful than truth

**[117]**

In the earliest times (as we call them — though doubtless the term is wrong.) every thing written ~~all~~ at all was poetry.— To write ∧any how was a beautiful wonder.— Therefore history, laws, religion, war, ∧were all in the keeping of the poet.— He was literature.— It was nothing but poems. Though a division and subdivision of subjects has for many centuries been made since then, it still prevails very much

**[118]**

as in those early times, so called.— Every thing yet is made the subject of poetry — narratives, descriptions, jokes, sermons, recipes, &c &c

---

vast and tremendous is the scheme! It involves no less than constructing a ~~state~~ nation of nations — a ~~state whose integral~~ state whose grandeur and comprehensiveness of territory and people make the mightiest of the past almost insignificant — and

(back *

**[119]**

Could we imagine such a thing — let us suggest that before a manchild or womanchild was born it should be suggested that a human being could be born — imagine the world in its formation — the long rolling heaving cycles — can man appear here?— can the beautiful ~~animal~~ vegetable and animal life appear here?

**[120]**

Washington House
Central st. Lowell

---

or 13 ⎤ No 11 Massachusetts Corporation
or 25 ⎦ Jane & Rebecca Horton

---

John I. Storms
Big Creek P.O.
Shelby county Tenn.

**[121–130 *cut away, some isolated numerals and letters still visible.*]**

**[131]**

Chapman
147 Atlantic st.
bet Henry & Clinton

102 Reade st

Talbot
Wilson st.
between Lee & Division av.
two squares east of Bedford av

14 2 11

**[132 *back cover*]**

# *you know how*[5]
# [ca. 1855]

**[1, *cover*]**

**[2]**

**[3]**

~~As~~ ^you know how the one brain includes those ~~diverging and converging variety of~~ beautiful wonders the perceptions or senses, ~~and~~ — ^includes also ~~what we call mind, and~~ the subtle ~~faculties~~ ^processes of thought and reason and causality, ~~with~~ ^~~also~~ and an infinite variety else, so diverging and converging as to either ~~enfold~~ ^~~wind its fingers around~~ ~~the whole world~~ or ~~analyze~~ make much of the finest thread of silk~~;~~ — ~~in some sue~~ or wind its fingers round the world.—

**[4]**

Well the one ~~obligation~~ duty under which a man or woman ^is bound to himself or herself, is the enfolder ~~or~~ of ~~all else~~ every bit that follows.— ~~O All~~ That ^~~our duty~~ is the only ~~love and~~ ^independent, ~~life~~ living entire obligation.— ^As small pipes from the aqueduct main, The rest are ~~par beautiful~~ parts that flow out of it. If ~~as small pipes from the aqueduct main~~ ~~though~~ they come ~~from~~ not ~~from it~~ thence, are only so [*illegible*]

**[5]**

dead ~~and ghastly~~ arms ~~and~~ or legs, ghastly ~~p~~ perhaps galvanised into ^a little motion, but having no ~~connection with the~~ vitality ~~of~~ from the ~~lungs and~~ heart — ~~and taking no start thence.~~ ~~And these are what the world is calls its duties.~~

¶ You have ^for instance ~~heard~~ ^been warned through your ~~h~~ whole life, week days and Sundays, ~~of~~ ^to pay your ~~duty~~ devoir to God.— ~~I know of no such thing.— I know~~ ~~if it were the main matter,~~ as under the name of [~~pray?~~] ^Religion the original and main matter. Really there is no such thing.— What is called such, even accepting the most florid and

**[6]**

?

large description of it, is but one ~~little~~ item in the ~~illimitable~~ sum of that boundless ∧ account ~~budget of~~ which a man ~~must~~ should be ~~ready to pay~~ ∧ always balancing with his own soul~~d~~

~~I can be~~

~~I can be I know nothing more melancholy dismal and bleak~~ and ~~shrunken~~ ∧ ~~and shrivelled~~ ~~than~~

I have seen corpses ~~sunken an~~ shrunken and shrivelled — I have seen ∧ dismal mannikins of abortions, still-births ~~hideous~~ ?

**[7]**

~~and~~ so small ~~enough to~~ that the ~~he~~ ∧ doctors preserved ∧ them in bottles — But no corpse have I ~~t~~ seen — no minnied abortion — that ~~sem seems~~ appears to ∧ me more ~~more~~ shrunken, ~~away~~ from comparison to the fullest muscular health of some fine giant — ~~seems to me more~~ more inert and ~~shining and~~ blue and fit for the swiftest burial — ~~more pain painfully~~?

**[8]**

~~dead and in the way of~~ more awfully a corpse because a [~~some?~~] ~~its heir~~ a ~~beautiful~~ ∧ ~~strong and~~ perfect shaped and affection ate youth, in living strength and suppleness, stands ~~there~~ ready to take his ~~horse~~ room when the ~~bier~~ hearse carries the ~~coffin~~ defunct away — then ~~all~~ the whole and the best of what ~~has been called~~ ~~for three times a thousand years~~ over this great earth has been called, and is still called, Religion, seems to me in comparison

**[9]**

with the ???? devotion worship ∧ extatic as the ~~emb~~ closest embraces of the god that made ~~this globe~~ it ~~which was~~ stronger than the propulsion of this globe ~~in its~~∧ — fiercer than the fires of the sun around which it ~~t~~ eternally swings — more faithful than the faith that keeps it in ∧ its company and place — divergent and vast as the space that lies beyond — which belongs to ~~eve~~ any well developed man. ^loving ~~and [as?] gentle as the~~ in a sort worthy that immeasurable love ~~and gentleness of that that is~~ are the

**[10]**

~~spark~~

which is the great law whence spring the ^l~~a~~esser laws we call Nature's

---

Of the Poet.

From each word, as from a womb, spring ~~twenty~~ babes that shall grow ^to giants and beget ~~a larger and more~~ superber breeds upon the earth.

---

Consecration of priests in Trinity Church — interlinking of hands.

**[11]**

The life car — the ? to shoot the rope over the ship — the ? on which the life car runs — and the process of passing them ashore

He drinks up quickly All terms, all languages, and ~~words.~~ meanings.— To his curbless and bottomless powers, they ~~are as~~ be like ~~the small~~ ponds of rain water to the migrating herds of buffalo ~~when they spread over~~ ~~occupy square miles and~~ who make the earth ^[~~*illegible*~~] miles square. look like a creeping spread.— ~~Look~~ See! he has only passed this way, and they are drained dry.

**[12]**

You break your arm, and a good surgeon sets it ~~at~~ and cures you complete; but ~~nor~~ no cure ever [~~n~~?] avails for an organic disease of the heart.

**[13]**

Your mighty religious and political improvements — good enough as far as they go — are still but ~~Most of the reforms of the world are~~ partial reforms — a good ~~arm —~~ back — a well shaped foot — a fine head of hair — a a ~~good~~ nice ear for music — or a ^peculiar faculty for engineering.

I ~~would~~ give you the entire health, ^ both of ~~mind~~ spirit and flesh, the life of ^ grace and strength and action, from which ~~as from~~ all else flows, ~~as from an a never-failing spring.~~— ~~It~~ What I give you, I know, cannot be argued about, and will not attract men's enthusiasms and interests

**[14]**

* shall uncage in my breast a thousand ~~great armed~~ [*illegible*] ^ ~~winged broad~~-wide-winged strengths and unknown ardors and terrible extasies — putting me through the ~~paces~~ flights of all the passions — dilating me beyond time and ~~space~~ — air — — startling me with the overture ~~to~~of some unnamable horror — calmly sailing me all day on a ~~broad~~ bright river ^ with lazy slapping waves — — stabbing my heart with myriads of forked distractions more furious than hail or lightning — lulling me drowsily with honeyed ~~opium~~ morphine — ~~writhing~~ tight'ning the ~~coils~~ fakes of death about my throat, and awakening me again to know, by that comparison, the ~~only~~ most positive wonder in the world, and that's what we call life.

**[15]**

**[16]**

~~I want that untied tenor, clean and fresh as the Creation, whose vast pure volume floods my soul. I want that tenor~~ ^ ~~[large and fresh as the creation?] the [*illegible*]~~ ~~parting~~ ~~of whose~~ ^ ~~[dark?] and orbed~~ ~~mouth shall [*illegible*] for me~~ ^ ~~lift behind over my head~~ ~~the sluices of Paradise all~~ ^ ~~the delight~~ ~~in the universe. that is~~ I want that tenor, large and fresh as the creation, the ^ orbed parting of whose ~~orbed~~ mouth shall lift over my head the sluices [*illegible*] of all the delight ~~there is.~~ yet discovered for our race.— I want the soprano that ^ lithely overleaps the stars, and convulses me like the love-grip of her in whose arms I ~~lie~~lay [*illegible*] last night.— I want ~~a sublime~~ an infinite chorus and orchestrium, wide as the orbit of ~~the farthest~~ ~~stars~~ Uranus ? ~~reliable as immortality falling in truly~~ true as the hours of ^ the day, ~~and night,~~ and filling my capacit~~y~~ies to receive, as thoroughly as the sea fills its scooped out ~~valleys.~~ sands.— I want the chanted Hymn whose tremendous sentiment, *back

**[17]**

shall uncage in my heart a thousand new strengths, and unknown ardors and terrible extasies ~~put me through all the~~ my ~~paces and powers,~~ — making me enter intrinsically into all passions — dilating me beyond time and space — ~~soothing~~ ^ ~~lulling me away drawing~~ ~~with the sleep of honeyed ? —~~ calmly sailing me down and down ~~over~~ down the broad deep ~~sea~~ river.— — startling me with the overture ~~of~~ to some unnamable horror — ~~tearing~~ ~~wrenching~~ stabbing me with ~~the wild elks~~ ~~horses~~ ~~of~~ ^ myriads of forked distractions ~~that leap through my bossom~~ [*illegible*]s more furious than hail hail and lightning.— ~~that leap~~ lulling me drowsily with [*illegible*] honeyed opium morphine — ~~and uncaging~~ ~~waking in my heart all~~ ~~a thousand~~ ~~terrible~~ ~~new~~ ~~*strengths* and~~ ^ [~~sin?~~] ~~ardors and~~ ^ ter ~~extasies.—~~ writhing around me the ~~folds~~ coils of collapsing death, and awakening me again to know, by that comparison, the only positive wonder in the world, and that's what we call life.—

**[18]**

~~We~~ I want ~~the~~ a sublime ? of Hymn ~~out some vast~~ chorus and orchestrium, ~~whose strain is~~ wide as the ~~world,~~ orbit of suns, reliable ~~pure as Jesus and sweet as the kisses of Hea[ven?]~~ ^ [~~runs out~~ surpass?] immortality, and filling ^ all my capacity to receive as ^ [*illegible*] the sea fills scooped out valleys. (tr +I want the boundless tenor ~~that~~ ~~which~~ ~~swell~~ clean and fresh as the Creation — whose vast pure volume floods my soul. I want the soprano ~~that that thrills me like kisses of Heaven, that~~ that ^ over=leaps ~~unfaltering~~ [~~illeg~~] the stars.+

**[19]**

For this huge harmony have you nothing to give us but one feeble note, and that a false one?

The ox is too ~~d~~tired — he rests standing

The attraction of gravity is the law under which you make your house plumb but that's not what the law is specially made for

**[20]**

Acc't of the accident to Charly Phillips

**[21]**

**[22]**

do not ∧more than symbolize the reflection of the reflection, ~~from~~ of the spark ~~from~~ ~~of a~~ ~~some~~ thrown off a spark, from ~~a~~ some ~~coal in the some~~ [*illegible*] emanation ~~of some of those pettier attributes~~ of God.— which ~~we~~ out ~~the greatest~~ Even these the greatest of the [*illegible*] great men of the world, can in their ~~happier~~ ∧best moments

**[23]**

Love, Reality, and Immortality ~~and~~ are the triune reins wherewith the Driver of the universe

**[24]**

delicious as the kisses of God.—

All the ∧~~computation~~ vastness of Astronomy — and space — systems of suns+++ [*illegible*] carried [*illegible*] in to ∧their computation to the ~~very bound~~ farthest that figures ~~will~~ are able or that the broadest ? mathematical faculty can hold — and then multiplied in geometrical progression ten thousand million fold (back

**[25]**

~~even~~ Though to this reflection the dazzle of ~~unnumbered~~

All such vastness and reality does not satisfy ~~the soul~~ and shou[t?] worthy

**[26]**

The air which furnishes me the breath to speak is subtle and boundless — but what is it compared ~~th~~ to the things it serves me to speak — the meanings —

**[27]**

**[28]**

# *Autobiographical Data*[6]
# [ca. 1848–56]

[*]

Autobiographical Data

From the middle to the latter part of Oct. 1844 I was in New Mirror —
We lived at Vandykes 4th of July 1826
We lived in Adams st in Brooklyn, 1827
I was in Lawyer Clarkes office in 1830 —
We moved to Brooklyn in May 1823
Moved to Cranberry st 1824
Moved to Johnson st May 1st 1825
Moved to Tillary st (Martin's) 1st May 1827 — moved to own house Nov lived there till Nov 1831
We lived in Henry st the winter before the first cholera summer (1830–1831?)
I was at Clements printing office in the summer of 1831 —
I went to Spooner's in the fall of '32.
I was at Worthingtons in the summer of of '32
I was at Spooner's when father moved in the country in 33.
We lived at Norwich in 1834.
I went up to Hempstead from New York 1st of May 1836 — went to Norwich to teach school in June same year.
I kept the school west of Babylon the winter of 36–7
At Long Swamp the spring of '37
At Smithtown the fall and winter of 37 —
Went to Huntington the spring of 38 —
We moved to Dix Hills in May 1840
We moved from Hempstead to Babylon in 1836, August
I went from Huntington to Babylon in 1839 (Spring)

Came down to New York (after selling Nina) in the summer of 39
I went to Woodbury to teach school in the summer of 40
Fall and winter of 1842 boarded at Mrs. R. in Spring st.
Spring of 1843 boarded at Mrs. Bonnard's in John st.—
Also at Mrs. Edgarton's in Vesey.
Summer of '43 at Mary's and at Brown's in Duane st.
October 1843 commenced with the Winants'
Edited *Tattler* in summer of '42
Edited *Statesman* in Spring of '43
Edited *Democrat* in Summer of 44
Wrote for *Dem Review, American Review* and *Columbian Magazines* during 45 and 6 — as previously.
About the latter part of February '46, commenced editing the Brooklyn *Eagle* — continued till last of January '48.
Left Brooklyn for New Orleans, Feb. 11th '48

**[*]**

I am not glad to-night. Gloom has gathered round me like a mantle, tightly folded.
The oppression of my heart is not fitful and has no pangs; but a torpor like that of some stagnant pool.

2

Yet I know not why I should be sad.
Around me are my brother men, merry and jovial.
The laugh sounds out and the beautiful sound of the human voice a sound I love.
No dear one is in danger, and health shelter and food are vouchsafed me.

3

O, Nature! impartial, and perfect in imperfection!
Every precious gift to man is linked with a curse — and each pollution has some sparkle from heaven.
The mind, raised upward, then holds communion with angels and its reach overtops heaven; yet then it stays in the meshes of the world too and is stung by a hundred serpents every day.

4
Let fools affect humility in the strength of their conceit: this brain (?) feels and claims the divine life which moves restlessly (?)
Shall a clear star deny the brightness wherewith the Hidden has clothed it?

5
Thus it comes that I am not glad to night.—
I feel cramped here in these coarse walls of flesh.
The soul disdains its
O Mystery of Death, I pant for the time when I shall solve you!

[*]

Subjects for articles

Rapid and temporary mann[*illegible*] of American changes of popula[*illegible*] for eminent statesmen.— (inst[*illegible*] of Crawford) (reverse instance, Pi[*illegible*]

—

Answer the objection that de[m?]ocratic forms of gov. not energet[ic?] enough in cases of emergency. (Commonwealth of England — direct[*illegible*] of France.)

[*]
5

4

---

[*illegible*]
6
[*illegible*]
[41?]
[*illegible*]

---

164

[*]
[~~*illegible*~~]~~dling~~ persons
[*illegible*]grades
[*illegible*]onal
[*illegible*].— Why
[*illegible*] meanness
[*illegible*]a
[*illegible*]ity — to
[*illegible*] from an
[*illegible*] who
[*illegible*] and
[*illegible*] soil.

[*]
Give us turbulence, ^give us excitement, give us f the rage and disputes of hell, — any thing rather than this lethargy of death that spreads like a ^the vapor of decaying corpses over our land —

only great because it
involved a great principle

Why what was it — that little thing that made the rebellion of '76 — a little question of tea and writing paper

---

The next worst thing to having such enormous outrages put into laws and acquiesced in by the people without any alarm, is to have them practically carried out.— Nations sink by stages, first one, and then ~~th~~ another,

I come not here to flatter

[*]
Why confine the matter to that part of ~~the~~ it involved in the Scriptures?—

—

The influence of the
gallows fails

There is invariably this fact about superior natures; they understand each other, and ^with similar sight behold the ^soul, the universe, immortality, and ~~the fallacies of~~ all the aims and arts of men.—

---

1 * The constitution covenants that [*~~illegible~~*] the free states shall give up runaway servants — that we all know.— But by by the letter and spirit of its most important provisions, we hold the right to decide how to do it, who the runaway servants are, and to ~~settle~~ perform the whole ~~thing~~ obligation as we perform any other obligation by due process of law and without any violent ~~or unlawful~~ intrusion from abroad.—

**[*]**

"O, liberty," said Madame Roland, "what crimes hae been committed in thy name!"

"O, Bible!" say I, "what nonsense and folly have been supported in <u>thy</u> name!"

Calvin burned Servetus at Geneva and found his defence in the Bible.— Henry 8th Edward 6th and the bloody Mary offered up scores of victims, at the stake and gallows, for religious opinion, and found their defence in the Bible.— The Inquisition also and St. Bartholomew's horrid massacre ~~are~~ discover ample authority in the Bible.—

**[*]**

I know that ~~timidest~~ America is strong, and supple, and full of growth.— I know we are on good terms with the world, and on extra good terms with ourselves.— ^Treaties we make with Europe; steamships paddle ^the sea Gold comes from California, and trade is brisk, and the jobbers are busy nailing up goods, and sending them off to customers, and the railroads [~~go?~~] run loaded, and all goes ~~gay and~~ thriftily.— These things I do not expect to see ~~grow~~ less [*~~illegible~~*] ^of ~~n~~[*~~illegible~~*] but more, ~~for~~ and if any one suppoes I am at all alarmed about the prospects of business ^on this continent he misunderstands me, for I am not — ~~not~~ no I see its way clear for a hundred years.— But with all [~~this?~~] ^such decking ourselves [*~~illegible~~*] in the robes of safety and gain, there ^at the gate sits Mordecai the Jew and we know that

^terrible sign that either [*illegible*] we r[*illegible*]~~t h~~[*illegible*] are to have his life, or he is to hang the best part of us on the gallows high.—

What are all ~~your~~ these business prospects, ~~your~~ these steamships, ~~your~~ these fat sub-treasuries and ~~your~~ our profitable trade? [*illegible*] I do not want these want brave and large souled men, ~~wicked~~ men ~~if~~ not X

[*]

~~If this~~ ^Are these ^two or three drops ~~be~~ any ~~prophecy of~~ sample [~~held?~~] ~~any prophecy of the requirements of the g~~[*illegible*] of the storm that is cooking for us? If I thought it was, [men?] of

I should ^advise all live Americans to get on their killing clothes, for there would be a little butchering to be done

these would be no days of dalliance or of ease ~~and~~ or talk.— They would be days ~~of~~ for all live all Americans to get on their killing clothes

---

~~I was years ago present at~~ Years ago I formed one of a great crowd [*illegible*] that rapidly gathered where a building had fallen in and buried a man alive.— Down somewhere in those ruins the poor fellow [~~*illegible*~~] lurked, deprived of his liberty, ~~and either in in danger~~ perhaps dead or in danger of death.— How every body worked! how the shovels flew! — And all for black Caesar — for ~~black~~ the buried man wasn't any body else.—

[*]

Our country seems to be threatened with a sort of ossification of the spirit. Amid all the advanced grandeurs of these times beyond any other of which we know — amid the never enough praised spread of common education and common newspapers and books — amid the universal accessibility of riches and personal comforts — the wonderful inventions — the cheap swift travel bringing far nations together — amid all the extreme reforms and benevolent societies — the current that bears us is one broadly and deeply materialistic and infidel. It is the very worst kind of infidelity because it suspects not itself but proceeds complacently onward and abounds in churches and all the days of its life solves never the simple riddle why it has not a good time.— For I do not believe the people of these days are happy. The public countenance lacks its bloom of love and its freshness of faith.— For want of these, it is cadaverous as a corpse.

**[*]**
[*illegible*]eamble or
[*illegible*]prised in
[*illegible*] with it
[*illegible*] being, ~~the~~
[*illegible*]othing at all
[*illegible*]at the top.
[*illegible*] the rest
[*illegible*][leys?] and
[*illegible*][able in?] just
[*illegible*] the sound

**[*]**

Going among a large collection of blind persons — the wish that they could see and have all the blessings and knowledge thence — would it make your sight any less valuable to you?

---

As to the feeling of a man for a woman and a woman for a man, and all the vigor and beauty and muscular yearning — it is well to know that neither the possession of these feelings nor the easy talking and writing about them, and having them powerfully infused in poems is any discredit . . . . but rather a credit.— No woman can bear clean and vigorous children without them.— Most of what is called delicacy is filthy, or sick, and unworthy of a woman of live ∧rosy body and a clean ~~rosy~~ affectionate spirit.— At any rate all these things are necessary to the breeding of robust wholesome offspring.—

**[*]**
[*illegible*] Indian

---

[*]

In the cheerful performance of the task of presenting some reflections ~~about~~ on Temperance, ^and its advantages to all who practice it,

---

[*]

What can be a more admirable aim for the most exalted human ambition, than the wish and resolve to be perfect?— Though the carrying out of this resolve requires some mental purification, the most of it, I think is of a physical nature. How many faults have I! — How many weaknesses! — Ah, if the flesh could but act what my rational mind, in its moments of clear inspiration aspires to, how much better I should be! — Faint not, heart! — Advance stoutly and perseveringly!

---

I went to edit the Aurora in April 1842.

In Jamaica first time in the latter part of the summer of 1839. In the winter succeeding, I taught school ~~at~~ between Jamaica and Flushing — also in February and spring of '40 at Trimming Square.—

In summer of 40 I taught at Woodbury.

Was at Jamaica and through Queens co. electioneering in fall of 1840.—

[*]

By the article of Sidney Smith (1826) it appears that at that time certain high orders of criminals had not the privilege of being heard by their counsel in their trials — jury

"I have myself," says Mr Scarlett, the English Barrister "often seen persons I thought innocent convicted, and the guilty escape.

Sidney Smith
essays

"Folly, sanctioned by antiquity."
Sidney Smith

---

Winter of 1840, went to white stone, and was there till next spring.—

Went to New York in May 1841, and wrote for "Democratic Review," worked at printing business in New World" office boarded at Mrs. Chipmans —

— Went in April 1842 to edit[?] Aurora

Wrote for "sun," &c

J. W. died at Dix Hills Sept 8th 1845

**[*]**

There is a quality in some persons which ignores and fades away the around the hearts of all the people they meet.— To them they respond perhaps for the first time in their lives — now they have ease — now they take holiday — here is some one that they are not afraid of — they do not feel awe or respect or suspicion — they can be themselves — they can expose their secret failings and crimes.— Most people that come to them are formal or good or eminent — are repugnant to them — They close up their leaves then.

**[*]**

The Pretender," son of James II appeared in Scotland.— [his?] [*illegible*] no avail

1727 George II. (Sir R. Walpole [*illegible*])
[~~*illegible*~~] two successive reigns

1745 Charles Edward, the Young Pretender came to Scotland, advanced to Edinburgh, was proclaimed king there, Battle of Culloden blasted all his hopes — after which, for six months, he wandered in disguise from cave to cave, and at last escaped to France

Adm. Byng executed.—

1764 George III. (grandson of George II)

1768. Middlesex election. Wilkes' case. Wilkes was three times chosen, and refused by the house.—

1772. dismemberment of Poland between Germany, Prussia and Russia.

1778. Earl of Chatham died, being seized with illness in the house of lords while speaking.

1789 French Revolution (Bastile taken)

1790. Disruption of Burke, with Fox ~~and Sheridan~~ (Pitt, younger, minister)

[*]

1791 Another quarrel of Burke with Fox, as he had formerly quarrelled with Sheridan in the House.—

French Revolution. The king by his weakness extortion and tyrany had incensed the people the States' general had assembled — the commons wished one body made of the three orders, and assumed the title of national assembly — Paris was (1789.) environed by a royal army of 50,000. The popular minister, M. Necker was removed, and then the insurrection broke out, the Bastile was destroyed, the king (17th July) visited the hotel de Ville and surrendered himself to the people.— In June, 1791, the king attempted to escape from Paris.— He was caught and brought back National assembly completed a new constitution, which was accepted by the king in Sept. the same year.— The Nat. As. then dissolved, and a new one was chosen, to the exclusion of every member of the former.— (Duke of Brunswick's proclamation 2nd page.) Sept 21, 1792, new Convention met, and decreed the abolition of royalty, and the formation of a republic.— Since the deposition of the king, the prisons had been filled, with suspected persons; on the 2nd of Sept. they were found open, and a horrid massacre took place.— In Dec. 1792, the Convention tried the king, convicted him, and on the 21st of Jan. 1793 he was beheaded.—

[*]

Shakspere born in 1564 died in 1615

Sir W. Raleigh born in 1552 was beheaded in 1618, under James $1^{st}$

Francis Bacon, Lord Verulam, born in 1561, died in 1626.

Algernon Sidney born in 1617, died in 1683 on the Scaffold. [*illegible*] bold champion of liberty — was beheaded under Charles II.

Dryden, born 1631 died 1701

Tillotson, born 1630 died 1694 archbishop of Canterbury, writer of sermons.—

Sir Wm. Temple born 1629 died 1700

John Locke born 1632, died 1704

George Farquhar, Irish, born 1678, died in 1707. writer of comedies.—

Addison, born 1672 died 1719.

Congreve, Irish, born 1672 died 1729. comic writer

[*]
Sir Richard Steele, Irish, born died 1729. commenced "Tatler" in 1709 — followed by "Spectator" and "Guardian".— When George I came to the throne, he received the honor of knighthood.—

Swift, Irish, born 1667 died 1744 author of "Tale of a Tub," "Gullivers Travels."

Swift, Rabelais, and Voltaire, have been accounted the three greatest wits of modern times.

Pope, born 1688 died 1744. (Queen Anne)

Sir Robert Walpole, born 1676, died in 1745. (George I)

Isaac Watts, born 1674 died in 1748 (a dissenter)

St. John, Vicount Bolingbroke, born 1672, died 1751.— At George 1st, he withdrew to France, joined the "Pretender." — Impeached of high treason, was pardoned, and afterward returned to England. He married a niece of Madame de Maintainon

Camoens, a Portuguese, contempoaray of Tasso, Italian.— C's poem on the first discovery of East Indies by Vasco de Gama

[*]

Britain

Little known before time of the Romans.— About the beginning of Christian era — Had rude forces, infantry and horses — Cesar first visited the island.— Claudius was the emperor, under whom it was subjected. Caractacus sought to free his country, was taken prisoner and carried to Rome.— "Alas! he said how is it possible that a people possessed of such magnificence at home should envy me a humble cottage in Britain?" — Boadicea, a Briton queen, [*illegible*]d by the Romans, fought, led her own armies, was routed, committed suicide by poison.— Romans left, after being masters for 400 years.—

After Romans abdicated, the British were so annoyed by the Picts and Scots, that they invited the Saxons, to come [*illegible*] from Germany, and protect them.— They came under Hengist and Horsa, brothers.— Vortigern was their king.— Treachery of the Saxons.— Prince Arthur a native Briton took up arms against them.— Es-sex Sus-sex, ^Wes-sex &c. Saxon kingdoms.— About 400 years after the arrival of Saxons, they having founded different kingdoms, and, quarrelled — all were united under Egbert of Wessex, who was crowned king of England. At this time St Gregory, (Pope) (St George?) sent missionaries to convert them. (Saw some children for sale in the slave market at Rome)

Danes now invaded England, and committed great ravages. "Alfred the Great" fought against them.— Edward, Son of Alfred

[*]

Ethelstan, son of ~~Alfred~~Edward.— Edmund.— Edred. Edwy.— Edgar.— Edward II.— Ethelred II.— Edmund Ironside. (Danes, under Canute [*illegible*] invaded Eng.) Canute and Edmund, keeping the kingdom in constant war, the nobility obliged them to divide the empire.— Soon after Edward was murdered, and Canute thereby came into possession of the crown.— Harold, son of Canute.—

Hardicanute, another son — Danes deposed, and Edward the Confessor, ^a Saxon, king.— Harold, son of a nobleman.— His pretensions were opposed by William, Duke of Normandy.— The crown had been left William by Edward the Confessor.— Pope in favor of William. William entered England, fought

Harold, defeated him, and gained the crown. End of Saxon dynasty, after 600 years.

1066. William the Conqueror
1087 William Rufus, son "
1100 Henry I. (Beauclerk, son of Wm Conquer or
1135 Stephen (nephew of Henry)
1154 Henry II. (son of [*illegible*] [of their?] quarrel with Thomas a Becket Ireland conquered.) Fair Rosamund
1189 Richard I (Coeur de Lion son of Henry II) (Crusades)
1199 John (Magna Charta, at Runnimede)

## *women*[7]

## [ca. 1854–60]

**[1, *front cover*]**

**[2]**

[*illegible*]women ~~creat~~[~~*illegible*~~] [~~*illegible*~~] c[*illegible*] Yet Homer [sup?] [*illegible*] earth was [*illegible*] surrounded [*illegible*][its?] dist[*illegible*] [borders?] [*illegible*] [interspersed?] [*illegible*]ts.

---

Osirtasen 1740 B C
Joseph
Abraham 1970 B.C.
Oldest [monuments in Egypt?] [*illegible*]d [Wilkinson?] [*illegible*] world are the pyramids [of?] Memphis 2010 B. C. [*illegible*]

**[3]**

[*illegible*] [ho?] [*illegible*]
of Egypt [*illegible*] [*illegible*] is [*illegible*]

**[4]**

Memorials — if they were timid and receptive he ~~had~~ made his chisels cut the granite with ~~the~~ tokens ~~of~~ feminine. He is the first after Osiris.

**[5]**

Troy taken 1184 B.C.

[p. 78?]

Dr. Abbott tells me that [Lepsius?] told him of finding monuments [through?] Ethiopia with inscriptions and astronomical signs upon them. [*illegible*]

**[6]**

be sure ^of the district where the trouble is — they wait thus perfectly still and in splendid postures —

---

The ^children's dancing school at Dodworth's

**[7]**

The difference is only the [*illegible*] difference of an inch.— But it is the difference between cutting [~~off?~~] the rope ~~that holds us~~ we cling to 100 feet above the land.— whether we cut it an inch above or an inch below where our hands hold on for life

---

[*illegible*] # [people?]

**[8]**

M. Winel.

A prince in Polish Austria ^near Hungary on his estate on the highway, puts up a perpetual inn where all wayfarers are entertained free of charge; this he keeps always open, and gives meat and bread and lodgings — and sometimes comes to amuse himself with the guests.

**[9]**

I have been asked, Which is the greater, the man or the woman?— Yes, I tell you, with the same answer that I tell whether Time is greater than space — and wh[*illegible*]

**[10]**

The life of man on earth is the chef d'ouvre of all things.— What then! is it a suck?— Has God ~~tried~~ conceived a joke, and tried it on, and is it a small one?

**[11]**

Of the poet
He walks with perfect
    ease among a congress
    of kings,
And one king ~~saith~~ says
    to another, Here is
    our equal, ^ a prince whom
    we knew not before
Then the great authors
    take him for an author
And the great soldiers
    for a captain
The sailors know
    that he has followed
    the sea,
The English believe that
    comes of Saxon stock

**[12]**

And the Italians f[*illegible*]
The
O laugh when my eyes settle
    the land
        T
    The bluey spoon-drift, like
a white race-horse of
brine, speeds before me

**[13]**

~~such~~ such a thing as ownership here any how.— ~~The Chief B[*illegible*]~~ ~~[*illegible*]~~ ^ ~~was~~ is ~~the [primal democrat?]~~ ~~[*illegible*]~~ ~~[*illegible*]~~ ~~of his~~ one of the laws ^ [*illegible*] that ~~[*illegible*]~~ from the moment ~~any~~ a man takes the smallest page exclusively to himself and tries to keep it from the rest [f]rom that ~~[*illegible*]~~ moment it begins to wither ∧under his hand and ∧[~~lose~~?] its immortal hieroglyphics ∧presently fade away and become blank [*illegible*] ~~and dead.—~~

---

stonecutter's tools

tooth-chisel — jib for the thumb

**[14]**

Of writers there are plenty who pay all demands upon them, if folks are willing to take notes, or paper acceptances of any sort; but only one out [*illegible*] centuries who gives ready ∧solid cash.-

**[15]**

It is a terrible sign of the human soul that it will not own any limit, even the widest.— The moment we knew the diameter of the earth to be eight thousand miles, it became no great thing to us.— With all the appalling grandeur of astronomy, if we could fix the line beyond which there was no more material universe, our soul, I think, would pine away and begin its death sickness

**[16]**

Rameses the Great, over 30 centuries ago

Solomon born 1032 B.C.

" ascended throne, 1015

Pharaoh, from phre or phra the sun

Wilkinson

Moses born 1571 B.C.

Exodus of the Israelites from Egypt 1491 B.C. 430 years after the arrival of Abraham in Egypt.—

Homer about 907 B.C.

Rome founded 753 B.C.

**[17]**

☞ over leaf

~~The [*illegible*] Nature is an ethereal mirror deep deep and floating~~
The mirror that Nature holds ^ and hides behind is deep and floating and ethereal and faithful.—
in ~~[*illegible*]~~ it ^ a man ^ always sends and sees himself in it — from ~~it~~ himself he reflects ~~his~~ ^ the fashion of his gods and all his religions and politics and books and art and social and public institutions — ignorance or knowledge — kindness or cruelty — grossness or refinement — definitions or chaos — each [*illegible*] is unerringly sent back to him or her who curiously gazes.

**[18]**

There is a fullsized woman of calm and voluptuous beauty. . . . [*illegible*] the ~~unspeakbl~~ unspeakable charm of the face of the mother of many children is the charm of her face . . . . she is clean and sweet and simple with immortal health . . . she holds always before her [*illegible*] what has the quality of a mirror, and dwells serenely behind it.—

**[19]**

When ^ out of a feast I eat only corn ~~bread~~ and roast potatoes ~~fo~~ for my dinner, through my own voluntary choice it is very well ^ and I much content, but if some arrogant head of the table prevent me by force from touching any thing but corn and potatoes then is my anger roused.—

---

Every one that [*illegible*] speaks his word for slavery is himself the worst slave — the spirit of a freeman is not light enough in him to show that all the fatness of the earth were bitter to a bondaged [*illegible*] neck.—

**[20]**

In the respect of happiness or extasy, the beautiful gas ~~is~~ pervades the air continually, and we only need to be rightly tuned and conditioned, in order that it may catch to us ? ?(like gunpowder catches to fire) and ~~pass~~ ∧flow into us like one river into another.

———

The schooner is ~~reefing~~ hoisting her sail she will soon be down the coast.

———

river pirate old junk shop

———

**[21]**

I do not seek those that love me, I would rather seek ~~out~~ after some that hate me

———

The village on the highland, seen from afar at sunset — the sun sh[~~*illegible*~~] ining on the ∧red white ∧[~~*illegible*~~] or brown gables ∧red, white or brown

———

the ferry boat ∧ever plying ~~forever and~~ ever over the river

———

the schooner sleepily dropping down the tide the ~~little~~ small astern towed by the rope,

**[22]**

In the open market place the barrels of apples, the flour and meat, and f[*illegible*] ~~product~~ ? in bunks and [bins?].

———

The deckhand of the steamboat in his red shirt.

———

The hayboat and barge — ~~flee~~ the two boat ~~with~~ bring her bevy of barges down the river

———

the

**[23]**

picture of the [New York customs?]

---

passage in poem
middle aged?? ‸single woman ? seeing from day to day for many years a man whom she deeply loves — never flagging — and eventually dies.—

---

The test of the goodness or truth of any thing is the soul itself — whatever does good to the soul, soothes, refreshes, cheers, inspirits, consoles, &c.— that is so, easy enough — But doctrines, sermons, logic ? ?

**[24]**

Do you know what I well know
Do you it is to
be loved as you pass in
the street?
Do you know what it is to
Do you know what it is
to have men and women
crave the touch of
your hand and the
contact of you?

---

~~Th~~ not — — must be the poets I would have The poets I would have must be a power in the state, and an engrossing power in the state.

**[25]**

**[26]**

If you have sons ~~habit~~ custom them
to be drivers of horses
I knew six brothers drivers
of horses

Why should I do much

The capitol, the president,
the laws,
I [dem?]

There was never any more inception
than there is now
Nor any more youth or age
And will never be any more
perfection
Nor any more heaven or hell

**[27]**

The few who write the books and preach the sermons and ?keep? the schools — ~~I do not think ther~~ are they so much more than those who do not teach or preach, or write ~~All~~ This we call literature and science is not so very much — there is enough of unaccountable importance and beauty in every step we tread and every thought of [*illegible*]

---

Literature to these gentlemen is a parlor in which no person is to be welcomed unless he come attired in dress coat and observing the approved decorations[?] with the fashionable

**[28]**

Poem — illustrating (good moments)
soul in high glee all out (exquisite state of feeling of happiness —
some moments at the opera — in the woods —

---

Criticism

He leaps over or dives under for the time, all the reforms and propositions that worry these days and goes to the making of powerful men and women.— ~~These~~ With these he says, all reforms, all good, will come.— Without these all reforms all good, all outside effects, are useless and helpless.—

**[29]**

Poem

"Bridegroom"
? for recitation
(tremulous with joy
Mario's voice
quivering)
(bring in a Death

We want no reforms no institutions, no parties — We want a living principle as nature has, under which nothing can go wrong.

— This must be vital through the United States, fit for the largest cases and actions and the [widest?]

**[30]**

~~If the~~
Do you think I have written
all this for my own
good?
Well perhaps I have . . . .
but ~~it is~~ not in the
your ~~you think,~~ imagine,

---

No one can realize anything
unless he has it in him . . . .
or has been it
It must ^certainly tally with what is
in him . . . . otherwise it is
all blank to him.
The annals the past, light, space
— if I have them not in
me, I have them not at all
The future is in me as a seed
or nascent thought.

**[31]**

If the general has ~~not the~~
best a good
army in himself
he has ~~no~~ a good army . . . . otherwise he has ~~a poor~~ no army worth mentioning.
If you [~~poor?~~] — are rich in
yourself you are rich . . . .
otherwise you are ^wretchedly poor
If you are located in
yourself you are well
located . . . . ~~if not~~ [~~while?~~]
you can never be ~~are~~ [*illegible*] dislodged or
moved thence
If you ~~can be~~ are happy out
of yourself you ~~can~~
~~be~~ are happy . . . . ~~for~~ but I tell
you cannot be happy
~~through~~ by others any more
than you can beget
a child ~~through~~ by others
. . . . or conceive a child
~~through~~ by others.

**[32]**

I write not ~~the~~ hymns
I see ~~th[*illegible*]~~ the [building?] [of?] churches to
God . . . .
If I build a church it
shall be ~~the~~ a church
~~of~~ to men and women
If I write hymns they
shall be all to men
and women,
If I become a devotee
it shall be to men
and women.

**[33]**

[*illegible*] [shorty?]
Brownie
Deadbodies
Hamlet's Ghost
Letloose
Graball     Punch
4th of July
Christmas Johnny
Doughnuts
Poggy — Shortey
Pochuck
Bonehardener
Codmouth
Black Jack
Broadway Jack
Dressmaker
Harlem Charley
Blow[er?] B[e?]ll
[*illegible*]

**[34]**

Dry Dock John
Raggedy
Jack Smith's Monkey
Emigrant
Wild man of Borneo
Steamboat
Elephant
Buffalo
Santa Anna
Blind Sam
Rosy
Baltimore Charley
Long Boston

Short Boston
Mannieyunk
Pretty Ike
Jersey
Mountaineer

**[35]**

It is not a labor of clothing or putting on or describing — it is a labor of clearing away and ~~not~~ reducing — for every thing is beautiful in itself and perfect — and the office of the poet is to remove what stands in the way of our perceiving the beauty and perfection

---

My final aim

To concentrate around me the leaders of all reforms — transcendentalist spiritualists, free soilers

**[36]**

flawless truth and put it in the windows of your [brains?]

A Man at auction

How much for the man
He is of ? value
For him the earth lay
preparing billions of
years without one
animal or plant
For him the things of the
air, the earth and
the sea
He is not only himself
He is the father of
other men who
shall be fathers
in their turn

**[37]**

A woman at Auction

How much for the
woman?
For her all
She [~~can?~~] is not only herself
she is the bearer of
of other women, who
shall be mothers,
She is the bearer of
men who shall be
[*cut away*]

**[38]**

For him all sentiments
~~For him~~
In his appointed day
he becomes a
God
In his appointed time
he reaches his
exstasy
He is the one loved
He is the master

**[39]**

(verse in each
pictures illustrating
a European
Asiatic
African

---

American opera

when a song is sung the accompaniment to be by only one instrument or two instruments the rest silent

— the ^vocal performer to make far more of his song, or solo part, by by-play, attitudes, expressions, movements, &c. than is ~~usual~~ at all ~~in the~~ made by the Italian opera singers —

— The American opera to be far more simple, and give far more scope to the persons enacting the characters

**[40]**

fiercely and with screaming energy

This great earth that rolls
in the air, and the
sun and moon, and
men and women — do
you think nothing more
is to be made of
than storekeeping and
books and produce
and drygoods and
something to pay taxes on?

**[41]**

^Who are the Three old men going slowly with their arms about each others' necks

Who are

**[42]**

This great round globe with
its rolling circles — and
time — and perpetual
motions — and all the
moving animals — men
and women — the sea

and soil — the plants
— thc curious emanations

Have you in you the enthusiasm for the battles of [*illegible*] ~~Re~~ Bunker Hill and Long Island and Washington's retreat?— Have you the heroic feeling for — —

— Look forth then ~~fo~~ – [there?] is still occasion for courage and [devotion?]

— Nature is not so poor but there is always occasion for courage and determined power and [defiance?]

**[43]**

Always ~~A truly~~ ~~the~~ any great and original persons, teacher, inventor, ~~poet or~~ artist or poet, must himself make the taste and by which ^only he will be appreciated or even received.

---

<u>for oration</u>

~~shall~~ ^must we be unchecked, un unmastered.— What real Americans can be made out of slaves? What real Americans can be made out of the masters of slaves?

---

Then you can say ^as to Nature [these?] words — send us O Nature as [much?] as you like — Send us the children of the poor, the [ignorant?] and the depraped — We are ready for them — we can receive them — for them also we have preparation and welcome — We have not only welcome for the [healthy?] [*illegible*] [strong?]

**[44]**

(Poem
<u>Bridalnight.</u>

one a quivering jelly of love
limpid transparent
[~~*illegible*~~] Limitless jets of love, hot
and enormous
Arms of love [lar?] strong as

attraction reach as wide and large
as the air
Drunken and crazy
with love, [swiming?] in
it is in the plummetless sea

**[45]**

~~Body~~ Loveflesh
swelling and
deliciously ~~throbbing~~ aching

whiteblood[?] of love

---

in dream
The architect that comes
among the stonecutters
and the heaps of
cut stone
poem describes how the
workmen, possessed with
an indescribable faith,
go on age after age in
their work — and at last
came architects and
used each in its place
the stones they
had cut

**[46]**

poem of a road

---

The snowstorm ~~or~~ rainstorm bunkroom stringteam the counterfeit detector the directory the ~~census~~ returns, the Presidents m[en?] and the [Governors?]

[*inserted from following page*] message and the ~~mayor~~ message of the mayor and the message of the Chief of Police

the blows of the fightingmen
  — the uppercut and onetwo[three?]

The bugle calls in the ballroom — the ~~dancers~~ gentlemen ~~lead out~~ go for their partners — the playing begins — the dancers bow to each other.

---

**[47]**

The swimming-bath
the [stinggah?]

The dishes on the daily table — ~~the coffee~~ the roast meat — the oysters — the coffee and cornbread and rye and wheatbread,

---

The questions are such as these
Has his life shown the true
  American character?
And does it show the true American
  character?
Has he been easy and friendly with
  his workmen?— Has he been
  the stern master of slaves?
Has he been for making ignominious
  distinctions?— Has he
  respected the literary classes and
  looked on the ignorant classes with [*illegible*]

**[48]**

If there be ~~animal~~ some brute ~~that is~~ very
  sagacious and intelligent
And a being of our human race
  no more sagacious and intelligent
  than that animal — is one
  preferred to the other?

Equality of all [rights?] and persons is [imperiously?] demanded by selfpreservation.— The cause of the ruin of all states that have been ruined has been that the whole body of the inhabitants without exception were not equally interested in the preservation of those states or cities — or that [a?] portion was degraded

**[49]**

form of a poem or the composition in which the opinions are expressed by different wise men or youths, as 1st wise man, 1st youth 1st woman.— or as expressed by Socrates, Christ

---

The expression of a perfect ~~well~~made man appears not only in his face — but in his limbs — The motion of his hands and arms and all his joints — his walk — the carriage of his neck — and the flex of his waist and hips
Dress does not hide him. The

**[50]**

quality he has and the ~~clean~~ strong sweet supple [*illegible*] nature he has [*illegible*] strike through ~~his the~~ cotton and woolen.— To see him walk ~~is a spectacle or a~~ conveys the impression of ~~to~~ hearing a beautiful poem.— To see his back and the back of his neck and shoulderside is a spectacle. Great is the body! — There is something in the ~~close presence~~ touch of any candid ~~and~~ clean ~~human being~~ person ~~. . . .~~— what it is I do not know . . . . but it fills me with wonderful and exquisite sensations.— It is enough to be with him ~~or~~ — with her.—

**[51]**

describe the perfect male body — pancratist — perfect in all gynasia

---

Poem of the Wrestlers

---

My respiration and inspiration
    . . . . the beating of my heart . . . .
    the passing of blood and air
    through my lungs.

Though it have all the learning and art of the schools if it has not life it is nothing ~~If~~ When you read or hear if it does[?] not call the blood leaping and flowing — [of?] —

We do not fall in love with statues — we have healthy love for them

**[52]**

American Opera.— put three banjos, (or more?) in the orchestra — and let them accompany (at times exclusively,) the songs of the baritone or tenor —

---

Let a considerable part of the performance be instrumental — by the orchestra only.—

---

Let a few words go a great ways — the ~~wo~~plot not complicated but simple — Always one leading idea — as Friendship, Courage, Gratitude, Love, — always a distinct meaning —

---

The story and libretto as now are generally of no account.—

---

In the American Opera the story and libretto must be the body of the performance.

**[53]**

The fingers of the pianist playing lightly and rapidly over the keys.

---

illustration

a man placing his ear

To place the ear flat on the breast of the motionless body to see if it has any life in it's heart.

---

Poem

The land where — —

[*illegible*]

The land where

**[54]**

The poor despised —
Irish girls ^and boys immigrants just
over

---

A fierce protective sweep
around shielding them
I am the poet of the shallow and flat and desp[ised?]

---

Any one ~~can~~ [*illegible*] may know that
the great heroes and
poets are divine
But

---

The woodman that takes his axe
and jug with him shall
take me with him all
day,

**[55]**

Poem

What endures

modify

I have no mockings ? and laughter
I have only to be silent and

---

man and woman at auction

---

Here is
I see — Adam and Eve again
I see the old myths
— the

---

poem picture of war
— (the hospital at Sebastopol,)

then the opposite — the inferences and results — what war does to develope and strengthen and make more energetic and agile humanity — and what it contributes to poetry, oratory, &c.—

**[56]**

~~all that~~

he does not lose by comparison with the orange tree or magnolia or with ~~the~~ fields that nourish the sugarplant or the cottonplant . . . . ~~all that~~ what strengthens or clothes adorns or is luscious can be had ^through subtle counterparts from him — from him ~~the~~[*illegible*] magnolias and oranges and sugarplant and cottonplant and all fruits and flowers and all the sorts and productions of the earth.—

**[57]**

Poem — addressed to a young man who has come ^of age and is in possession of immense wealth.—

---

address on literature

— you must become a force in the state — and a real and great force — just as real and great as the president and congress — greater than they

**[58]**

I am an old artillerist

I tell of some

---

On South Fifth st (Monroe place) 2 doors above the river from Sixth street — going toward Greenpoint —

---

On Wilson st

---

Green, corner Fifth & Grand

**[59]**

**[60]**

blatherers

The ~~wealthy~~ affluent man is he who ~~answers all the~~ ^ confronts ~~wealth~~ ~~whatever~~ the grandest show sees [*illegible*] by ~~its~~an equivalent or more than equivalent [~~in?~~] from the ~~depths~~ ~~bottomless~~ grander ~~riches~~ wealth of himself.—

Insouciance
een soo se áwnz

---

or the mettlesome action of the blood horse

---

and the unimpeachableness of the sentiment of trees

---

~~haughty~~ [&?] jealous and haughty instinct

**[61]**

## *In his presence*[8]
## [ca. 1850–55]

**[1]**

**[2]**

**[3]**

In his presence all the ~~crowns and see~~ Presidents and governors and kings of the world bend their heads —

All wealth and vaunted honor —

His eminence ~~makes~~ makes that all rank however vaunted

When he appears, Presidents and Governors descend into the crowd, ~~for H alone is has eminence; and in its company,~~ capitalists and bankers are cheap with all their golden eagles.— The learnedest professors,

**[4]**

and the ~~makers~~ authors of the ~~best~~ ^ most renowned books, ~~are~~ ~~becom~~ are baffled of their art, ~~and~~ having come to ~~the flowering~~ ~~sweetness blooming~~ of a great ~~fact~~ ^ fact embodying flower and fruit in nature, where ~~they and~~ the ~~bes~~ best of ~~them~~ themselves are but the ~~first twittering~~ ? sprouts, groping ^ feebly ~~out of~~ from the February ground.—

having come to a great fact in the orchard of nature covered with ~~perfec~~ flowers and fruit, where the best of themselves is but a feebly pushing through the February ground.—

**[5]**

The rights of property! Why what ^ build ~~foundation~~ substance is there ~~for the~~

[in any other] right of property than that which is built on the primal right — the first-born, deepest broadest right — the right ∧[of every human being] to his personal self.—

Every man who claims or takes the power to own another man as his property, stabs me in ~~that~~ the heart of my own rights — for

**[6]**

they ∧[only] grow of that first vast principle, as a tree grows from the seed

Why do we arrest and a thief of property.— Mainly because in stealing from another man he jeopardizes the principle by why you and I and all others hold our own?

**[7]**

The one scratches me a little on the ~~cheek~~ [forehead], the other draws his murderous razor through my heart

The one maugre all the snivellings of the [fash?] leaves the man as he found him solid and real as a — the other

**[8]**

If every man and woman ~~upon this which~~ [riding in] this ∧[huge ruined[?] car] ~~huge vehicle~~ that ~~wheels~~ [whirls] us through the universe, be not ~~interested in~~ touched to the vitals, by the ~~discussion~~ [question] whether another of the passengers~~, can [can?] safely~~ [shall] be made a slave, tell me O learned lawyer or professor — tell me what are they interested in?— What does touch them?— What comes home to a man, if ∧[the principle] the right to himself does not?— Is there in the wide world any ~~principle~~ [thing], that so evenly and so universally bears upon ∧[every individual of] our race, in all ages, in

**[9]**

tongues and colors and climates, and conditions,— Is there any thing that ∧[it stands us in hand —] all of us without one single exception, ~~are so~~ to keep the the rats and the ~~wolves~~ [moths] so carefully away from, as this — the warrantee deed, the original charter of the very feet ~~we stand on?~~ [that bear us up]

---

A good saying in the street

Only something from a gentleman ~~w~~$^{c}$ould insult me; and a gentleman never ~~can~~ would insult me.

**[10]**

☞ ~~Common~~ Good naturedly treat every thing — every sect — every dogma — every nation — ~~pen~~ refer to the heart of what goodness there is in them —

**[11]**

**[12]**

The difference is between the laws of a ^ just and equitable republic and the laws, even though be the same, that come from an irresponsible tyrant.—

**[13]**

I have heard of people who suggest as a choker upon (the right ? of freedom that all men are more or less slaves — some to gain, some to fashion, others to priests and superstition.— The hard-working mechanic, they say, is

**[14]**

**[15]**

I know there are strong and solid arguments against slavery — lawyer — practical man — arguments addressed to the great American thought Will it pay?— &c &c &c &c

~~These~~ Discourses ~~upon~~ in this channel entertain and instruct us well

— — —

But all these must be now left aside.— We will ascend to ~~that~~ tribunal of last resort — we will not waste words with messengers and secretarys.— We will ~~go directly~~ stand face to face with the

**[16]**

chief of the supreme bench. We will speak with the soul.—

The learned think the unlearned an inferior race.— The merchant thinks his bookkeepers and clerks sundry degrees below him; they in turn think the porter and carmen common; and they the laborer that brings in coal, and the stevedores that haul the great burdens with them?

**[17]**

But this is an inferior race.— Well who shall be the judge ~~who is the~~ of inferior and superior races.— The class of dainty gentlemen think that all servants and laboring people are inferior.— ∧In all lands, The select few who live and dress richly, ~~always~~ make a mean estimate of the body of the people.—

---

If it it be ~~right~~ justifiable to take away liberty for inferiority — then it is just to take money or goods, to commit rapes,

**[18]**

to seize on any thing you will, for the same reason.— ~~Would~~ Is it ~~be~~ enough answer to the crime of stealing a watch, that you stole it from an ignorant nigger, who dont know the odds between an adverb and three times twelve?— If you spend your violent lust on a woman, by terror and violence, ~~is~~ will it ~~balance accounts~~ receipt the bill when ~~who~~ you endorse it, nothing but a mulatto wench?—

**[19]**

But ~~free~~ as great as any worldly wealth to a man, — or ~~her~~ womanhood to a woman, — greater than these, I think, is ∧the right of liberty, to any and to all men and women.—

It is as logical to take the life or property of some poor fellow for his inferiority or color, as it is to take his personal liberty.—

**[20]**

Beware the flukes of the whale. ∧He is slow and sleepy — but when he moves, his lightest touch is death.— — ~~I think he already feels the lance, for he moves a little restlessly. You are great sportsmen, no doubt What!~~ That ~~black and~~ huge lethargic mass, my sportsmen, dull and sleepy as it seems, ~~has~~ holds the lightning and the taps ~~bolts~~ of thunder.— He is slow — O, long and long and slow and slow — but when he does move, his lightest touch is death.

**[21]**

The flukes of a whale they are as quick as light

---

The Poet

~~His~~ He has a charm that makes ∧fluid ~~the heart of~~ every thing in the universe however distant or however dense, and ~~when made~~ so he ~~breath~~ inhales it as a breath, and it is ∧all good air and arterializes vitalizes ? the blood ~~within~~ that goes squirting through his heart.—

**[22]**

The poet, having not a dime, has the good of all things. And men, indeed, only have the good of any thing, in proportion as they ~~enjoy~~ approach ~~the n~~ his nature

The mere rich man, whose draught on the bank ~~for~~ is good for scores of thousands, may be, indeed generally must be, a ∧blind and naked beggar in ~~the~~ the only real riches. ~~of~~

**[23]**

All the riches ? evoked into the world by ~~all the~~ inventors, by the industrious, and by the keen, ~~are~~ become bubbles when the true poet scatters the utterance of his soul upon the world.— To have the crops fail — to forego all the flour and pork of the western states — ∧to burn the navy, or ~~half the~~ a populous town were less to lose, than one of his great sayings to lose.—

[24]

Each word is sweet medicine to the soul.—
He sheds light upon the
sun,
~~He~~ On The darkest night he sheds an infinite darkness.

You can, to the poet, bring nothing which is not a curious miracle to him.—

[25]

Change all this to commendation

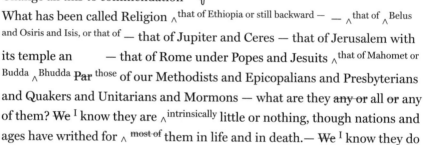

What has been called Religion ^that of Ethiopia or still backward — — ^that of ^Belus and Osiris and Isis, or that of — that of Jupiter and Ceres — that of Jerusalem with its temple an — that of Rome under Popes and Jesuits ^that of Mahomet or Budda ^Bhudda ~~Par~~ those of our Methodists and Epicopalians and Presbyterians and Quakers and Unitarians and Mormons — what are they ~~any or~~ all ~~or~~ any of them? ~~We~~ I know they are ^intrinsically little or nothing, though nations and ages have writhed for ^ ~~most of~~ them in life and in death.— ~~We~~ I know they do not satisfy the appetite of

[26]

the soul, with all their churches and their libraries and their priesthood.— Nevertheless let us treat them with decent forbearance. Mean as they are when we have ascended beyond them, and look back, they were ^doubtless the roads for their times~~;~~.— ~~and~~ Let us not ~~despise~~ too quickly despise them;— for they have ~~brought~~ sufficed to bring us where we are.—

Like scaffolding which is a blur and nuisance when the house is well up — yet the house could not be achieved without the scaffold.—

[27]

[28]

# *The regular old followers*[9]
[ca. 1853–55]

**[1, *cover*]**

**[2]**

**[3]**

---

The regular old followers of the law and traditions as plainly first expounded among the Mahometans are called Loonees

---

**[4]**

[*cut away*]∧[*illegible*] wonders

**[5]**

What is it to own any thing?— It is to incorporate it into yourself, as the primal god swallowed the ~~twelve~~ five immortal offspring of ~~Gaea~~ Rhea, and ~~added~~ accumulated to his life and ~~stren~~ knowledge and strength all that would have grown in them.—

**[6]**

* if he merely have all the care and ~~lifting~~ hauling and ~~hoisting~~ lowering and hoisting of them, and so goes on for a lifetime, and they never serve ~~to~~ his sinews and blood and senses ∧for food or for warmth.— The more of these he has, the more books to keep, the more he ~~must~~ stays indoors, the more he demeans and wilts ~~himself~~ and shins it, and deforms himself into the crooked. Will it pay?—

Just as much as the care-taker of beef and apples ~~who never eats thereof~~ and coal which never warm him nor enrich

**[7]**

into the soul and is the[?] strength and life and knowledge they evoke there.—

I will not envy a man who possesses [~~a?~~] sides of beef and barrels of apples or cubic rods of good coal *

**[8]**

**[9]**

him

**[10]**

Faith.— Becalmed at sea, a man refreshes himself by swimming round the ship.— A ~~little child seeing him~~ deaf and dumb boy is looking over ~~the~~ his younger brother and the swimmer, ~~lazily~~ floating lazily on his back, smiles and beckons with his head ~~for the babe to come.—~~

Without [*illegible*] waiting a moment the young child, laughing and clucking springs into the

**[11]**

Death Song

Joy Joy! O full of Joy

---

~~On the sea-shore~~ Away becalmed at sea one day
I saw a babe, laughing kicking, &c &c
And as a swimmer ~~passed~~ floated ~~idly~~ in the waves, he called the child.—
Laughing it sprang, and there

**[12]**

Black Bob and the young girl

When the ~~passengers~~ ship strikes, who thinks of a gold watch or earrings?—

---

When the San Francisco was wrecked, the most valuable jewelry lay about the cabin unnoticed on the floor

---

**[13]**

sea, and as he rises to the surface feels no fear but laughs and though he sink and drown he feels it not for the man is with him there

**[14]**

~~The Death~~, Disaster, and temptation, are the examiners ~~and measurers~~ of ^a man.— They take his weight and density; and thenceforward he can be labeled or stamped at so much value.

Agitation is the test of the goodness and solidness of all politics and laws and institutions [*illegible*] and religions.— If they cannot stand it, there is no ~~life~~ genuine life in them, and shall die.

**[15]**

Where others see ~~some~~ a ~~dolt, a clown, in rags~~ ^slave a pariah an emptier of privies.... the Poet beholds what ~~shall one day~~ be, when the days of the soul are accomplished ^shall be ~~be a mate for the greatest gods~~ ~~the~~ peer of god.

Where others are scornfully silent at some ~~one~~ steerage passenger from a foreign land, or black ^~~or emptier of privies~~ the poet says, "~~Good day,~~ My brother! good day!"

And to the great king "How are you friend?"

**[16]**

~~Hav~~ You have timidly waded close to the shore, ~~wading~~ holding a board

Come with me, ~~I~~ [~~and?~~] that I ~~learn~~ teach you that you be a bold swimmer, and leap from the          into the ~~open~~ ^[~~plain sou?~~] unsounded sea, and come up, and ~~laugh~~ shout, and laughingly shake the water from your hair.—

---

The poet is a recruiter
He goes forth beating the drum.— O, who will not join his troop?

**[17]**

**[18]**

**[19]**

The boat starts out from her slip, and finds a vast cake of ice reaching from one shore to the other. Five times she drives into it, and five times recoils and has to put back.— The sixth time she plunges ~~far~~ desperately on, the ice opens a crack as she advances, and so makes a chance for her just the very way she most wants to go.—

**[20]**

When a grand and melodious thought is ~~taken~~ told to men for the first time, ~~in~~ ∧down and within their hearts ∧~~they~~ each one says ~~in it down and within~~, That music! those large and exquisite passages! where have I heard them before?

**[21]**

**[22]**

a noble soul ~~shows~~ ~~off~~ often illustrates itself in what the world rates as trivial; the grandeur and beauty of the spirit making the commonest action more luminous than the sun.— I knew of a ~~poor~~ woman, in a little farm house in the country, who took a pair of ∧her home-knit stockings and exchanged them at the store for tea.— Coming home she stopped at her nearest neighbor's gate, and called to her that she had ~~tea,~~ ∧something good; and the neighbor ~~X~~ must fetch out a cup and go

**[23]**

~~half~~ halves; for both loved tea, ~~and had no money,~~ and were without for a some days, and had no money.—

**[24]**

Front windows on first floor,— lights 13 × 17 — Window five lights high — A sash of two lights across top — The other eight lights made in two door-sides, hung each with hinges

## *I know a rich capitalist*[10]
## [ca. 1854–60]

**[1, *cover*]**

**[2]**

**[3]**

I know a rich capitalist who, out of his wealth, built a ^marble church, the most splendid in the city; and when it was opened, he stood at the door, the first Sunday, and helped the sexton show people to seats.— He was the meanest looking person in the place, and proud ~~at~~ of his building and wealth.

**[4]**

The Elementary Laws do not get excited and run and bawl to vindicate themselves.— ~~Priests and~~ The doctors might all deny the attraction of gravity, and that sublime ~~law~~ power would never complain.— Be ~~thou~~ you like the grand powers.—

---

Exist.— ~~The Soul is larger than the~~ Do not trouble yourself to ~~set~~ soothe ~~satisfy~~ ~~soothe~~ sputterers and ~~babb~~ infidels ?.— (Manure ~~thy soul,~~ the fields of the heart, for it brings great crops.—) ~~As~~ Sure as the

**[5]**

most certain sure — ~~as~~ reliable as Immortality — ~~you~~ the effects ~~come when~~ appear after the causes ~~appear.~~ are born.

---

I see on the Egyptian head-rests the most hideous forms and combinations of groups as if they intended to scare away [unrest?]

[6]

[7]

The genuine Man is not, as would have him, like one of a block of city houses, that can't stand except as it is upheld in the midst of the rest

---

Greater than ~~b~~ wires of iron or treaties, or even strong mutual interests is ~~the~~ Sympathy.— When

Creighton ∧[~~re?~~]hove ~~too~~ to for many days and nights and rescued the wrecked thousand on the San Francisco

[8]

If a man spatter mud on his new clothes, by lifting a child or an old woman over the ~~gutter~~ slush let him nevertheless be content.— Mud like that strikes in and makes beauty spots

[9]

Pride of Birth.—

There is nothing in * nothing royal blood, or the ~~succession~~ inheritance through a direct line of the ∧name of the most ∧[~~*illegible*~~] historical heroes, or ~~in any~~ ∧tr * (the eminency of any office of President or Governor or Mayor,) ~~that begins to but~~ [*illegible*] that should make us carry our heads so high, ~~as~~ and so fill us with ~~more than imperial pride,~~ bulging pride ~~than ever spread itself in capitols, or courts,~~ as the consciousness that we are ~~hum~~ human souls.— Office, however ~~high,~~ exalted and wealth, however capacious, ~~∧may but~~ often show ~~many~~ a mean and starved nature

[10]

~~for their [domos?]; as the~~

The best of such distinctions abstractly amounts to little.— Toiled for, suffered for, lived for, as they are by the ~~vast~~ majority of men, their ∧only real charm is that they ~~but faintly~~ symbolize ∧afar off the unspeakable haughtiness and nob~~ility~~leness which~~, are grace~~ the ~~soul~~ personality of ~~every~~ man carries well, if he ~~but~~ once take the hint of his ∧own ~~inalienable~~ birthright.

[11]

Love is the cause of causes.— ~~W~~ Out of the first Nothing ~~and~~ — out of the ∧black fogs ~~of primeval~~ of the nostrils ~~Or originalVacuity,~~ of Death ~~that~~ which ~~vast and sluggish~~ ∧hung ebbless and floodless in the spread of space — it asked ∧of God with undeniable will, something to satisfy ∧itself [*illegible*] ~~itself.—~~ ~~immortal longings.—~~ ~~From its~~ By it then Chaos was staid with.— ~~Like A family~~ Like a brood of beautiful children came from them ∧~~whom we call~~ the Laws of Nature.—

[12]

Yes he is like a small boy who raises a big kite, and it pulls entirely too hard for him.— He had better let it go ere it carry him entirely ~~out~~ up in the air and out of sight

---

A coffin swimming buoyantly on the swift flowing current of the river

[13]

Yes I believe in the Trinity, — God Reality — God Beneficence or Love — and God Imortality or Growth.

---

He dives in the water for a ~~dead~~ drowned man and sees the body ~~and~~ with open staring eyes and the hair floating out and up from his head

[14]

Love is the cause of causes,
Out of the vast, first Nothing
The ebbless and floodless vapor
    from the nostrils of Death,
It asked of God with unde
    -niable will,
Something to satisfy itself.—
By it then Chaos was staid with
And duly came from them
    a brood of beautiful children
Whom we call the laws of nature

**[15]**

There are two ~~attributes~~ ? of the soul, and both are illimitable, and they are its north latitude and its south latitude.— One of these is Love.— The other is Dilation or Pride There is nothing so in-conceivable haughty as the The style of the most magnificent heroes or rulers is

**[16]**

? Nature is always plumb +

Loyalty of some flatterer of royalty who (latter) is brought to the scaffold

**[17]**

~~The reason that~~ Who do ~~the~~ we ~~turn f~~ look back, as century after century adds to the length of the road between us, — why do we ∧always turn with [~~living?~~] pleasure and curiosity to the sayings and doings ∧thirty centuries ago of wandering Jewish tribes, of little Greek communities, of half savage Rome, and of Ethiopia and Persia? There is something in those sayings and doings that effuses directly from the soul — Raw and bungling as they send it out, — they do not ~~give it f~~[*illegible*] send it out at second hand, but fresh and alive.—

**[18]**

* This Poetry, or aliment of the soul, we must have.— It is clamored for with the most irresistible longing.— Accordingly it is everywhere and ~~upon~~ each ~~objec~~ and all that our senses can

Children and simple people often ~~touch the~~ [*illegible*] ~~tune~~ make speeches that illustrate ~~this relation with~~ some of these relations, better

**[19]**

∧Much the largest portion of what rides jauntily through the ~~world~~ literary ~~world~~ avenues as poetry, and keeps the saddle for scores, perhaps fifties of years, is awkward and ~~ill-bouncing~~ [~~badly?~~] ill paced enough;—

~~Jingling~~ such as Love-~~songs~~ shambles, in long metre or short, ~~some very~~ some of them ardent, ~~and~~ but most of them very dismal and spavined, ~~; make up~~ — both styles ~~having~~ always ~~been ready and numerous~~ on the road;— and

**[20]**

* What stuff passes for poetry in the world

What awkward and ill-bouncing riders

---

What is printed in books or what not, and has rhymes attached to its tails, is but a very small portion of the poetry of

---

case of the driver who came in looking as natural as life, but was frozen dead and hard

**[21]**

A lawyer who had put off his case once, came in court and asked further delay, ~~in a tearf~~ with tears in his eyes stating the death of his mother. The Judge was just granting his request, with great commiseration, when an old lady from the gallery cries out "O _____ my son! how often have I whipped you for lying."

**[22]**

pork and pound cake ~~and things~~ and ~~things~~ ∧products that can be [stewed?] or ∧[worn?] put in the bank.— All ~~expr~~ that makes clear this relation, and ~~tracks~~ defines the road ~~between~~ between ~~any thing~~ conceivable objects and the human spirit, ∧and explains what those objects meaning, is poetry, coarse or fine.— Even if ∧the explanation be two or three removes off, ~~or~~ as most are, or ~~done at second and third hand,~~ ~~removes~~ ~~and~~ distantly suggested, ~~we are thankful;~~ folks take them and relish them well; for we are greedy of this sort of ~~feeding~~ diet, and ~~exceedingly voracious,~~ never get ~~weary~~ tired of stuffing *

**[23]**

pork

Friends.—

* I discover that among people whose company is pleasant to me, I almost invariably grow fonder and fonder of those ~~who without any~~ who ~~evidently~~ constantly like me ^and are not afraid to show it ~~steadily,~~ who and ~~are~~ good natured, ~~and~~ have no notably offensive ways,.~~, and don't blow hot and cold~~ (They may be ~~plain~~ ugly in the face; simple or slack in mind; and of common ~~po~~ employment.—) * tr

**[24]**

~~Pile up your~~

You shall go in some rich man's house, where the long suite of parlors ~~have~~ has been attacked and taken possession of by artists, ornamenters, makers of carpeting, marble mantels, curtains, ~~good~~ soft seats, ^and morocco binding for books.— ~~and marble mantels~~ What can be unbought; for the place yet ^looks very beggarly. The ~~worthy~~ gentleman who ~~has~~ footed the bills, ~~for all these,~~ has surely ~~omitted~~ forgotten something.— We remember that ~~hour~~ ~~^moment~~ first of April at the post office, when the young man in the linen jacket ^blotched with ink handed ~~us out of~~ through the window a

**[25]**

very rare envelope, promising great things, ~~when~~ and~~,~~ we found nothing at all inside but a piece of blank paper.—

---

* It is this which is the source of all Poetry; for there is ^in ~~all~~ men an instinct of the truth. ~~in all men There is a file~~ We have a saw-toothed appetite ~~^with~~ which restlessly hankers for ~~some satisfactory~~ food out of this immense and varied earth, ~~beyond men something~~ more ^satisfactory than

**[26]**

where the Congress meets is the sacred ? place.— If they adjourn from there to some log house or shed of hemlock boards

~~Ever~~ ^ The ~~heart~~ ^ kernel of every object thing ~~that~~ can be seen or ^ felt or thought of has its relation to the soul, and is significant of something there.— ~~This is the~~ He who can ~~put~~ tear off all husks and skins ~~aside and~~ and ~~[peel?] the~~ pierce ~~or~~ ^ straight through every stratagems of concealment, ~~and goes to the actual~~

*

**[27, *back cover, inside*]**

## *9th av.*[11]
## [ca. 1854–60]

[1]

$9^{th}$ av. cor 24th s
Dan Van Valkenb

---

Lot on Lawton st. near
Division av

W. McCormick
105 Byard st.
S. Wallin
8 LeRoy Place
Bleeker St

---

Silas Ludlan

---

Youmans
63 2d. av.

---

F. Bellew
70 West 27th St

---

Empire House —
Pennsylvania av between
3d and 4th street

---

Mrs. Harrison's Pennsylvania

[2]

Patrick Fleming, Jackson Hall [Alley?]
& Pennsylvania av

---

f[*illegible*]
Charles Drummond

Dr. Smith
140 York st cor Charles

---

Mrs. Tyndale
Germantown
cor Main and
High sts.—

---

Mrs. Chilton
69 Verick st.

(Phebe Ann
Wood
348 Grove

---

Mr. T. C. Leland,
77 Duane st.

---

Mrs. Walton
107 Dean corner
Hoyt

---

John W. Usher
Cor. Pensylvania av. & 14th st.
City Lunch

[3]

[4]

N.Y. Express, Oct. 21, 1856

"But for the American party, the Northern, sectional, geographical party of Wm H. Seward & Co. would, under Fremont, have swept the whole Northern country." (editorial.)

[5]

[6]

Proem.—

Proem of all
These are the candid
open-shown thoughts
of me, and of all
my body & soul
~~Lo, the amp free~~ open ~~amplitude~~
over and over
Lo the round globe, tumbling
Lo, friendly persons advancing,
tall, muscular, ^friendly with
sufficient hands and feet,
Lo — ~~the~~ great women ~~of~~ upon ~~of~~ the world
the New World and ~~the~~ lo
how they precede the beard-faced masters
~~of~~ upon the world,

---

[7]

[8]

Lo

Shall speak in the Presidents
Message from the porch
of the ^Federal Capitol, and in

the Governors' Messages
from the State Capitols,
and in the rulings of
the Judges of the
Supreme Court,

**[9]**

**[10]**

Commencement of Discourse
"Spiritualism"

Life is very great but there [~~f?~~] is something greater than life, absorbing life, namely Death.— When as we are in the midst of affairs, going to dinner, &c, we receive the news of the sudden death of — ⌜over⌝

**[11]**

**[12]**

Proem
^Preface of Endless Announcements

Toward the perfect woman
of ~~The~~ America
Toward the perfect man
of America
Toward the President
of These States, and
the members of
the Congress of These
States
Proem
Preface of Endless
Announcements

---

After all is said, it remains to be said, This too is great in its reference to death

**[13]**

**[14]**

Poem of Remorse

———

I now look back to the
times when I thought
others — slaves?— the ignorant?
— so much inferior to my self

———

To have so much less right
than myself

**[15]**

**[16]**

O you round Earth,
I

---

Savage and strong,
Free, luxuriant, im ,
I, from Mannahatta
speak up for The States.

---

O my body, that gives
me identity!
O my organs~~!~~ all and ~~each,~~ ^every one O that
which makes manhood!
O

---

A Savage and ~~luxuriant~~ strong
Primal
~~Am~~ Free, luxuriant, [~~f?~~]
in I, ~~come,~~
~~an Amer~~

from Mannahatta
stand ~~in the midst~~
of ~~The States~~
speak up for you and
for These States —

**[17]**

(Simply
Endless Announcements
nothing more
☝

**[18]**

Words of America
Free and severe words,
the master's words

---

The mother's, father's,
husband's, wife's,
son's, daughter's words,

---

☞
The Proem must have throughout a strong saturation of America, The West, the Geography, the representative American man.

**[19]**

All that you do [g] gain
dissipates away
But all that you
do to your body,
mind, morals, lasts
in this sphere and
in other spheres

**[20]**

Shall grow in the manly
muscle of men and
in the greatness of
perfect women

---

I do not say that life
is not beautiful,
But I say that whatever
it is, it all tends to
~~dr~~[~~*cut away*~~] the beauty of death.

---

[*cut away*]

---

To you, ~~endless~~ endless announcements
~~To You~~ whoever you are, I
kiss you with lips of
^~~real~~ love ^personal

**[21]**

<u>Premonition</u>
(last verse
? To you, endless announcements!
? ~~To America~~
Whoever you are, For your sake, these
* Free, ^fresh and savage, ~~strong,~~
~~Cheerful~~ Fluent, luxuriant,
~~fluent,~~ self-composed —
persons

[*cut away*]

I was born fond
of the sea-beach,

~~In~~ ∧In ~~the~~ streets of Mannahatta's ~~I~~ streets walking
~~and sound thence~~
∧~~I sound~~ ~~the strong~~ ∧I make poems
~~of~~ ∧for The States.
In Mannahatta's streets walking
I make poems for The States.

**[22]**

---

*

Free, savage, strong,
Cheerful, luxuriant, fluent,
self-~~sufficient~~ composed – fond of
my friends, fond of women and children
☞ Fond of fish-shaped ~~Paumanok~~
Paumanok, where I
was born — fond of
the sea-beach,
From Mannahatta I send
the poems of The States.

**[23]**

**[24]**

O inter[~~sect?~~]twined lands!
O land of the future!
~~This~~
~~Ahold of hands~~
copious land
Washington's land
~~These I interhanded~~
~~The interhanded States~~
O ~~my~~ the lands!
~~The~~ O ∧copious the embracing, interhanded, ∧the many-armed, the
knit together, the

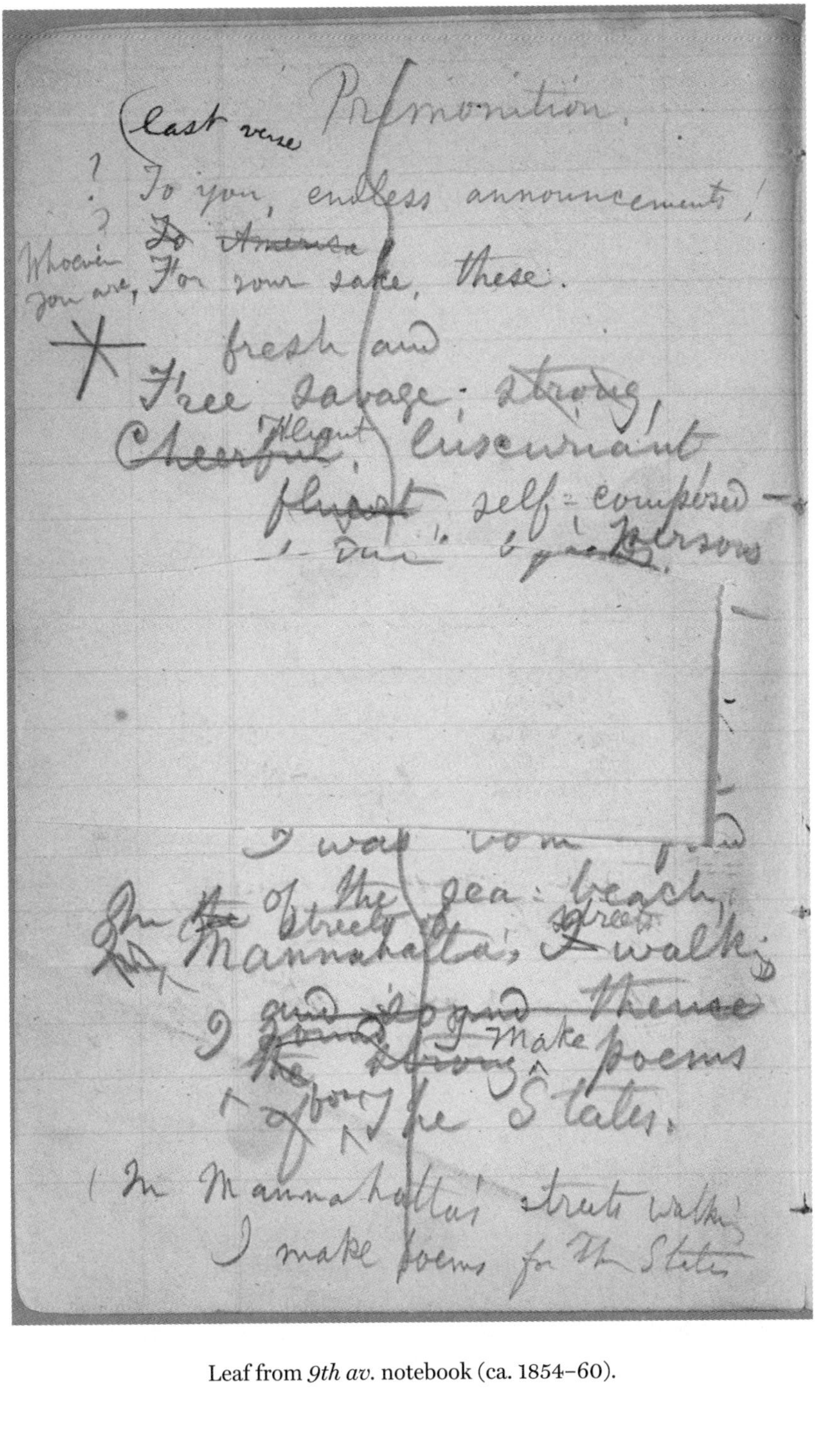

Leaf from *9th av.* notebook (ca. 1854–60).

passionate lovers, the
fused ~~ones~~ and clasped, ~~the equal~~
~~womb-offspring,~~ the
old and young brothers,
the ~~equal~~ ~~world~~ side by side, the
experienced sisters
and the inexperienced
sisters, the equal ones,
the womb-offspring, the
well-~~attached the~~
beloved of ages! ~~and of~~ ages! ages!
~~ages,~~ — the inextricable,
the river-tied and the
mountain-tied.

**[25]**

**[26]**

[*illegible*]
breezed, the Arc[*cut away*]
braced, the sea-bosomed,
the Mississippi-drained,
the fresh-breezed, the
ample-land, the wonderful,
the welcome, the inseparable
brothers!
O dear lands! O death!
O I will not ~~desert~~
~~you by death~~ be
~~death~~ be ~~divested~~ discharged severed
from you by death
O I ~~do not care!~~ cannot be severed! I
~~will yet~~ visit you [~~still?~~]
yet with irrepressible love,
O I ~~will visi~~ come
silently and invisibly
Again the

**[27]**

[*cut away*]

---

This then is life,
This ~~This~~ Here is what has ~~been~~ come ~~arrived~~ upon the earth, out of ~~then is~~ the earth,
~~and what has arrived~~
~~after~~ so many throes
and convulsions.—

How curious! How real!
Underfoot, the divine soil —
Overhead, the sun.—

~~Afford foothold to my poems,~~
~~you~~
Nourish my poems, Earth, and give
them roots, ~~you earth,~~
for they are your
offspring,
Bedew them, ~~dews,~~ you
spring and summer ^dews — — shelter

**[28]**

Philip Holmes

Adirondacks — to Troy — then in the cars to Moreau — then by stage to Glen's Falls — then by stage to Lake George — then to Scroon lake —

---

I will visit the Texan
in

---

The ~~wal~~ jaunt over the
prairies as welcome as
ever

~~The banks of the~~ long ~~sail voyage~~ the
~~Missouri~~ up ~~the~~
~~Mississipp~~

Shine upon them, sun, for
they

**[29]**

them; winter snows, for
they ~~are~~ would make you

~~Help~~
Favor them, ~~to yo~~ all you
laws of materials, and
~~all ponderable things~~
~~all~~ of vulgar and rejected
things, for they would
make you illustrious
You mothers

You young women, for
they ~~p~~ ∧would announce you
~~as just~~ ∧forever as capable
and eminent as
~~the~~ young men

**[30]**

The ∧[p?] man or woman of Texas, the Lousianian
the Floridian, the Georgian
the Carolinian, the Mississippian
the Arkansian, the Californian
as much my friend as
ever, and I his friend
∧or her friend as much as ever,

Oregon as much mine as
ever,
^you Mannahatta! ~~Mannahatta~~!
~~Mannahatta! still~~ close,
as ever! O close! close to me!
~~O~~ The man of ~~Ohioan~~ and woman of Ohio as ~~close~~ real
to me as ever
The Kentuckian ~~my~~ for me and I for him as much as ever

Wisconsin, Iowa
Michigan, Illinois,
Indiana, Missouri,
Kansas, Nebraska, Utah,
^Minnesota! for me a ~~as much as ever~~ the same and I
for them ~~as much~~ the same as
ever!

**[31]**

You old man and old woman;
for they ~~know see~~ would show that
you are no less
admirable~~,~~ than any

You sexual organs and
acts, for they ~~behold~~ are determined to tell
you with glad
courageous loud
voice, to make
you illustrious,

**[32]**

The Tennessee-man and
the Tennessee-woman
— ~~the same as ever to me~~ no less to me than ever
Pennsylvania, New-Jersey,
Delaware, Maryland,

Virginia, yet travelled
by me,
~~The~~ Maine, New-Hampshire,
Vermont, Massachusetts,
Connecticut, Rhode Island,
New York, yet dwelt
in by me,

---

~~Huron, Erie Mie~~
Ontario, Erie, Huron,
Michigan, Superior,
yet sailed upon
by me
[*cut away*]

**[33]**

**[34]**

---

To you endless an
To you, these, to
report nature, man,
politics,          from
an American
point of view.

**[35]**

**[36]**
These are the words of the
master
These

**[37]**

These shall live abide,
Shall grow in
Shall walk in the streets
Mannahatta
Shall climb the Alleghenie[*cut away*]
and
[*cut away*]

**[38]**

---

As long as the earth
 is brown and
 solid

---

Free, savage, strong
Cheerful, luxuriant, fluent, self-sufficient,
~~Out from~~ ¥ fond of ~~the sea-beach, from~~ ~~fond~~
 of slender Paumanok where I was
 ~~born,~~
~~From Manhattan~~ ^ fond of the sea-beach ~~Island I~~
 send the poems of the States.

**[39]**

**[40]**

Listen to me,

Out from Paumanok, where
 I was born, and ~~I recite~~

---

All is in yourself,
~~The All things, all thoughts,~~
 Things, thoughts, the stately
 shows of the world,

the suns and moons,
the landscape, summer
and winter, ~~the~~
poems, endearments,
All

---

Free, Savage, and strong,
~~Primal~~, ^ ~~arrogant~~ coarse luxuriant, ~~coarse, and~~
~~combative~~, fluent self-sufficient,
^ ~~O From~~ Out ~~of~~ from Manhattan Island
I ~~make~~ send the poems
of The States,

**[41]**

**[42]**

---

Fille'd fill'd with such ~~wonders~~
Over-head, ~~how~~ the splendid ~~the~~ sun!
Under-foot, ~~how~~ the

O divine soil,

Under-foot, O divine soil!
Overhead, O

* How curious! — How real!
Under-foot, the divine soil!
Overhead, the sun!

~~How curious~~
~~How curious I myself!~~
Me,

**[43]**

**[44]**

I understand you, you
bards of other ~~ages and~~ lands
I ~~understand you,~~ bear you in mind, you
ancestors of men.—

**[45]**

How curious is the brown
~~wo~~ real earth!
How curious, how
spiritual is the water

---

Politics

On the one side pledged
to — — —
On the other side to
— — —
— On the one side — — —
[*illegible*]

**[46]**

**[47]**

Lo! ~~the~~ ships sailing!
Lo, ~~the the interminable~~ intersecting
streets in cities, full
of living people, coming
and going!
Lo, ~~where~~ iron and steam
so grand, so welcome!
Lo, [~~th?~~]

---

[48]

[49]

Forever and

Thy soul!

~~To cons~~

Forever and forever, ~~as long~~ longer
as the than ~~soil~~ ground is brown and solid, ~~as~~ longer
~~as~~ than water ebbs and
flows
They ~~gi shall~~ duly give place, ^in ~~a few~~ ^their order of millions of years — but
you O my soul shall never
give place!

---

* Life, — how curious! how real
Space, ^and time, filled with such
~~easy~~ wonders!
To walk, to breathe, how delicious
The ~~daylig~~ day! ~~these~~ the
~~curious! divine,~~
animals! identity!
eyesight!
Underfoot, the divine
soil,
Overhead, the sun.

[50]

[*illegible*]
~~to~~ ^~~shall ought to~~ deserves ~~receive~~ more than
you, and never can deserve
I do not ~~forget~~ fail to
salute you with my hand and neck, you
poets of all ages
and lands,
I do not forget ~~to bless~~

any one of you, you fallen
nations, to bless you — — nor any
one of you, ~~you~~
ancestors of men

**[51]**

---

How real is the ground!
Come let us ~~p~~ set
our feet upon the
ground;
How perfect and beautiful
are the animals!
~~How vas~~
How much room, and
splendor! How inevitable
How ~~vast and~~ spacious!

**[52]**
[*illegible*]
~~my~~ ancestors ; of man
Nor ~~you, you~~ you ~~the~~
old poets

I do not forget to salute
you, ~~you old~~ you poets,
of all ~~times~~ ages and
lands,

**[53]**
Do you not know [that?]
~~the~~ your soul has brothers
and sisters, just as
much as the your body
has?

**[54]**

This then~~,~~ is life, and
This the earth, —

How curious! How real.
Underfoot the divine soil, —
~~O~~ o verhead, the sun

Surround ? ~~these~~ my poems, you
east and west, for
they are for you
And you north and
south, for they are
for you,
Imbue them, nights, for
they are (of you, and)
for you,
And you, days, for they
are for you.—
Lo

**[55]**

Great ideas dominate
over all —

---

What has Shakespeare
done to England?

---

Not — — not — — —
are of any account
compared to the
few men of great
ideas

---

Even One great idea vitalizes
a nation

---

— Men of great ideas

**[56]**

**[57]**
~~You~~
Personality!
Your Personality! You
~~and~~ whoever you are?
O you coward that
dare not ~~claim~~
be audacious ~~for~~
~~your own sake!~~
O you liar that
~~falsely~~ assume to
be modest and
deferential
O you slave
— O you ∧tongueless, eyeless, earless,

— O you that
will not receive me
for your own sake

**[58]**

**[59]**
Personality!
You! whoever you are!
without one single
exception, in any

part of any of These
States!
I ~~seize~~ ? you with ~~st~~
free and severe ~~you~~
hand — I know well,
whoever you are, you are my equal,
and the President's
equal,— and that there
is no one on this
globe ~~and~~ any ~~better~~
~~g~~ greater than you —
and that there is
no existence in all
the universes any more
immortal than you~~rs~~,

**[60]**

**[61]**

In Poem

The earth, model of poems ~~that is my~~
~~model~~ — ~~I do not~~ ? none need
discard what I
find in the theory
of the great, round diversified
earth, so beautiful, ~~and~~
so rude.

The body of a man,~~—~~that
~~I~~ is my model — I do
not reject what I
find in my body — I
am not ashamed — Why
should I be ashamed?
The body of a woman,~~—~~
that is my perfect
model — I believe

in all the body of
the woman — I believe
the perfect woman
shall even precede
the man

**[62]**

**[63]**
<u>Poem of Maternity</u>

---

O my dear child! My
Darling

(Now I am maternal —
a child bearer —
I ~~bea~~ have from
my womb borne
a child, and
observe it

~~For great ideas!~~
The life that is not
underlaid by great
ideas is — —

**[64]**

**[65]**
For friendship:
— — —
For immortality:
— — —

**[66]**

Dwelling ~~neighbor to the~~ nigh the Ohioan
and Kentuckian, a
friendly neighbor,
~~W~~ Sauntering the streets of
Boston, Portland,
long list of cities
[*cut away*]

**[67]**

* National hymns,
The freeman's and freewoman's
songs,
The master's words, ~~strong~~ arrogant,
~~lawless,~~ fluent, severe.—

**[68]**

**[69]**

? For your own sake

To stand fast by me!
To stand unshaken, ~~and~~
tenacious, — ~~to~~

~~To believe in me — no~~
~~matter~~

---

**[70]**

**[71]**

---

Have you any doubt of mortality?
I say there can be no more
doubt of immortality than
there is of mortality

[72]

[73]

The observer stand ~~some~~ clear day on the northeast height of Washington Park, some ~~y~~ clear day in the year 1900, (the ~~of~~year of These States,) will look on

[74]

[75]

Primer of Words
~~and Th~~ and
Thoughts — (none of these suit
Ideas
Principles

[76]

[77]

American songs,

— in which prose (to be spoken — with a low, or other musical accompaniment,) is interlineated

[78–82 ***are blank***]

[83]

I had rather have the good will of the butchers and boatmen of Manhattan Island than all the nominations approbation rewards of the government — literats elegant persons

~~Jake~~

[84]

**[85]**

\ Sam Matthews /

Walt Whitman stands to-day in the midst of the American people, a promise, a preface, an overture a

Will he fulfil the half-distinct half-indistinct promise?— Many do not understand him, but there are others, a few, who do understand him? Will he justify the great prophecy of Emerson? or will he too, like thousands of others, flaunt out ~~the~~ one bright commencement, the result of gathered powers, only to sink back exhausted — or to give himself up to the seduction of

**[86]**

"Ancient Hebrews"
by Abm. Mills
A. S. Barnes & Co.

---

"Glimpses of Life and Manners
in Persia"
by Lady Sheil
with notes on Russia, Koords,
Turkomans, Nestorians,
(refers to 1849)

---

Mrs Tynedale
at Mrs. Manning's
~~at~~ in Clinton av.
near De Kalb
nearly opposite the church

---

Dr. Draper's Physiology
(Harper
last 2 no's
Harper)

---

Brownlow's Map of the Stars
184 Cherry st.

[87]

A. Brownson Alcott
Oct. 4th '56

---

Jas. Metcalf
79 Warren st. (station house)

---

Mr. Held
4 Boerum
near Fulton av.

---

Clerke's Rudiments
& Practice
1 vol.

---

Comic Blackstone

---

Prof Wines'
Commentaries on the
Hebrew Law

---

Montesquieu
Spirit of the Laws

---

Robert Hunt's
"Poetry of Science"

---

Poetry of the East
Pub. Whittemore, Niles, & Hall
Boston

16th Sept — b

---

J.L. Metcalf
3d district station house
~~3d ward~~ 79 Warren

---

Organism of Language
Becker's
Translated into English

---

Grimm's work in German Language

---

W. Gibson
363 Sixth av

---

Middlesex House
Concord, Mass

---

Dr Ruggles
24 East Warren

---

Wilson
4 Greene
near Cumberlan
1 door

## *The scope of government*[12]
## [ca. 1855–56]

**[1]**

~~That~~ The scope of government is always to be kept very broad ~~and ample~~ — The questionthat ~~is to~~ must premise ~~all~~ enactments must ~~is~~ be [*illegible*] Will this appeal apply to ~~universal~~ men and women universally? ~~Has~~ Does it ~~reference~~ directly or indirectly ~~to preserve~~ defend the rights to life, liberty, and property, of each ~~and all men and women~~ uncriminal man and woman, without any exception whatever?

Whatever is not that broad

**[2]**

**[3]**

*

The government to suit these states is no government of lawyers, ~~dilletanti~~ [~~or?~~] — nor a government of dilletanti.— either.— In ~~government~~ politics, in poems, in war, in behavior, one thing tells forever — and that is ~~approp~~ ability the fit ability fitness purpose capability — Not gab, not being genteel, not plenty of money,— none of these ~~will~~ save a ~~man~~ country.—

---

The substratum on which the American constitution is based, is, that every uncriminal person is endowed with the right to ~~liv~~ his or her life, liberty, and the equal pursuit of happiness.—

**[4]**

**[5]**

*

In what respect does the ~~A~~ government of this land represent the strong live — — ~~American~~ people of this land, this day, or any of these days?— ~~Not~~ Is there one.— ~~It is Where is A~~

Is this melange A crowd of ~~dyspe~~ attorneys, feverish ~~men~~ southerners ~~dyspeptics~~,—
owners of slaves

seekers of contracts
bleeders of the treasury,
bullies without courage,
angry dyspestic~~als~~ ~~speakers~~ from the north,
supple human hinges from the same,
(are they this great America?
this ~~Pres scum~~ this poor scum
that has floated somehow into the presidency —

these supple

**[6]**

**[7]**

secretaries — these ^ milliners of diplomats (sent ~~forth~~ in their ~~milliner's~~ poppy-show liveries to ~~speak show~~ dance for us in ~~foreign lands~~ — the cotillions of distant courts) —

— these are they America?— Are they the great nation? of ~~thirty-two nations~~

**[8]**

**[9]**

Go back to first principles — re[*cut away*] nothing through parties. I h[*cut away*] [that?] man a slave who, [*cut away*]ts day ~~lis swallows receives~~ obeys the ~~commands~~ authority of any party, ~~whatever~~ no matter how specious their pretensions.— Listen to all, learn from all, consider well what they have to offer, but obey yourself only.— ~~These~~ They who ~~pull the~~ fabricate the creeds and commands of these parties, are all infidels ~~and scorners of you~~ — they have no faith in man — they do not dream of any other way to success

**[10, *sketch of three leaves*]**

**[11]**

~~but~~ except schemings, caucuses, ~~lies~~ lying, ~~not~~ not one lie, but all lies — not one face, but a face for every different section interest.

I tell ^you these men are all using you.

---

The ~~business~~ performances of government must be reduced to minims.

---

~~Two~~ Out of ~~any~~ thirty ~~laws~~ enactments passed by the ~~state legislature~~ Congress of these States, or by the legislatures, twenty-nine are for petty personal objects, in which the people have no broad interest whatever.—

**[12]**

**[13]**

Obey no man

Learn

Think upon all subjects for yourselves.— (Learn from

all sides but decide for yourselves

The remedy is not in authority but in the throwing off of authority.—
~~Then~~ Then when ~~false usurper~~ that which abdicates, ~~is replaced by after his work is done~~ and was an usurper allowed to do certain work, ~~comes~~ the true power comes into possession.— ~~I say~~ It is not this or that party who is going to save America, and make it justify the mighty prophecies and promises which are all that it has hitherto been.— It is in countless breeds of great

**[14]**

**[15]**

individuals, the eternal and only anchor of states.—

I have been informed that it is expected ? that those who address the people, ~~Are expected to~~ will flatter them.—

I flatter none.— I ~~come to rebuke~~ think I could taunt you rather than to flatter you.—

What have you been about, that you have allowed ~~these~~ that scum to be floated into the Presidency?

What have you been about that

~~What do you send~~

~~Can you find nothing but~~

~~Do you think nothing~~ Your Congress is filled with little but gab, ~~college-stuffing~~ book-knowledge and ~~tailors~~ tailors clothes, ~~is~~ ∧ever ~~wanted in your Congress blather~~ doughfaces and ~~blatherskites?~~ puttyfaces?

**[16]**

**[17]**

Do you think ~~the experiment of~~ liberty and equality have ~~has~~ now done with America? That the work is finished, and the dwelling is ∧henceforth secure?— ~~No~~ Believe it not? No

---

~~Where are you represented~~ What representative have you — what single representative ~~have~~ of you ∧is there in the Capitol? Where ~~in the~~

**[19]**

The insects.

get from Mr. Arkhurst a list of ~~just~~ American insects —

---

? Just simply enumerate them
with their sizes, colors, habits,
lives, shortness or length of life —
what they feed upon

(A little poem, of a leaf, or two
leaves, only)

I dare not be
too assuming over them.

~~end the insects~~ —
First enumerate the insects —
— then end by saying
I do not know what these are but
I believe that all these

are more than they
seem
I do not know what they are
I have advised with myself . .
. . . I dare not consider
myself, ~~in~~ any more for my place, than
they are for their places

**[21]**

That [*cut away*]
know there ~~excuses~~ [*cut away*]
which I do not know,
~~That~~

---

~~Assurances a~~ I
I need no assurances . . . I am
he who is pre-occupied

**[23]**

I ~~think~~ ~~know~~ do not doubt that
From under the very steps, ~~and~~ hands ~~and~~ eyes
~~That besides what I~~ eyes am
cognizant of, are ~~th~~
~~calm and~~ looking faces I
am not cognizant of —
calm and silent faces.
~~That~~
I do not doubt but there
is far ~~more in myself~~
~~more in my poems than~~
more in myself than
I have supposed . . . and
more in all men and
women . . . and more in
my poems than I
have supposed,

**[25]**

I do not doubt that there
are ~~more~~ experiences
and growths for me
through, time, and
through the universes,
of which I cannot
have the slightest
inkling or idea
I do not doubt the
universes are limitless
. . . in vain I try to
fancy how limitless
I do not doubt it is
~~eternally~~ safe for ~~the~~
~~mighty~~ orbs and systems
of orbs to ~~play~~ play their
~~swift~~ eternal ~~plays~~ sports through

**[26]**

the air — and that I shall
one day be eligible to
do as much as they, and
more then they,
I do not doubt, ~~that~~
whatever can possibly
happy through any of the
worlds is provided for,
in the ~~nature~~ inherences of things,
I do not doubt, [*illegible*] whatever
can happen in this
world, interior or exterior,
in America, in the ~~other~~
remainder of the ~~centuries~~ earth,
~~as in pol~~ among affairs,

politics, children, failures,
~~deaths~~, murders, wrecks,
degradations death defection ~~is~~ each and all
amply provided for

**[28]**

~~I am in fear~~ [*cut away*]
~~I do not believe~~ [*cut away*]
I do not see how ~~the~~
~~earth~~ nothing but maladies
can be ~~buried~~ resolved back in
the earth, and ~~I~~ return
otherwise

**[29]**

**[30]**

I ~~do not~~ am amazed how
the earth ~~can remain~~
~~so~~ vital and calm

~~I do not think see how~~

~~Billions of~~ Behold!
~~Here~~ This ~~in this~~ is the compost ~~are~~ of
billions of diseased premature corpses,
Perhaps every ~~grain~~ mite has once
formed part of a sick
person
Yet behold! ~~The shorn erath!~~
~~Behold how~~ The grass grows
upon the prairies!

**[32–33, *cut away*]**

**[34]**

Not bring to me ~~some~~ a single one ^ of the ~~vile~~ diseases that have ~~continually~~ forever ~~each discharge relieve themselves up~~ laved themselves in it?

How can you keep sound, you
quadrupeds? ~~That feed upon~~
~~crop~~ I see you are

I ~~will~~ cannot not believe ~~myself~~,
yet awhile,

I do not see how there can
be any thing but disease
~~and~~

**[35, *cut away*]**

**[36]**

distempered

morbid

No, all is fresh,
The ~~fruit~~ berries in the gardens,
— how juicy and cool
they are!

~~The~~ The fruit of the ~~out of the~~ Apples-orchard and that of
the orange orchard — ··· ~~the~~
mellons, grapes, peaches,
pears — I feared they would
poison me, but they do not.
As I lay reclining on the
grass, ~~I thought every~~
~~spear rose out of the~~
~~manure of diseases~~
how can I not catch

some disease? . . . ~~for~~ for probably ^ ~~perhaps~~ every
spear of grass rises out of
what was once some
catching disease

**[37]**

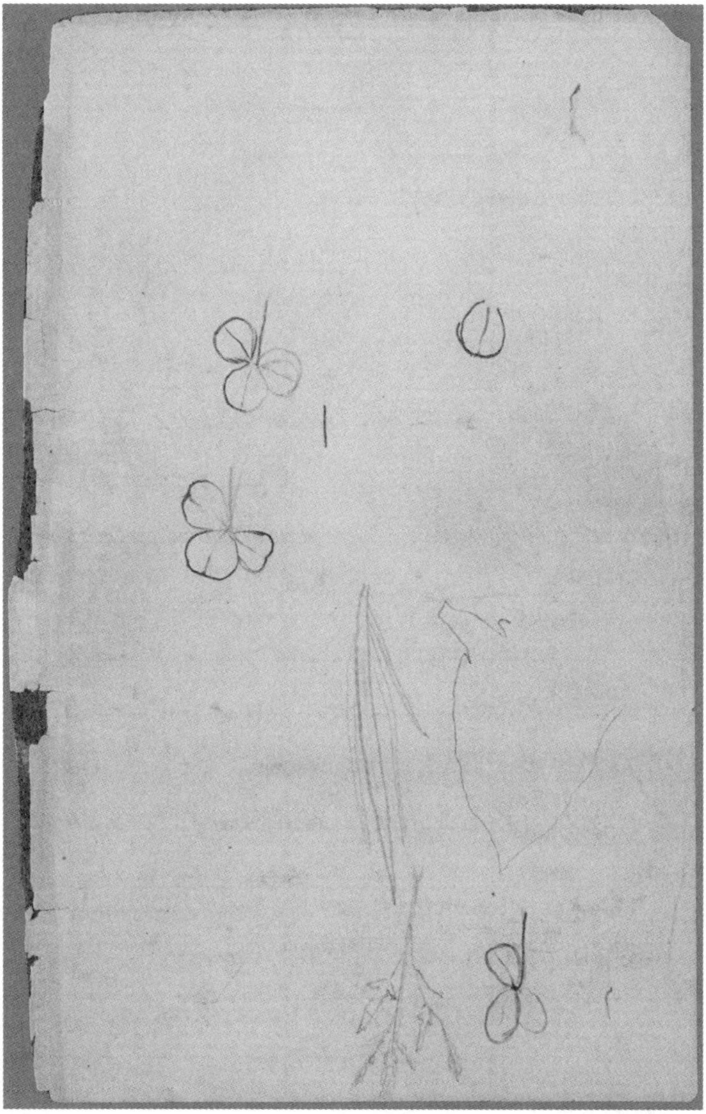

Leaf from *The scope of government* notebook (ca. 1855–56).

[38]

What is ~~wa~~ now wanted in these states — and what will ~~always~~ be wanted, a hundred years hence, and ~~every~~ ever so many hundred years hence — is clear-eyed, well-informed, healthy-brained, bold-mouthed men,— ~~able~~ men possessed of such native ~~firmne~~ resolution, that they readily ~~sink~~ part aside ~~all~~ authority, law, custom, officers, popularities, [*illegible*] and to walk sternly on with their own divine conviction of what is right.—

[39]

**[*Here, Whitman flips the notebook and writes on the backs of certain pages, upside-down*]**

[31]

An item for conversation
everywhere —

---

To be simple, nature, <u>as native as animals are native</u> — dismissing all the chat, talk of business or money, meaningless talk, criticizing acquaintances and their faults —

To be silent unless something must be said that cannot be left unsaid.

Never to attempt to be witty, or strive after effects — <u>not</u> <u>one</u> <u>any</u> how

To dismiss the usual amiable acquiescence also —

[27]

O Mother did you think there
could ever be a time
when I might not

I walk forth amid the calmness
of grass and foliage

—

But after a little time I
will return among men —

**[24]**

~~The bot~~ Buds ~~bud form~~ swiftly form upon the
vines
~~The dews rains of April~~
The she-birds ~~of morning and~~
~~evening, carol~~ build
~~their~~ nests or brood
on ~~their eggs~~ them, — the he-birds
carol on the trees,
mornings and evenings,
The ~~animals young~~ young
of ~~fowls~~ poultry [*illegible*] break
through the hatched
eggs,
The ~~animals~~ new born of animals
appear — ~~the from~~
~~cow the cow~~ the calf

**[22]**

is droppedt from the cow, and the colt from the mare,
~~The The~~ [*cut away*]
[T?] [*cut away*]

**[20]**

~~Yet You are very patient,~~
O I am terrified at the
earth — it is ~~so~~ that calm
and patient!
It ~~does~~ gives such ~~things~~ values ?
to men, and receives
~~those~~ such leavings ~~what they men~~ bring
~~themselves~~ at last!
It ~~covers up such~~ ~~receives those foul~~
[*illegible*] ~~corruptions, and~~
grows ~~blossoms and~~

~~grass thence~~
such sweet things
out of such corruption,

**[18]**

It ~~never tires of~~ turns ^so stainless on its axis with ~~for~~ all those
successions of diseased
corpses,
It distills ~~such its~~ such winds
and perfumes out
of ~~such bequeathed~~ such infused
~~maladies~~, fœtor,
It renews so ~~faithfully~~
with such unwitting looks its
~~su~~ prodigal annual ^sumptuous crops,
It gives such divine
materials to men, and
receives such leavings
~~in return~~ at last !

## *George Walker*[13]
## [ca. 1856–65]

**[1, *front cover, outside*]**

**[2, *front cover, inside*]**

Joseph Velsor 130 Suffolk

5 × 6 × 12 [×?]

— with moderate arch

Mechanics Coffee & Reading Rooms

corner 10th st Avenue D.

---

Hewett's pamphlet
"on the uses of
iron"

Miss Libby
cor Willoughby & Duffield

---

49 Madison st.

---

Shirting Mr. Rhodes
244 Bleecker

---

Map of Mountains & Rivers
wholesale 90cts.
Wells, 140 Nassau st.

---

Map of the world

---

wholesale (90cts)
The world's standards & costumes
Charts in sheets wholesale colored 38

[3]

70 in paper
5 in cloth & gilt.
Nov. 23

"For Sailors of All Nations"
(Inscription on the Mount in Evergreens Cemetery — a simple round column with a square cap supporting a representation of the globe on which the seas and the shores of the continents are outlined
thy hills of Abyssinia
The beautiful, strong, black
active Abyssinian

[4]

"Sight & Hearing"
C Scribner

---

"Stories of the Italian
Poets," by Leigh Hunt.

[5–6, *cut away*]

[7]

Full poem
~~add~~ For the dying
treating them and talking to them
courageously —

---

no whining or praying or tears

---

I have all lives, all effects,
all hidden invisibly in
myself . . . they proceed
from me.

---

Gist of my books

To give others, readers, people, the materials to decide for themselves, and know, or grow toward knowing, with cleanliness and strength

[8]

Stillman & Durand
care of F. W. Christern
763 Broadway

— Sunday Courier 15 Spruce
— Sunday Mercury 22 Spruce
— Sunday Times 162 Nassau
— Daily News 129 Nassau st 2d story
— Irish American 116 Nassau
— Sunday Leader 25 Chambers st
— Leslie's Illustrated News
12 Spruce st
— Young America 98 Nassau
— Citizen, 10 Spruce
Police Gazette, 103 Nassau
— Ledger 120 Nassau
— Yankee Notions 98 Nassau
— Harper's Magazine, Franklin
square

[9]

I have seen at night from the foundry chimneys

Where the fires ^into the night burn high
and glaringly and cast
strong contrasts of

darkness and wild
red and yellow light
over the tops of
the houses, and
down into the
clefts, ~~of~~ the streets.

---

— Picayune, 114 Nassau
Clipper, 102 Nassau
Observer, 138 Nassau
Churchman
rooms 40 Trinity Building
111 Broadway
American Celt
cor Ann & Nassau
Independent
22 Beekman

**[10]**
O days of the present
will attire you
in beauty
I will attire you in
as much beauty as
the days that arc
past

---

— NY Sun
N.Y. Sunday Herald
Journal of Commerce
Courier & Enquirer

**[11]**

Full poem

~~There is something~~ Theme — that which

involves gladness, joy — all out —

---

Edward H Dixon

Editor Scalpel

42 Fifth av

---

oilworks,— candle making

**[12]**

American society literature is settling itself, ~~as if for good~~ in utter defiance of American principles.

It is settling itself in accordance with European principles, and on a far larger scale than the European scale — as much larger as the American proportions are larger than the European proportions.—

The modes on which it arranges itself involve the idea of caste — involve servants, masters, superiors inferiors.

---

Under the American forms much, ~~if not~~ something most that is expressed is the European idea of caste,

inferiority[?]

**[13]**

Poem — comprehending the ~~idea~~ sentiment of saluting

Helō!

Halo~~w~~! Hellō!

Halow!

**[14]**

For ~~battle-a~~ broad-ax — See acct of the sack of Rome in 1527 "sweeping on with that horde of Spanish bigots and German unbelievers and Italian brigands to the sack of the old great city

---

I see The telegraph lines of
the earth

---

the crowbar, ^pickax shovel, spade,
~~shovel,~~

the flail,

**[15]**

axe — Firemen using the axe to cut in floors or partitions, when the fire is under the floor — or using the axe anyhow.

---

**[16]**

Catlin's Indians plates
Leggett's 88 Nassau
Valentines NY
same place

**[17–18, *blank*]**

**[19]**

In conversation, discussion, intercourse, &c — not to take the position (or drift the talk that way,) of one wanting compliments — this must be real, because if the wanting compliments exists it will show out some how

---

**[20–21, *blank*]**

**[22]**

The best Only first rate poems have the quality of arousing in ~~those~~ ^men and women who hear them or read them those thoughts effects that no words can even describe — effects which themselves cannot be described — great effects, proportioned to the ideas, ~~cha~~ images, and characters of the poem.—

**[23]**

**[24]**

[*cut away*]~~with~~

[*cut away*]sed

**[25]**

[*cut away*]

Che[*cut away*], cucumber[*cut away*]

— tree) mulberry,

**[26]**

[*cut away*]

---

He ~~sees~~ so looks at men through the telescope that they are enlarged — while all others reverse the telescope and ~~lo~~ behold ~~Man~~ minnikins

**[27]**

axiom for laws, for punishments —

---

No punishment shall be provided for the sailor, soldiers, or without its being strictly eligible to be inflicted on the officers, even to the commander in chief.—

**[28]**

**[29]**

Poem

holding in terrorem over the heads of men the sure results of all evil

---

I see Christ eating
his last supper,
with thc young and
older men around him,

**[30]**

Where the women enter the
public assembly the
~~same as the men~~
Where ~~the~~ women walk in the
~~streets in~~ great processions,
in the streets the same as the men,
Where the enter the
public assembly and
take their places the
same as the men,
and are appealed to
by the orators the same
as the men

**[31]**

The water-carriers on a
stooping-trot —

The [*illegible*] three-year-old child
sweeping

---

Where women ~~mixing~~ mix in ~~wth~~ healthy games, the same as men —
Where they run, leap,
ride, swim, ~~lead,~~
play at out-door
plays, the same as
men,

**[32]**

I think ∧the genius our continent has complacently gone to sleep, these years, satisfied with having produced the men of the times

**[33]**

The cities confer with
each other from across
~~oceans~~ two thousand miles — the continents
~~are~~ talk under the
~~bottoms~~ waves of
seas

---

Lesson for beginners.—

Write every thing — especially poems — well.— ~~Doing~~ mostly because doing well passes into a habit — the best habit of art.—

**[34–35, *blank*]**

**[36]**

I [see?]
The Spanish dance
with castanets in the
chestnut shade to the
rebeck and guitar
— The courage of and
nimbleness of the
ma~~d~~tador
I hear ∧by the the ∧careless song song
of the muleteer loading
his panniers with
grapes
I see the lithe ma~~d~~tador in the arena at Seville
I see the Brazilian
v~~q~~aquero on horseback with his
lasso coiled on his
arm

**[37, *light sketch of unknown object*]**

**[38, *blank*]**

**[39, *pencil sketch of the layout of "M Kibben St" in Brooklyn, with "R R" and "bay" also labeled*]**

**[40–43, *blank*]**

**[44]**

There is more ~~ado~~ hullabaloo ~~raised about~~ made for the ~~unlawful~~ hourly whims of these 350,000 slaveholders, than, ~~than would be made about~~ has ever been made, or ever will be made, about the ~~whole~~ ~~whole~~ lives on earth, and the eternal lives afterwards of the ~~thirty millions of~~ ∧whole main ~~m~~ body of the inhabitants of these states, ~~the~~ ∧the good thirty millions of men, women, and children.—

**[45–47, *blank*]**

**[48]**

* What the earth is and
    where the earth is will allure me

Not more spiritual, not
    more divine and beautiful
        than this earth,

---

say to Slavery
Go, and return no
    more,

---

To young men for artists —
(sarcastic)
To Rome!— Go study the human figure — study anatomy — study it along the wharfs and levess, the 'long shoremen, ~~pulling r~~ hoisting and lowering cargoes — study the pose of the drivers of horses —

[49]

Would you like to know what to produce? Produce great persons . . all the rest will surely follow

---

Missing vessels, (ships) at sea — never heard of — The Schooner of Uncle Dan's sons.

---

The Pacific

[50]

What made ^~~the best~~ home where her
presence was
What the performance of
all the housekeeping duties,
What made the mother
of ~~the best children~~
~~. . .~~ brave and athletic
children,
What made the love that
clung to her through
through the growth
and marriage of her
children, and their old
age just the same
She was - - -

[51]

[52]

More than
Her wholesome and

She was silent and at
them

Yet she loved them when
she saw them or
passed among them.—

What made ~~a~~the healthy girl ~~and~~
What a ^made the sensible sweet tempered woman
that men so love,
What makes[de] the best daughter
and the most beloved of her
parents,
What makes[de] the best wife,
the chaste equal of
the husband, fully bearing her
share,

**[53]**

**[54]**

They did not wound her
. . . . she was possessed of herself . . . .

. . . . she received them
as the air received them,
or as the laws of nature
received them,
She too ~~too~~ ^~~herself~~ was a law in
nature . . . . she was

as great as any . . . .
~~the greatest law . . . .~~
[*cut away*] was maternity
[*cut away*]

**[55]**

**[56]**

Full Poem — indicating, any way, (loosley) the illustrations of the true female character.

The violent oaths ~~of the drivers~~, the ~~blackguard~~ hiccupping song of the drunkard, the smutty expression, the quarrel, .... none of these annoyed ~~heard~~ her,
She heard them .... she
heard the taunt, the
accusation, the rank words,
She knew ^as she passed the thoughts of
the young men .... nothing
was concealed from her,
.... she was aware ....
she saw the doers of all
these, .
She was not the less
considerate or friendly
toward them,

**[57]**

**[58]**
Where ~~the~~ the great renunciation
is made in secret, that
will allure me,
Where personal love reaches
toward me, that will
allure me .... to the
prisoner in his cell,
or the slave, or the
^solitary sick person, it will
certainly allure me,
I ^do not know what is waiting for
me to be – ~~nor what the being~~
~~of it shal will exhibit~~
But ^I know that I shall be
~~I know~~, in great form and nature
I cannot prove it to you
or any one .... but I
know it is so. *

**[59]**

"I greet you at the
beginning of a great
career"
~~W~~R. W. Emerson

**[60]**

I believe whatever happens
I shall not forget
this earth,
I believe I shall walk
and walk among
men and women.—
Wherever I go I believe
I shall often return
There are many words and
deeds that will happen
that will [r?]allure me.
~~That~~ Where any one thinks of me
or wishes me ^[*illegible*] that will allure
me,
Where the happy young
husband and wife
are, and the happy
old husband and wife are, will allure
me.

**[61]**

I say the land that
has a place for
slaves and the
~~me~~ owners of slaves
has no place for
freemen.—

As to her
She is mine — ma femme

**[62]**

Tighter yet may the bands
be drawn,
What thought you have of
me, I ~~have~~ had as
much and more than
as much of you,
I have laid up ~~great~~ in my
stores in advance —
for I ~~have thought~~
considered ^long and friendlily
of you before you
were born.—

---

Who knows but all shall come
home to my soul?
Who knows but, there are
consequences ^~~coming~~ to me seasons
and centuries afterward
Who knows but I ^am looking
at you now, for all
you cannot see me?

**[63]**

The area of pens of
live pork — the
killing-hammer — the
men in their oil-skin
overalls — the hog-hook
— the scalder's — tub ~~the~~
— the cutter's cleavers —

the gutting ~~gutting, cutting, packing,~~
— ∧the packer's maul, and the plenteous winter
~~work of pork packing~~

mufti
ulema

**[64]**

∧You ~~that are~~ wayward, vain, ~~a blabber~~,
blabbed, blushed
resented, was ∧shallow, ambitious,
curious, fearful, lied,
stole, adulterous,
~~emerged from~~ a
solitary committer,
greedy, grudging,
/ — the wolf, the snake,
the hog not altogether wanting ~~emerging at~~
the covetous wish — the
frivolous word — the
cheating look —

had guile, lust, ∧hot wishes I dared
not speak.
Refused my love to those that gave
me theirs.

---

It is not you alone who ~~are all~~ know what it is to be these —
I too knew what it was to be these.—

**[65]**

~~I am~~ Of me the good comes
by wristling for it,
I am not he bringing
ointments and soft
wool for you,

I am he with whom
you must wristle
. . . . I am

~~T~~ The good of you is
not in me . . . . the
good of you is
altogether in yourself.
I am the one who
indicates, and the
one who provokes
and tantalizes

**[66]**

drenched with joy,— had my friends, loved them, was loved by them,— was irritated,— saw hundreds of men and women I loved, yet never told them so, Had my hopes and dreams,— laughed, slept, had my friendships,— approaching or passing,
I too ^was called ~~too~~ by
name by the clear
prompt voices of ~~my~~ ~~the~~ my friends
~~I who~~ as as they saw me ~~as~~
~~I~~ passing or approaching

**[67]**

He does not
I do not (wish to) spend
my life in a corner
I do not ~~bee~~ go among
conspicuous persons
either

---

to produce such a public that great performances will not be received with noisy applause but as matters of course.

**[68]**

That I am is of my
        body, and what I am
        is of my body

~~That I~~
* What belongs to me . . . . that
        it does not yet spread
        in the spread of the
        universe, I owe to my body
? tr up * What ~~soul~~ identity I am, I owe
        to my body . . . . what
~~What~~ soul I owe to my
        body,
Of all that I have had,
        I have had nothing except
        through my body,
Of the make of my body
        was not my mortal experience
        only,
My body makes my immortal experience

**[69]**

Idea to pervade largely

---

Eligibility — I, you, any one
        eligible to the condition
        or attributes or advantages
        of any being, no matter
        who,—

---

3d Feb. Make no puns

| | |
|---|---|
| funny remarks<br>Double entendres<br>"witty" remarks | nothing to<br>excite a<br>laugh |

ironies
Sarcasms
— only that which
is simply earnest,
meant, harmless
to any one's feelings
— unadorned
— unvarnished

silence
silence
silence
laconic
taciturn

**[70]**

I ~~also~~ too lived,
    I too walked upon
    the solid earth,
    and bathed in the
    sea

But I, wearied, wavered,

I too was ~~cohered~~ struck from the
    float eternally held
    in solution,
I too was cohered and received
    identity ~~by~~ through my body,
Of all that I had, I had
    nothing except ^through my body
Of all that I have or
    shall have, it is the
    same

**[71]**

They exfoliate

---

pork packing

slaughter[ing?] pork — the
The ~~heaps of the~~ [hanging?] carcasses
of pork ~~the~~ slaughtered
~~slaughtering~~ — the men
in their oil-skin
overalls — the
~~scalding rooms —~~ scalded —
— the packing —

The killing hammer — the
hog hook — the gutting

☞ over

**[72]**

(Full poem

I too have — — —
have — have —

I too have — — —
felt the curious
questioning come upon
me,

In the day they came
In the silence of the night
came upon me,

What is it now
between us?— ist
it a score of years?
or a hundred years?
or five hundred years?
Whatever it is, it avails
not . . . . . distance avails not
and place avails not.

**[73]**

In the best poems appears the human body, ~~fully formed,~~ well-formed, natural, accepting itself, unaware ~~that~~ of shame, loving that which is necessary to make it complete, proud of its strength, active, receptive, a father, a mother,

---

**[74]**

The continual and hurried crowd of
men and women crossing
The reflection of the sky
in the water — the ~~white~~ blinding
dazzle in a track from
the [almost?] declin~ing~ed sun,
The lighters — the sailors
in their picturesque costumes

— the nimbus of light
around [*illegible*] ~~my~~ the shadow of my
head in the [*illegible*]
[*cut away*]

**[75]**

Convey what I want to convey by models or illustrations of the results I demand.— Convey these by characters, selections of incidents and behaviour.

This indirect mode of attack is better than all direct modes of attack.

☝ The spirit of the ☝ above should pervade ALL my poems.

☞ Avoid all the "intellectual subtleties," and "withering doubts" and "blasted hopes" and "unrequited loves," and "ennui" and "wretchedness" and the whole of the lurid and artistical and melo-dramatic effects.— Preserve perfect calmness and sanity

**[76]**

The ~~dancing~~ edged waves, the
~~but~~ scooped cups,
and the dancing
motion,
The yellow masts,
the pilots in their pilot-houses,
the sailors at work in the
rigging,
The swift current, the ~~b~~ white
~~brack~~ frothy wake left by the paddles
of the steamboats
The gray walls of granite
storehouses near the
docks — the ~~swift~~ quick tremulous motion
of the flukes of the
wheels
The flags on the tops of the

**[77]**

You may have but a few to (fully,) understand you.— Nevertheless that few is to rule rules the world.—

**[78]**

I have ~~ga~~ looked toward
the lower bay to
notice the arriving
ships,
~~To~~ I have looked on the
white sails of the
~~el~~ clean [*illegible*]
[*cut away*]

**[79]**

The newer better principle through all my poems.— (dramas? novels? compositions of any sort.)

---

Present only great characters, good, loving characters.—

Present the best phases of character, that any one, man or woman is eligible to.

Present noble phases of character for young men

---

A Combination

I must combine the tenderness and trembling sympathetic manliness of Jean Paul with the strength of Homer, and the perfect reason of Shakespeare.

**[80]**

I too ~~have crossed~~ many and
many a time have crossed
the ferry
I have watched the
sea-gulls flapping
their wings — ~~I have~~
I have seen ^them floating with
motionless wings high
in the air at
sunset, just oscillating
their bodies,
I have seen the ~~bright~~ glistening
yellow light parts
of their bodies and
~~leave~~ the rest in
strong shadow
I have seen them
~~thus~~ high up ~~afa afar off~~
slowly wheeling in
circles, edging slowly to the
south

**[81, *bracketed words at bottom were cut away, are now a separate fragment*]**

(Poem or passage)
the scenes on the river
    ~~Po O~~ as I cross the
    Fulton ferry

---

Others will see the flow
    of the river, also,
Others will see on both
    sides the city of
    New York and the city
    of Brooklyn
A hundred years hence others
    will see them,
Two hundred years — many
    [hundred years hence
    others will enjoy the flow
    of? the?]

**[82, *bracketed words at bottom were cut away, are now a separate fragment*]**

Cursed is that age or
    nation that does not
    realize itself, and
    esteem itself,
Wretched is that man
    who does not esteem
    himself

---

Put "Manhattan" for
    New York all
        through

[English Johny (49th St Jockey cap) Sam — (49th st round shoulders light clothes]

**[83]**

What is there you can
        conceive more wonderful
        than what you see
        around you?

Nothing can be conceived
        of by the fancy that
        can be more wonderful
        than what we see.—
[*cut away*]

**[84]**

for Gymnastic and Athletic

---

I heard to-day of a young ~~man~~ man who was bequeathed $600,000[?] and wasted it — There are young men who are bequeathed more than that and never put it to good —

[*cut away*]

**[85]**

~~You~~ It is mentioned that the Irish and German and other foreigners mix in our politics.— Gentlemen with perfect respect I say you you can think what ~~wh~~ you choose about this;— It is a credit to men and no disgrace to them to take an eager interest in politics.—

---

Amherst White, attorney
        cor Barclay & Broadway

---

A. J. Davis
        137 Spring

**[86]**

Gentlemen, I will be very plain with you.— I see in my country many great qualities.— I see in America not merely the home of Americans, but the home of the needy and down kept races of the whole earth.— I know just as well as you the terrible ł effects of ages of degradation and caste.— It is a real truth — it is a black and bloody lesson —

---

A. Baker. Boots

15 Ann st

Stout boots $4

Double water proof $4.50

**[87]**

Not only American literature, but ^the structures of American social intercourse are household life, are growing up in ~~utter scorn of~~ total severance from the roots and trunks and branches [*cut away*] growth

[*cut away*]

**[88]**

The gross and soiled she moved among and was without repugnance did not make her gross and soiled

[*cut away*]

**[89, *back cover, inside*]**

George Walker

Edward Smithson

John Swinton (Lewis his bro.

Sam (with black eyes & cap)

Henry Hearne

William Meeker

William Phillips

George P. Morris

Leo

Pete Dempsey

Henry Post (Fulton op. Eagle office
Nick (black eyes 40th st.— small
Joe (Canadian Montreal)
Bill Young (milkman & driver)
George Applegate (tallest)

**[90, *back cover, outside*]**

## *Dick Hunt*[14]
## [ca. 1856–57]

**[1, *front cover*]**

**[2]**

([Medium?]
[1/6 size?]

Dick Hunt
68 Stanton

---

(The Human Body by Wilkinson)

---

Mrs. Hicks, widow
75 — wooden house
Columbia with pillars

---

Audubon the Naturalist (-75$^{cts}$) C. S. Francis
Diamond Atlas

12mo.— Morse & Gaston
pub

---

Young's Political History, U. S.— Derby & Jackson

---

Lieut Maury in "Open Arctic Sea"
Brooklyn Institute Sat. Dec. 20

---

Mrs. ^Cornelia Ridgeway —
147 South Sixteenth —
Philadelphia

Washington Medallion
Steel Pen

Presbyterian Quarterly Review Dec
M. W. Dodd

Is there any English translation
of Schlosser's "History
of the Ancient World
and its cultures."

German — 1826 - 34

**[3]**

1/8 entree stampede, canard coupee (duck)
roturier (plebian)

History of Ancient Art
translated from German of
Winckleman
2 vols. 8vo. sold by [*illegible*] & Phinney

Home Journal — [Shaks?]

Spirit of German Poetry
by Joseph Gostick

French Literature — Chambers pub — Spanish Lit

Italian Literatures — Chambers pub.

Schlegel's
History of Literature
viz. Lectures on the Literature of All Nations

Trees of America (serial)
by R. W. Piper, M.D.
Boston, Munroe & Co.

---

System of Physical Geography,
By J. M. Warren, 4to 92 pages
pub by H Cowperthwaite & Co

---

Adventures in the Wilds of the U.S.
and British America by
Chas. Lanman 2 vols 8vo.
Phil. J. W. Moore

---

Capt. Clias
Elementary Course of Gymnastics.
trans.

---

N.E. Historical & Genealogical
Register A. R. Phippon 310 Broadway.

**[4]**

Mrs. Rose
72 White St.
or 74 — husband
engraver
name on the
door

---

Look after Arnold Talfourd's "Ancient History"
10 vols. comprising the political, social,
literary & Philosophical Histories
of Egypt, Assyria, Rome,
Greece, &c. (English ed.
Dix & Edwards 321
Broadway

Look (same place)
at Cyclopedia of Geography
Chas Knight. 4 vols. quarto

---

Frank Bellew, 70. (or 90) West 27th st.

---

Youmans, 63 2d av.

---

Mrs Price
31 Hicks

---

~~R.B. Kimball~~
~~cor First Place, Clinton st.~~
~~7th~~

---

McDonough
16 Hanover place

---

Mrs. Chilton, 69 Varick st

**[5]**

Hank Pierce (4th av
Charley (black hair & eyes — round face) 4th av.
Albert, (Mrs. Jones's son.)
Jack (— 4th av.— now in a N.Y. Express wagon
Frank (Beeswax)
Anson W. Turner 29 (oyster Fulton Market)
Charles Brown (Broadway Brownie)
Storrs King (or "Fulton" with Jack Garrison
John Schoonmake (Lawyer around
City Hall
remember Ben Carman
Jakey (James) tall, genteel friend
of Brownie)
Jay (5th av.) — 139
Bill (Moses) 5th av. 137

Bill - (big, black round eyes — large
coarse) formerly Madison
Jo — (smallish gallus, on Fort Greene
— (Irish descent playing ball).

playing [*illegible*] ball
- Abe (round red pleasant grayish
keeping tally
- John Campbell, round light complex
lymphatic, good-look[?]
- John (light complex — light gray eyes
light hair
- Tom Gray — smallish (legs) [*illegible*]

**[6]**

Edward Smithson (20) full-eyed genteel boy I meet often at the ferries Irish or English
Jack Swinton ([*illegible*] English, (23) at Showery's porter [*illegible*]
Lewis " (in Bangs & Platts)
William Phillips — (large, light, No 8 engine) (26)
Leo (22) No 8 engine (in Showery's)
Henry Post (stout, mechanic, (26)
George Applegate (tallest)
Bob Fraser (28) policeman (5–6), slow, mild Cor Myrtle & ~~Hudson~~ Raymond
Tom Haynes (26) driver, Myrtle – mild –
August (Gus) Dutch boy (16) with cake
Bill (23) round faced, blue eyes, light Irish skin (5th av) 7th av
Harry, conductor Myrtle — (Jamaica Academy)
Jim (new policeman) Irish, (round shouldered
Oscar Clark (4th ave liquid eyes now clerk in R.R. Company)
Ed. F. Underhill — Tribune
193 — 23d st.
Mrs. (lady we hired of in Skillman st 17 Johnson st
4th av. Tracy (26) ~~rath~~ genteel jovial "Judge"
Tom Harvey (5th av.) smallish, timidish, Irish
"Victory" 13
- James Dalton (20) round faced, lymphatic lost front teeth
- Jack — (20) ☉ head more length

[*pasted-in advertisement for new steamer located at Fort Hamilton, NY*]

**[7]**

[*cut away*]

---

William Davis, (thin from Portland 23d st
Bob,— (hermaphrodite[?]
Long Jack (7th av.)
James Clark (Drunkard cor Raymond)
George Whittock, (Tall carman South ferry
Jake (75 Broadway 49th
William Nash, boy light hair
Jim Cunningham, (boy without thumb)
Johnny Rose

**[8]**

**[9]**

4th av.) Brownie, (looks something like handsome Mike hackman
Jack (policeman round, full-sized lymphatic, (eating peanuts night cor Classon & Myrtle
Wm Wilson (Broadway —
Charles Fuller
Johny (round faced — full eyes) liquid in Dunbar's and engine house
Pete (smallish — looks a little like 5th av Billy Folk
Wm Vanderbergh, (young fellow, sick, sandy complexion Fulton ave near City Hall
Tom Riley (handsome Irish fighter
John Kiernan (loafer young saucy looking pretty good looking

**[10]**

**[11]**

Dave. (rich, (white hat.) rides on Broadway line)
Jack, (big young fellow, ^sits corner Adams & Myrtle
4th av. } Arthur, big round sandy hair coarse, open
Peleg, round head & face, young
Wallace, (sailor boy English
was in Japan)
John Stoothoof, (police South ferry smallish sized)

Pete Dempster, (Cor Kent & Myrtle open faced — gay)
Charles Held (boy son of Mr. Held tuner
Mr. Banks, (Lobscouse)
Bill, (engineer Union)
124 4th av
4th { Jo (red hair large red face
Teunis — tall — (Yankee)
Pete — not driver }
Felix M'Cluskey, California
Landon Lennon
about 325
John Davenport — (Classon tall, genteel)
Charly Smith, 119 or 20, 4th av
Jay 815 (about)
or 812

**[12]**

Wm Culver (boy in the bath (18) gone to California
James (lame boy in front of Savings bank (13)
Johnny, ("steel trap)
Jim (boy with Johny Gray)
Charley (Mr Rider's boy
Mike Talley (or Dally) the thinnest 25
Pete "
Tom Egbert 85 (conductor (sailor open neck (24)
Percival de Clifton
Robert (Dad)
Milton (light complexion, (Ohio) 5th av.
Ben Wallis — (grocery cor Clermont & Myrtle
Northport boys { Edmund Bryant — elder
Melville " }
Henry Taylor (Johny Sackback)
Johny Williams (policeman at Fulton ferry N. Y.
Aleck (friend of Andrew.)
Charley Van Dwyne (13) boy on the Nassau sometimes

Mr. Mason — (shoemaker (saw him in Andrew Rome's)
Frank (kindling Wood)
Reuben (in the Grand St. frame shop — now driver)
Charley Quail — (policeman)
David Stewart — (No. 12)
Peter Ridley (apple pedlr
Abe Debevoise (young boy)
Johny Nevin (22) small quiet, carpenter
Dave Rogers
Jack (5th av.) full brown black beard — '(25) brown faced, Feb. 16 '57
Jerry Boerum small, smiling, friend of George,
Phil Stokey (policy player)
Jim Johnson, (saloon & Book)
Woodhull Woolsey

Union Ferry —
- Al (carpenter, Union ferry shop — close by George Wright's bench
- Ansel Ketchum (with Tom's bench
- Alphonso — new — light haired — Amity st.

**[13]**

at Police Station —
- Charley — police ropemaker
- Jerrys — police — looks like Jake Beasly

---

- Charley — -elderly Classon av round[?] white hair
- Dave. coachman Halseys

---

4th av. Mrs. Jones —
- Ed, small, black eyes & brows
- Bill, big bony Yankee linen coat
- Bill big dark complexioned, St. Helena
- George, (sulky head sideways
- Jim, (looks like Chatman
- Johnny (red faced, small chunky
- Mr. Ferris, starter[?]

Johny Mullen red hair, pipe

Irish contractor, Jackson [hallo?]

Lefferts Laidlaw

4th av. — Jack (Davis) light-eyed light haired [~~*illegible*~~] drunk at Pat Newman's
George, coarse complex low forehead pock mark 4th av.
A1 Yankee, thin, medium, black moustache now 5th av
Elisha Jones — foreman

Ab'm Litchalt, small, formerly police now market

Hiram Kellum

Billy Stevens

78? Pat (young, neat jockey cap 8th st.—

Charley — filmy eyes, 4th av

Jim (Jubal Cain)

Tom Van Brunt

Eugene

Tom Hyer, Irish 4th av.

**[14]**

Joe Downing (boy, often at segar store

Oliver (tall, (25,) conductor Myrtle come up in carriage,

Justin (Chousey) boy — (16) blacksmith — come up in the carriage

George Lavallette (tipsy) son of surgeon in Naval Hospital

Jim Allen (44) met at Dominick Colgan's told me he was with me in Hablock's school.)

(Wm Stewart, police captain tall)

Jack Gill, (elder)

Tom "

Bill McCue (Irish — 49th st., snub nose

Tom — policeman, cor William & Frankfort sts

Little Dominick (Dominick Colgan's son) 29

Adolphus Davenport (actor) old boy friend of Ansel Jenning's

Dave Ackerman, (loner)

Charles Edwards, foreman in Lockitts Myrtle

Wm Mosscrop — oyster shop Myrtle & ~~R~~ Ri[*illegible*]

Sam Adams — 63 Broadway large light com[?]

Frank (30) 4th av. fat round face looks like Louis Cost.

Cornish (tow head) 4th av.

Bill (36) Dunham from Phil. dark face stocky frame

Jim Le — — young fellow light longish hair out by Cannon

Jack (5th av.) with the beautiful beard black

Edward (28) young Brooklyn man printer in N.Y. Times)
(ask Tom McEvoy the name of the boy [with?] Geo. Leland
Pat — 203 (Eighth st)

---

Met cor Myrtle & Washington and Marsh —
Teunis — round faced brown ^24 with moustache
Sam — looks some like Bill 49th india ink on his hand
Mike Dally.
24

Mike Butler, boy (18) in stone cutters Kent av.
George Applegate (tallest)
Dan shorter (Myrtle av. market.

**[15]**

George Wright 16 (boy 16 in plaster ornament shop, Myrtle n Ryerson
Charley 22 (fireman in the new drab clothes — 18 NY.
Martin Evans (36)
Ben (19) (tall bony big nosed boy for Hendrickson's express
William 35) tall dark eyed, moustache, ? German formerly Madison av. now Broadway
Martha, (15)(in Burroughs
George (22) (18 — tall mild
John Baulsir (28) (pilot Nassau)
John Evans (30) red beard, wrote notice in Woodbury[?] Times
Chris Pike (30) in office Fulton av. cars
Thos Shephard (30) pol. 7th w.) smallish grey eyes pleasant
Patrick Corr 26 (new pol. Irish boy good looking)
George Moore 21 (tall, thin, works sewing machine)
George Matthews 20 — (in feed store Graham
Ike Debevoise 20 (black eyes & hair)
Pete Clayton 36 (fat round face cor Myrtle & Fulton Brooklyn police
Charly Held 12 — (boy)
Justin 17 (boy, blacksmith from Jersey was the g[*illegible*]
Oliver 21 (tall conductor, slender was in the carriage
Hiram Kellum (25)

[16]

W C. Holley D.C. Holly Real Estate

~~5~~ ~~3~~ Nassau

3 or 5 on the ground floor

---

W Griffith 83 Prospect

---

A. J. Davis, 137 Spring st.

---

Dr. J. D. Whelpley

at Mrs Hildreths

cor. Bleeker & Wooster st

---

Welsh Church

11th st near 3d av.

---

McDonald 335 Broadway

room 39

---

Mrs Bloom

57 High

---

Geo Wheeler

79 55 ~~79~~ Mercer

[17]

Soiree dansante

---

Aleck (big, young, (26,) gets out cars at Prince St.

Quaker Ed. (4th av. (33)

Sam [~~Matthews~~?] (young fellow I met in Dominick Colgan's

John Cunningham — tall thin face No 18

Pete (young married man No 18) bad teeth, good eyes

Tom Lambert (tall young man, Mason Myrtle Av

Revand K Field

Valentine Carman
Hank — (in Geo Douglass coffee & cakes)
Bill (~~tall~~ stout, (Dunbar's) small mouth fat light blue eyes)
George Golder (black eyes & hair — deaf one ear 49th st)

Met with Mike Dally March 24 Myrtle n. Washington:
- Teunis — (25) round, brown face, moustache met at Garry Van Dynes
- Sam — dark complexion, full eyes, (large figures in india ink on left hand
- Mike Dally —

Henry Sinslam[?] hat shop, Myrtle n Canton
Charley — 131 (4th av)

---

Wm Husted (young man in Myrtle near Clinton)
Sandy (5th av.) fancy, "hallo Walt.)
Tom (foreman (13) "Victory" Wmsburgh
David Barnet (boy) (18) in lawyer's office op. City Hall
Billy (138, 4th av) thin consumptive

**[18]**

- Elisha Jones
- Bill " — the sailor
- Dave "

4th av:
- Jack — red faced — marked mouth
- Tom (looks something like Frank with Mrs. Hibbard

5th av. Luther Calvin Davis — (coarse red face
Jack MCoon (boy 20 went in Castle Garden with me April 20)
George Rogers 4th av. has been west 3 years
Stephe (boy with Charley Palmer, black moustache)
Henry Hyer (32) Madison av. thin, bony bilious — told me of Chinese women
Johny (24) 4th av (white teeth) round clear face, brown eyes
John Van Lear (5th av.) fat, lymphatic, no beard
Bill (4th av.) 27 — medium, dark comp & hair — & eyes — ? Dutch
Billy (tall young, walked up to Gold St. with, night N. H. firemen's procession
Elias B. Pierson (32) 5th av. been in the rebel army in China
Jo (Lane) starter Madison av. Wall st.
Aleck (tall (34) — 7th av. seen him in Clason av. Sunday.

George (not Jo) ("Brushmaker") 4th av (thin face superb sonorous voice
Wm Craig 90 (young man — Kent av)

**[19]**

Saml. D. (or E.) ~~Etten~~ Van Etten
Milford, on the Delaware river
Pennsylvania

Go on the N.Y. & Erie R.R. to
Port Jervis (fare $2.00
thence by stage to Milford
(fare 50 cents)

---

son (Charley Etten)

---

Charley Hicks (16) boy clear gold complexion & hair — fat — son of Hicks, in "Fulton's" engine room
Gus White (25) at Ferry with skeleton boat with Walt Baulsir — (5ft 9 high — round — well built
Timothy Meighan (30) Irish, oranges, Fulton & Concord
James Dalton (Engine — Williamsburgh)
Charley Fisher (26) 5th av. (hurt, diseased, deprived)
Ike (5th av.) 28 — fat, drinks, rode "Fashion" in the great race
Jack (4th av) tall, slender, had the French pox (moderate in talk)
Franklin Sivall (4th av) tallish, gaunt
Mike, (Irish) tallest of the two boys at Newman's
Dan " least tall

**[20]**

G W Hill
cor 18th St & 8th ave
George Waldo Hill

---

Talbot
600 Broadway

---

Brittan
333 Broadway

---

Mr. Ives
cor. 4th & South Third
over Savings Bank

---

Every Monday evening — (soirees.)

---

Geo $^{H}$ Riblett
319 2$^{d}$ avenue
near 21$^{st}$

**[21]**

Who was the Greek poet
Pindar?
Who Merlin?

---

Stop at Fowler & Wells and
get paper with "Broadway" article.
also Prince's catalogue

---

Engagement at Harrison's
Wednesday 3d June

---

Moses Stern (tailor)
446 Grand st. N.Y.

---

Mr. Goodfellow
65 — Tenth st

---

R.P. Cooke, M.D. Dentist.
3 Great Jones st

**[22, *italicized words are not in Whitman's hand*]**

*E D Carpenter*
*134 ½ W. 19th St*

Swinton
51 Macdougal st.

---

Dr. Ruggles
24 Warren

---

Charley Goin (pier 20)

*A. Brisbane*
*Irvington N.J.*
*Take Newark train at 3 or 5 get out at Market st Depot in Newark, and get into the Irvington omnibus*

**[23]**

Chicago Magazine
Ross & Tousey

---

Rangers & Regulators of the
Tanaha
Rob't DeWitt

---

Lectures on Human Voice
Eveng's of } Monday 23d March &
Thursday 26th "
at University Medical
College next to
Opera House 14th st.

---

? savoir vivre
good manners — breeding — gentility —
— high-style

[24]

James Gillan (24) driver Myrtle — large country — open faced

Albany Bill (Madison av. tall black eyed)

Billy (beautiful — 1 Bleecker st 8th av)

Jackson L— — / 4th av young fellow from Philadelphia

Jack (tallish, young,* Bleecker & 2d st)

?Charley (tallish and goodsized liquid eyed 4th av — new hand

Charley (East Broadway formerly in Brooklyn

Jack (5th av German birth, black eyes & hair now Madison av.)

Jo Baker (23) fine head — 4th av

Mike Morrow

Mike — (Bdway) was at Mrs. Hoyts with Dressmaker)

John Brownie — (4th av.) tall, genteel)

? (Jack) Riley

Henry Nelson Hannah (

William (Bdwy) (brother of George, formerly 4th av)

playing ball { Pete (Myrtle & Clermont &c 19 or 20 looks something like George
Dave — black eyes .25
George Wood (small moustache }

---

Ike (boy Myrtle) gray eyes) 13

[25]

[26]

---

Geo. Wheeler
79 Mercer
one door above
Spring

---

Hector Tyndale,
707 Chestnut St.
above 7th St.

---

Mrs Sarah Tyndale,
corner Main & High st,
Germantown;

(Germantown Depot
corner 9th & Green sts.)

**[27]**

Clairvoyance (viz clear seeing

---

E. C. Jones

---

go over Jersey City ferry
take the Morris & Essex
RR
for Drakesville
N.J.
Lake Hopatcong
45 miles from
N.Y.

---

Sam Bonnard
South 6th St. near Grove
Jersey City
Inquire for J. B. Forrest
engraver

**[28]**

Truman & Spafford
Cincinnati
O.

---

Robley
cor 18th st & 9th av.
Greenwood

---

**[29]**

[*cut away*]

Meserole st.
near Bushwick av.

---

Schneider's

---

Building an iron steamboat
foot of North Fifth st.
Wm McConnell
sub-contractor

---

five sts. north of Grand

---

**[30]**

**[31]**

(to women — sternly)

Do you suppose you have nothing waiting for yourselves to do, but to embroider, to clean, ~~and~~ to be respectable and modest, and to not swear or drink?

**[32]**

(Spooney)

William Place
(a public house on the Delaware
frequented in the spring by
raftsmen)
Go to Port Jervis ($2)
thence by stage to
William Place's on the
route to "Bushville" (Pa)

[33]

"bold robber"

women rely on men

---

the spiritual influence of
women, & sex —

Mrs. Tyndale's
theory

---

* (That no State shall be
subject to another but
each, shall ~~be free to~~ itself ~~the~~
~~form~~ ^ ~~sole judge of~~ ~~its own institutions~~
have the sole control of
its own institutions,
That there shall be real
tr up)* and continual comity between
~~The States~~, the whole of
them, or any two of
them,

[34]

Questions for Swinton

To tell me of Etruria

[35]
Hemp, corn, and tobacco,
(in Missouri & Kansas

---

Hold fast by me!
I know very well ~~that~~
~~they~~ ^ these ~~must be~~ may have to be ^ searched ~~sought~~ ~~read~~ many

times before they ~~will~~
come to you, and comply with you ~~?— But~~
But what of that? Has
not Nature to ~~read~~ be ~~sought~~ searched
many times?

---

I know they must be
persuaded many times a long while

**[36]**

Miss Ellen Grey
Bowery Theatre
Cor Hicks & Amity
before 1st May
tall high house
free stone.

---

Wm G. Metzler
Tuskilwa
Bureau co
Illinois

**[37]**
word

rifacciamento

Bat-ra-chom a óm a chy

**[38–40, *blank*]**

**[41]**

Oude, (the oldest city in
Hindostan) pop. 10,000

in Names of Pieces

some may be called Poem
(as Poem of W.W.
an American)

some " " Hymn
(as Hymn of
the Body)

" " " Song as
(

" " " simply as
(To a Common
prostitute

" " " Poemet
(as

**[42, *italicized text is a pasted-in business card, with address written in a hand not Whitman's*]**

Scoville
Maiden lane
above William st.

***Mr. S. Emlen Randolph.***
*Room 229 St. Nicholas*
*or 123 South 9th ^ Phila*

**[43–44, *cut away*]**

**[45]**

Noon trains from New York
arrive at Rutland
at 9 o'clock at night

[46]

[47]

That is profitable great to you which
you carry with you
after death

I will carefully earn ~~all~~
~~the~~ riches ~~which I~~
~~can~~ to be carried with
me after the death
of my body.
Poem

I will . . . . .

[48]

[49]

All poems, or any other expressions of literature, that do not tally with their writers actual life and knowledge, are lies.

**[50, *two pasted-in business cards. Only the last line is in Whitman's hand.*]**

*also Southington Highland*
*Plainville Station Conn*
*Hartford Fishkill RR*
***James Richardson Jr.***
*256 Asylum Aven*
*Hartford*

*Edward H. House.*

*Boston Courier*

228 Astor House

**[51]**

I will make a song that
there is no imperfection
in man or woman
And I will make a
song that ~~there each~~
~~thing is~~ no one thing
in the universe is
inferior to another, and
that all are equally
miracles,
And I will make a
song that there is
nothing more beautiful
than death.
And I will make a
song that whatever
happens to any one
may become beautiful

**[52]**

**[53]**

And I will make a new
song of riches, namely
the riches of the body
and the spirit, which
are before death
and after death

---

☞ Every Poem of any thing must enclose and express the spirituality and joy of that thing — (of the train of that thing) — (of those things) — not be a mere didactic

**[54]**

**[55]**

[*cut away*]

Finally after all the physical greatness of the city is attained — after the architecture of the house is finished — then ∧what of the man in the house ∧city? ~~or~~ ∧What of the woman?— What is a ∧great city, or a ∧great house, without great men? great women?

**[56]**

**[57]**

Poem of Prophecies —

— There shall be

(containing prophecies — of all
that will probably be in
fifty, a hundred, two hundred, &c years
hence —

---

doctrinaire — theorist

---

Strong conviction
☞ Not to volunteer, interfere,
or ask questions —

---

Always reality — no "funning"
no wit — no ~~"imagination"~~
~~or~~ ornament

**[58]**

**[59–64, *blank, partially cut away*]**

[65]

~~Poem of (after Death)~~

☞ The eliptical
style for orations
operas
I will be the originator
the inventor

---

That the extasy of
the pythia, the
oracles
— the divine rage afflatus
— that of Christ Hercules &c
are just as eligible now

[66]

[67]

? Poem of Wise Books
Poem of the Library
— (bring in all about the
few leading books.
Literature of Egypt,
Assyria
Persia
Hindostan
^Palestine
Greece — Pythagoras Plato — Socrates — Homer — Iliad Odyssey
Rome,— Virgil
Germany — Luther
Christ
Bible
Shakespeare
Emerson
Rousseau — ("Social Contract")

**[68]**

**[69]**

Motto for all
political ~~philos~~ action

Walt Whitman's terrible
Motto.

No nation, once ∧fully enslaved, ever fully recovered its liberty.—

**[70]**

**[71]**

(Poem of the Library

— first a respectful word to those who in ~~all~~ ancient times, ∧and in all times, in unknown nations, have written wise words, or taught them —

---

wisdom comes mostly back to the projecter, teller — no matter if no record —

---

All my poems do. All I ~~do~~ write I write to ~~fo~~
arouse in you a
great personality

**[72]**

**[73]**

I must not fail to saturate my poems with things, substantial, American
scenes, climates, names, places, words, ~~fa~~ permanent facts (include
☞ every important river and mountain
animals
trees
crops, grains, vegetables,
flowers

**[74]**

**[75]**

Celebrate sing the great ^ante-conditions of the globe, the gaseous, watery (granitic) vegetable ~~periods~~ stages —

---

Poem of Precepts

☞ <u>Poem of Joys</u>
<u>and Works</u>

**[76]**

vegetable
in its natural state,
~~to eat~~ not to eat
grows ^not in US. foreign production
not a fruit
not a wood
sea
sold at drug stores
soft.

**[77]**

The greatest thing about a city is — its people

**[78]**

vegetable

Bet it ~~the same~~ as if I were
with you — Be not too
certain but I am
with you

**[79]**

Poem

poem to one
three centuries
hence or thirty
centuries hence

~~To~~
~~To~~ I, alert, full ∧ ~~formed~~ visible compact, of
life, thirty eight
years old,
To you, yet unborn,
these.
~~As~~ When you read these,
~~Now~~ I that was
visible am ∧ become invisible,
Now ∧ it is you ~~are~~ compact,
full of life, realizing
~~my~~ my ~~these~~ ~~my~~ poems,
If I were ~~here~~ ∧ with you ~~doubtless~~
~~it~~ may be we would
love another

**[80]**

**[81]**

What would be thought of a surgeon or physician who should be delicate ~~and modest, and treat of costumes and respect the~~ and know only the body as it appears in fashionable costumes?— What is more real than sex? What is there at all the facts of existence but procreation?— ~~Yet~~ These are the very things,— what misses these, misses all. There is just the same reason for my poems, and what they seek to do, to include sex and procreation, as there is for the ~~surg~~ physician to include them

**[82]**

[83]
between 9 & 12 (55 Greene
& 1 & 5

---

easy

[84]

[85]
Thomas the Rhymer — — Scotch (supposed about 80 years old)
died 1299
see p 195 — 6 — 7 — Scott's Poems

---

"the importance of the
individual — that is the
greatest ? saying
the — — — — — — that is
the
to — — — — — — that is
the

[86]

[87]
The idea of grades in the mental condition and development of people.—

---

The people ~~are~~ in strata — remember the vast, largest, most continued popular strata (? strats) — also the various other strata, those of criminals, those of ignorant persons.— Also, in other countries, under other religions and governments.— For instance, the common people, what they are, with their physique, their social customs, amusements, costumes, liberty, slavery, and the rest.

---

This ^The great fact of grades ~~comprehends~~ includes and explains a hundred subordinated facts; without ~~them~~ it, the included facts not well understood.—

**[88]**

vegetable & mineral
no tool, implement, or in-strument.
not in the room
 — larger than a foot
on land
is a fixture
 — outdoors
public spectacle
figure
chiseled
 — on top of a building
not on city building
on Broadway,
no place of amusement
bird
above
is eagle on top
above the St. Germain
on

**[89]**

Poem of Legacies

— including all that we have received from the past —
 — tables, languages, figures, measures, literature

**[90, *written upside down, italicized words not in Whitman's hand*]**

court plaster

---

all animal

---

~~vegetable~~

*~~no~~ not in the room*
*in town and country*

*smaller than your arm*
*not a mecanicks tool*
*not wood*
*not any Diet*
*not any tool*
*Groes in the ground*
*it Groes in the north*
*it Bares flowers*
*it is of a fiber*
*not groe on the vine*
*not in Bo[ston?]*

**[91]**

**[92]**

vegetable
not of diet
not wood
in this room
not a cigar
not sold
not about a person
does belong to the premises
not represent any thing
not dry goods
not on a level
not a cork
above the counter
fast & fixed
touches the wall
No paper

**[93]**

[*cut away*]

Book of Letters ? Poem

---

Letter ? Poem to a prostitute
Letter to felon
Letter to one about to die
(end letter to prostitute —
— "I salute you my love,
with a kiss on your
lips, that you do
not forget me —

**[94]**

**[95]**

? whether the right of voting, legal owning &c, (being "of age") should not be changed from 21 to 18 years —

**[96]**

**[97]**

? Poem of American Names

---

the ^ bookbinder's hammer, knife, shears, & folder

---

the standing press,
" ~~stamping~~ embossing press,

**[98]**

**[99]**

In Poem of Personality — incorporate all the ideas of the Personal Magnetism articles

---

? Poem of Large Personality.

(make this poem for women just as much as men)

**[100–102, *blank*]**

**[103]**

[*cut away*]

? (The Dutch parentage of
Manhattan, the English
of Massachusetts, the
~~G~~ Swedes of New Jersey

[*cut away*]

**[104]**

**[105]**

personality — pride
self-esteem
self-appreciation
egotism
elevatedness

---

the strap and paddle for the
punishment of slaves

---

the young heifer

**[106]**

**[107–112, *torn out*]**

[113]

Make A Poem (expressed in th[inks?] and ~~act~~ moving acts)
involving the idea, that in morals and mental results good, evil, &c, there is the same reciprocal play of effect and causes, as in the physical world.

---

When the original men of These States threw off the imperialism of Great Britain, then was dimly roused before the fathers, the vista of a noble government.

[114]

The Mayor this forenoon issued an order to the various Captains, directing them to call in the men at 4 oclock this afternoon and have them deliver up the city property — the Captains to hold on to the Station Houses till the further action of the Common Council

[115]

Poem of (my brothers
and sisters) artists,
singers, musicians

[116]

[117]

— 1, 2, 3, &c
an equal friend of
all The States.

[118]

[119]

The greatest s — — of for a Great City
— ~~The~~ A city may have great temples, avenues,
&c

but ~~it p~~ in its common people, their ~~knewledge~~ personality, heroism, ruggedness beauty & strength

**[120]**

**[121]**

The greater the reform, the
greater the personality
that is needed,

---

<u>Poem of Tears</u>

Can I not make a
poem in which
the tears drop
down in great
drops?

**[122]**

**[123]**

animal & mineral
about the person
not in sight
about not Sam
carried in pocket
moves on a joint
Belongs to Cale

this pencil I am writing with

**[124]**

**[125]**

1 — mineral
2 ~~l~~ more than a foot
3 not in the room

4 is ~~some~~ a conspicuous object in this city
5 is in an ~~elevated~~ ~~lofty~~ elevated position
6 in Broadway
7 private property
8 below Canal
9 in front of a house
10 below the first story
11 no figure of any thing

**[126]**

(stone mortar) stone stoop

~~12 below Worth~~
13 stone
14 above St. Paul's
15 about the door way
~~1~~16 at a hotel
17 Astor house stoop
18 not the pillars
19

**[127]**

Clinic, (or clinique)

relating to a bed, bed-ridden
— (the lectures, or treatment
of a surgeon or phys.
given off-hand, as
^he stands by the the patient, ~~is brought~~
~~to him~~)

**[128–129, *blank*]**

**[130]**
bevel

vegetable
not gritty
it is wood
manufactured
it is used as a tool
it is used by any of us in this room)
not used as a support
smaller than my arm
not require the mouth
carried about openly
less than a foot
has a handle
used to strike blows,
used by

**[131]**

the Ame

**[132]**
~~all~~[?]

| | | | | | | | |

---

mineral
manufactured
instrument
not iron
not a mechanic's tool
not used by us
not for hurt,
sold not at stores
bigger than my fist

not used in medicine or surgery,
not used by any public officer
no precious metal
not in this city
is in the U.S.
not in memory of any person
On land

**[133]**
not an edifice
not as a signal

**[134]**
Washington Monument
at 14t$^{h}$ st.

**[135–136, *torn out or blank*]**

**[137]**
poem of the ~~Indians~~ aborigines
— introducing every
principal aboriginal
trait, and name

---

☞ bring in ~~Indi~~ aboriginal
traits in poem of
(American) Materials

**[138]**
(square
Mineral
not in this room
manufactured

sold at stores
hardware stores / & drug stores
not taken in the stomach
∧sometimes used in surgery
iron and steel
not an edged tool of any sort
no application to persons
instrument
no handle
mechanic
Carpenters
sometimes more than 9 inches sometimes less.
smooth
~~one~~ points
Joint

**[139]**

---

Poem of Criminals
Now I ~~take~~ betake
myself from all
others, and go
among criminals —

**[140–144, *blank or torn out*]**

**[145]**

in Poems somewhere put in the Dutch liberty, conscienteousness and good natured tolerance — the settling spirit of Manhattan island — and its prevailing characteristic to this day

[*pencil sketch of connected polygons*]

**[146]**

**[147]**

America brings to the ~~judgem~~ test
  of characters and heroism
  ~~entirely far larger~~
  her own large and
  new standards

**[148]**

**[149]**

? A poem ^(or passage in a poem) giving an account of my way of making a poem
  Poemet
  Poemot

**[150–159, *blank or torn out*]**

**[160]**

[*cut away*]
grows both north & south
no shell
generally cooked
eaten at this counter
sometimes sold by the bushel
smaller or larger than Jack's fist
whitish meat

**[161]**

eat here every day,
grows in a lump,
(~~no~~ may be either mealy or not

**[162–163, *blank*]**

**[164]**

Mineral
quite certain not in the room,
something made through the use of fire
~~iron~~ steel
smaller
carried about one
not a part of another ~~at~~[?] article
not ~~a part~~ used about the toilet
used by any one
nothing to do with sound

**[165]**

**[166]**

It is ~~not any more~~ no more in the
rythmic legends than in
all else,

It is not in the ∧old books — it is not in ~~old books~~ the rythmic
legends,— nor it has not ~~in w~~
descended ~~to~~ in
~~the~~ books, any more
than all else,

**[167]**

? Poem of the past

~~What of the past~~
Poemet.
~~What is the poem of the Past~~
~~I was~~
I was looking ∧a long while for the poem
of the past and now
I have found it
It is the Present — it is

the this Earth to-day, and
~~all th Amer~~ this
America, and all
languages and inventions
It is the ~~long~~ broad show of
artificial things, ships,
~~international commer~~
~~exchanges, books,~~
and the interchanges
of nations

**[168]**

**[169]**

animal & vegetable
in this room
not used by drivers
worn above the waist
not the neck
complete in
~~it's~~ a

---

Poem expressing the sentiment of the joy of old age — of an old person — (? or in the poems of Joys.)

O my old ~~age~~ manhood! — my
joy!
^My children and grandchildren! My white hair and
beard! My ~~calmness~~ largeness majesty
^calmness and ~~peace~~ majesty from
~~many~~ many years!

**[170]**

handsome room, gilt chandeliers

---

white-neckcloths — — quaker looking horse-shoe, line of men —

homily of a reverend gentleman —

room about one-quarter full

a regular Yankee Dyspeptic faced speaker, with awkward, see-saw gestures

very dry speech, the usual platitudes

**[171]**

[*cut away*]

O the ~~exquisiteness~~ joy of
    ~~my~~ womanhood! — O ripened
    happiness at last!

~~I am my breast have~~
~~suckled many so~~
I am more than ~~seventy~~ eighty
    years of age, in perfect health — ~~my~~
My hair ~~also~~ too is ∧pure white —
    ~~I My~~ I am the most
    venerable mother ~~in~~
    ~~perfect health~~ — I am complete in myself
To me ~~also~~ all people ~~are~~
    ~~drawn more than~~
    draw nigh — ~~they~~ I f
    attract ∧with more than ~~I am~~
    the attraction of my youth.—

**[172–176, *blank*]**

**[177]**

12 — no legs
13 — houses commonly have these things in them
14 ∧mostly in the Kitchen, parlor and bedroom

15 not used about the fire, nor in preparing any thing for the fire.
16 no water
17 — no instrument
18 no kind of a box
19 neither a handle nor handles
20 not pliable

**[178]**
foil

Mineral
manufactured
in sight
used not with food
one complete article
not any vessel
not as large as my hand
no matter about the weather
not about the person
above four feet height
not for sale
not hung up
not handled
not on shelf or counter
driven in horizontally
nail

**[179]**
Hindostan, from the
western sea.—

~~Mother~~
^I look on the Mother, at far removes, ~~even~~ of
These States,
Mother of ~~religions~~ languages

— mother of the great
idea of ~~the~~ avatars,
~~of~~
~~Like~~ As a child looking over [~~*illegible*~~] I look
I turn seeing
~~his~~ afar at the ~~my~~ house ~~the place~~ house of
maternity, the land
of migrations.
~~As I~~
I ~~stand~~ look on ^the shores of my ~~the~~ western sea ~~to~~ behold the
~~There there is the~~ old mother
of me. (I
~~We~~
I come westward From the Himmalehs, from
the vast plains, from
the north, ~~and~~ from
the flowery islands, ~~how~~
~~long it is since! how~~
~~many generations!~~
~~Here~~ The circle is circled,
tr up (We face home again, as ~~from~~ after
long travel, growth & sleep

**[180]**

| | |, | | |, | | |, | | |,

**[181]**

**[182, *back cover*]**

# *Calamus-Leaves* ~~*Live Oak, with Moss*~~[15]
## [ca. 1859]

**[1]**

#14
p. 360

Calamus-Leaves.
~~Live Oak~~, ~~with Moss.~~

I.

Not the heat flames up and con-
sumes,
Not the sea-waves hurry in and
out,
Not the air, delicious and dry, the
air of the ripe summer, bears
lightly along white down-balls
of myriads of seeds, wafted,
sailing gracefully, to drop
where they may,
Not these — O none of these, more
than the flames of me, con-
suming, burning for his love
whom I love — O none, more
than I, hurrying in and out;
Does the tide hurry, seeking some-
thing, and never give up?— O
I, the same, to seek my life-long
lover;

O nor down-balls, nor perfumes, nor
the high rain-emitting clouds,
are borne through the open air,
more than my copious soul is
borne through the open air, wafted
in all directions, for friendship, for
love.—

**[2]**

Calamus 20
p. 364

II

I saw in Louisiana a
live-oak growing,
All alone stood it, and the
moss hung down from the
branches,
Without any companion it grew
there, glistening out ~~with~~
joyous leaves of dark green,
And its look, rude, unbending,
lusty, made me think of
myself;
But I wondered how it could
utter joyous leaves, standing
alone there without its friend,
its lover — For I knew I could
not;
And I plucked a twig with
a certain number of leaves
upon it, and twined around
it a little moss, and brought
it away — And I have placed
it in sight in my room,

2

**[3]**

It is not needed to remind
me as of my friends, (for I
believe ^ lately I think of little
else than of them,)
Yet it remains to me a
curious token — ~~I write~~ — it makes
~~these pieces and name~~ me think of manly love,
~~them after it~~;
For all that, and though the
~~tree~~ ^ live oak glistens there in Louis-
iana, solitary in a wide
flat space, uttering joyous
leaves all its life, without
a friend, a lover, near — I
know very well I could
not.

3

**[4]**

(131) — 357

III

When I heard at the close of
the day how I had been
praised in the Capitol, still
it was not a happy night
for me that followed;
~~And else,~~ Nor when I caroused — — ~~Or~~
— ^ Nor when my ^ favorite plans were accom-
plished — ~~it was well enough~~ — was I really happy,—
~~Still I was not happy~~;
But ~~that~~ ~~the theat~~ ^ that day ~~when~~ ~~when~~ I rose
at dawn from the bed of
perfect health, electric, in-
haling sweet breath,

When I saw the full moon
in the west grow pale and
disappear in the morning light,
When I wandered alone over the
beach, and undressing, bathed,
laughing with the waters, and
saw the sun rise,

4

**[5]**

And when I thought how
my friend, my lover, was
coming, then O∧ I was happy;
~~O~~ ~~tThen~~ ~~e~~Each breath tasted
sweeter — and all that day my
food nourished me more — And
the beautiful day passed well,
And the next came with equal
joy — And with the next, at
evening, came my friend,
And that night, while all
was still, I heard the
waters roll slowly continually
up the shores
I heard the hissing rustle of
the liquid and sands, as directed
to me, whispering, to congratulate
me,— For the friend I love lay
sleeping by my side,
In the stillness his face was in-
clined towards me, while the
moon's clear beams shone,
And his arm lay lightly over my
breast — And that night I was happy.

5

[***Beneath a paste-over is an earlier version of the concluding stanzas above, with no strikethroughs***]

And that night O you happy
        waters, I heard you beating
        the shores — But my heart
        beat happier than you
        — for he I love is returned and
        sleeping by my side,
And that night in the stillness
        his face was inclined toward
        me while the moon's clear
        beams shone,
And his arm lay lightly over my
        breast — And that night I
        was happy.

**[6]**

Calamus 23
p. 367

IV.

This moment as I sit alone,
        yearning and pensive, it
        seems to me there are other
        men, in other lands, yearning
        and pensive.
It seems to me I can look
        over and behold them, in
        Germany, France, Spain — Or
        far away in China, ^India, or ~~in~~
        Russia — talking other dialects,
And it seems to me if I
        could know those men~~, better~~
        I should love them as I
        love men in my own lands,
It seems to me they are as

wise, beautiful, benevolent,
as any in my own lands;
O I ~~know~~ think we should be
brethren — I ~~know~~ think I should
be happy with them.

6

**[7]**

8 [amplitu?]354
8

V.

Long I thought that knowledge
alone would suffice me — O
if I could but obtain
knowledge!
Then ~~my lands~~ the Land of the Prairies engrossed me — —
the south savannas engrossed me —
For them I would live — I
would be their orator;
Then I met the examples of old
and new heroes — I heard ~~the~~
~~examples~~ of warriors, sailors,
and all dauntless persons —
And it seemed to me I too
had it in me to be as
dauntless as any, and would
be so;
And then to finish all, it
came to me to strike up the
songs of the New World — And
then I believed my life must
be spent in singing;
But now take notice, Land of
the prairies, Land of the south
savannas, Ohio's land,

7

**[8]**

Take notice, you Kanuck woods
— and you, Lake Huron — and
all that with you roll toward
Niagara — and you Niagara
also,
And you, Californian mountains —
that you all find some one else
that he be your singer of songs,
For I can be your singer of songs
no longer — ~~I have passed ahead~~ —
I have ceased to enjoy them.
I have found him who loves me,
as I him in perfect love,
With the rest I dispense — I sever
from all that I thought would
suffice me, for it does not — it
is now empty and tasteless
to me,
I heed knowledge, and the grandeur
of The States, and the examples
of heroes, no more,

8

**[9]**

I am indifferent to my own
songs — I am to go with
him I love, and he is to
go with me,
It is to be enough for each
of us that we are together —
We never separate again.—

---

8 ½

**[10]**

Calamus 32 p. 372

VI.

What think you I have
        taken my pen to record?
Not the battle-ship, perfect-
        model'd, majestic, that I saw
        to day arrive in the offing,
        under full sail,
Nor the splendors of the past
        day — nor the splendors of
        the night that envelopes me —
        Nor the glory and growth of
        the great city spread around
        me,
But the two ~~young~~ men I saw
        to-day on the pier, parting
        the parting of dear friends.
The one ~~who~~ to ~~remained~~ remain hung on
        the other's neck and passionately
        kissed him — while the one
        ~~who remained~~ to depart tightly prest the
        one ~~who remained~~ to remain in his arms.

---

9

**[11]**

10 — 356

VII.

You bards of ages hence~~,~~! when
        you refer to me, mind not
        so much my poems,
Nor speak to me that I pro-
        phesied of The States and led
        them the way of their glories,

But come, I will inform you
who I was underneath that
impassive exterior — I will
tell you what to say of me,

[*illegible*] 9 ½

**[12]**

Publish my name and hang up
my picture as that of the
tenderest lover,
The friend, the lover's portrait, of
whom his friend, his lover,
was fondest,
Who was not proud of his songs,
but of the measureless ocean
of love within him — and
freely poured it forth,
Who often walked lonesome walks
thinking of his dearest friends,
his lovers,
Who pensive, away from one he
loved, often lay sleepless and
dissatisfied at night,
Who, dreading lest the one he loved
might after all be indifferent
to him, felt the sick feeling —
O sick! sick!
Whose happiest days were those, far
away ^through fields, in woods, ~~or~~ on hills, he
and another, wandering hand in
hand, they twain, apart from
other men.
Who ever, as he sauntered the
streets, curved with his arm
the manly shoulder of his

friend — while the curving
arm of his friend rested
upon him also.

---

10

**[13]**

(9) 355

~~IX.~~ VIII.

Hours continuing long, sore
and heavy hearted,
Hours of the dusk, when I
withdraw to a lonesome and
unfrequented spot, seating
myself, leaning my face
in my hands,
Hours sleepless, deep in the night,
when I go forth, speeding
swiftly the country roads, or
through the city streets, or
pacing miles and miles, stifling
plaintive cries,

11

**[14]**

Hours discouraged, distracted,
— For he, the one I cannot
content myself without —
soon I saw him content
himself without me,
Hours when I am forgotten —
(O weeks and months are
passing, but I believe I am
never to forget!)

Sullen and suffering hours —
(I am ashamed — but it is
useless — I am what I am;)
Hours of my torment — I
wonder if other men ever
have the like, out of the
like feelings?
Is there even one other like
me — distracted — his friend,
his lover, lost to him?
Is he too as I am now? Does
he still rise in the morning,
dejected, thinking who is lost to him?
And at night, awaking, think who is
lost?
Does he too harbor his friendship si-
lent and endless? Harbor his anguish
and passion?
Does some stray reminder, or the
casual mention of a name, bring
the fit back upon him, taciturn
and deprest?
Does he see himself reflected in me?
In these hours does he see the
face of his hours reflected?

---

12

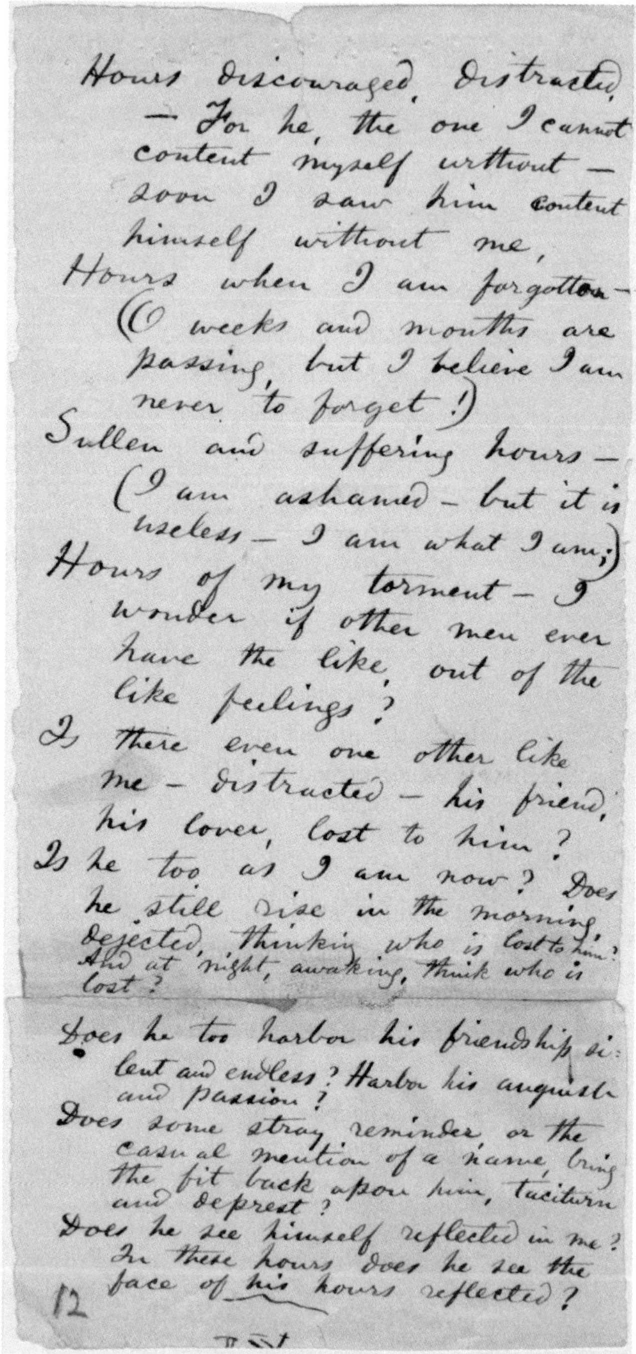

Hours discouraged, distracted,
— For he, the one I cannot
content myself without —
soon I saw him content
himself without me,
Hours when I am forgotten —
(O weeks and months are
passing, but I believe I am
never to forget!)
Sullen and suffering hours —
(I am ashamed — but it is
useless — I am what I am;)
Hours of my torment — I
wonder if other men ever
have the like, out of the
like feelings?
Is there even one other like
me — distracted — his friend,
his lover, lost to him?
Is he too as I am now? Does
he still rise in the morning,
dejected, thinking who is lost to him?
And at night, awaking, think who is
lost?
Does he too harbor his friendship si-
lent and endless? Harbor his anguish
and passion?
Does some stray reminder, or the
casual mention of a name, bring
the fit back upon him, taciturn
and deprest?
Does he see himself reflected in me?
In these hours does he see the
face of his hours reflected?
12

Leaf from *Calamus-Leaves* ~~*Live Oak, with Moss*~~ manuscript (ca. 1859).

**[15]**

Calamus 34

p. 373

IX.

I dreamed in a dream of a
city where all the men
were like brothers,
O I saw them tenderly love
each other — I often saw
them, in numbers, walking
hand in hand;
I dreamed that was the city
of robust friends — Nothing
was greater there than ~~the~~
~~quality of~~ manly love — it
led the rest,
It was seen every hour in the
actions of the men of that city,
and in all their looks and
words.—

13

**[16]**

Calamus 43 . p. 377

X

O you whom I ∧often and silently come
where ~~I~~ you are, that
I may be with you,
As I walk by your side, or
sit near, or remain in
the same room with you,
Little you know the subtle
electric fire that for
your sake is playing
within me.—

14

**[17]**

Calamus 36

p. 374

XI.

Earth! ~~My Likene~~ss! Though
you look so impassive,
ample and spheric there
— I now suspect that
is not all,
I now suspect there is
something terrible in you,
ready to break forth,
For an athlete loves me,
and I him — But toward
him there is something
fierce and terrible in me,
I dare not tell it in words —
not even in these songs.

15

**[18]**

To a Western Boy

Calamus 42

p. 377

XII

To the young man, many
things to absorb, to engraft,
to develope, I teach, that
he be my eleve,
But if through him ~~rolls~~ speed
not the ~~red~~ blood of
~~divine~~ friendship, hot
and red — If he be not

silently selected by lovers,
and do not silently select
lovers — of what use were
it for him to seek to
become eleve of mine?

16

# *W. Whitman Portland av.*[16]

# [ca. 1857–62]

**[1, *front cover*]**

**[2]**

W. Whitman
Portland av. near Myrtle
Brooklyn

**[3]**

~~Mrs. Case, 296 Bleecker~~
Hines, 174 $10^{th}$ av. bet. $21^{st}$ & $22^{d}$
Miller, 205 $8^{th}$ av.
Geo. Potter, 137 West $16^{th}$ st.
~~Swinton 154 West $26^{th}$ st. bet. $7^{th}$ & $8^{th}$ av.~~
Mrs. Rose, 95 Prince
Peale, 15 Hudson [*illegible*], 2d story,
over drug store.
Billy Anderson, 74 [*illegible*] st

---

86 West $42^{d}$ st. Ada Clare
near $6^{th}$ av

---

John J. Irwin, Grocer,
Putnam av. bet. Franklin &
Classon

---

Houghton (Boston) Knickerbocker

---

George,     23$^{d}$ st. large (rooms on 6$^{th}$ av.

---

Bub Cooper 41 Troy st
Mrs Bloom, 27 Schermerhorn st
Mike Lawn } 23$^{d}$ st No. 7
Pete Lawn } 14th No 7
Aristides — 5th av

---

Mrs. Case. 54 Greenwich av. 3$^{d}$ floor

---

Al. (No. 5 4th av) Jan 3$^{d}$ '62

---

Jack $_{\text{Abbott}}$ } 467 $_{\text{No 7}}$ Bowery & [*illegible*]
Bultz cor. 12$^{th}$ st & av. C Eatin Saloon

**[4]**

**[5]**

Mary Hart ( ~~No~~ )

---

10 Washington street
— 1$^{st}$ Floor — husband $_{\text{is a pedlar}}$
Thomas Dougherty

---

**[6]**

**[7]**

No 9 — 5th av.
Saturday ^$^{\text{21st inst}}$ — ~~3$^{d}$~~ 2$^{d}$ trip
down
— ~~Corner~~ $^{\text{to near}}$ 9$^{th}$ st ~~in~~
in Broadway
Henry Taylor

[8]

[9]

James Metcalf, 3d district Station
House, Chambers st.

---

Dec 28 — Saturday night Mike Ellis — wandering at the cor of Lexington av. &
32d St.— took him home to 150 37th street, — 4th story back room — bitter cold night — works in Stevenson's Carriage factory.

---

letters for Burnside Ex
left at
Col. Frank E. Howes store
203 Broadway

[10]

ξ

[11]

<u>The two vaults</u>

Subject — Poem

---

The vault at Pfaffs where the
drinkers and laughers meet
to eat and drink and
carouse,
While ^on the walk immediatey
overhead, passes ~~all~~
the myriad feet of
Broadway

---

As the dead in their
graves, are underfoot ^hidden

And the living pass over
them, recking not of them,

Laugh on laughers!
Drink on drinkers!
∧Bandy the jest! Toss the theme from one
to another!
[~~Sm~~?] Beam up — Brighten up
bright eyes of beautiful
young men!

**[12]**

**[13]**

Eat what you, haveing
ordered, ~~is~~ are pleased
to see placed before
you — after the ~~w~~
work of the day, now,
with appetite, eat,
Drink wine — drink beer —
raise your voice.
Behold! ~~Welcome~~ your friend, as
he arrives — Welcome
him, where, from the
upper step, he looks
down upon you
with a cheerful look

**[14]**

**[15]**

~~Behold the company~~
Overhead ~~passes~~ rolls Broadway
— ~~over~~ the myriad
rushing, ~~Broadway~~

The lamps are lit — the
shops blaze — the
fabrics and jewelry are seen through
the plate-glass ~~in the~~
windows ~~are [*illegible*] the~~
~~show of the art and~~
~~fabric of the~~ [earth?]
The strong lights from
above pour down
upon them, and [~~po?~~]
are shed outside
The thick crowds, ~~with~~
well-dressed — the
[~~unceas?~~] continual crowds
as if they would never end

**[16]**

**[17]**

The curious appearance
of the faces — the glimpses
first caught of the
eyes and expressions,
as they flit along.
(~~O~~ You phantoms! ~~how~~ oft I
~~stop~~ pause, yearning,
to arrest some one
of you!
Oft I doubt ~~your reality~~ your reality ~~whether~~
you are real, ~~and~~ — I
[~~must?~~] suspect all is
but a pageant.)
The

**[18]**

**[19]**

The lights beam in the
first vault — but
the other is entirely
dark

---

In the first

---

get at Library
Schiller's complete Works

---

English with new translations
by Dr. C. T. Hempel

---

New York City during the
Revolution, $4^{to}$; 195 pages
— published for ~~by~~ the Mercantile Library
Association

---

**[20]**

**[21]**

Anne E. Green
in Care of Dan'l Hathaway Livery stable keeper
Columbus
Franklin co. Ohio

---

drawers factory
Grand street, near Attorney

---

**[22]**

[23]

Presbyterian Church of
Jamaica — 200th
anniversary <Tuesday afternoon 3 oclock

7th & 8th of January

---

The congregation have just erected two mural tablets — set in the walls of the Church, — on which are inscribed the names of all the deceased ministers — 19 ministers altogether —

[24]

[25]

Exercises on Tuesday.

Prayer by Rev. Nicholas Everett Smith —

Scriptures read out of a Bible older than 1776.

Hymn ^read and from Sternhold & Hopkins, printed in 1714, — before Watts was born

Stones inaugurated by Rev. Mr. Oakey — 5 or 6 minutes — object of stones, and welcome.—

**[26]**

**[27]**

Rev. James M. McDonald
of Princeton, N.J.
~~fo~~ stationed at Jamaica

---

Ecclesiastes 1st ~~4~~,
"One generation passeth
away, and another
generation cometh,
but the earth abideth
forever."

---

— subject — relation of
the permanent to the
transient, ^~~especially~~
or the gains over the
losses in history

**[28]**

**[29]**

dwelt briefly on the
transient nature of
earthly thing

---

Removed as we are from
Greece, Egypt, &c we still
find engrafted to-day
on our own affairs,
all that is valuable
belonging to them, such
for instance as the
family institution.

---

Change the form, but
the substance always
remains

---

progress has been made
no matter how slow.

**[30]**

**[31]**

the Church has come over sea to us —

---

drawing from the very decay of the past, a vigorous life for the future.

---

Picture ~~of~~ a bird's eye of the history of the ~~civilized~~ world at the time of the settlement of this island 200 years ago.— England — Russia, Holland, France &c. Louis 14, Cromwell,

**[32]**

**[33]**

No English copy of scriptures had yet been — John Eliot's Indian testament had been printed in

---

The Dutch church in Brooklyn existed.

---

In 1657 there were but three schoolmasters on Long Island. Rich Jones.

---

Scho. of Jam was arrested

---

1656 Jamaica was settled
1644 Hempstead " "

**[34]**

**[35]**

~~Salut au Monde~~

Yemacah Indians — were found here from thence the town was named.

---

Tribes here were subdued by Capt. Underhill & others.

---

how very 200 years ago
humble — thatch & log
the appear houses

---

in imagination enter one of the houses here — of 200 years ago —
— food venison & fish — bread scarce — dinner indian pudding

**[36]**

**[37]**

minute description of domestic life here on Long Island at that time

---

gun killing wolf

---

Costume — of man & woman of the time

---

picture of the whole domestic life of people of Jamaica

---

| | |
|---|---|
| no of heads in Jamaica | 87 |
| in 1683 | 5 |
| whole pop. | 435 |

---

Danl Denton's celebrated History of New York
1670, pub in London

---

Denton was the first town clerk in Jamaica town

**[38]**

**[39]**

During 7 years preceding 1688,

there were 27 marriage

71 baptism

23 burials

in a pop of ~~14~~50

---

picture in imagination

— entering a home here 200 years ago —

— conforming [~~bu?~~] to the historical facts as

---

— conversations

some had been in Cromwell's & Charles' battles

---

some had seen a witch burnt — or told stories of witchcraft.

**[40]**

**[41]**

— 1670 — account of a witch at that date here

---

imagine also the scene presented here on a Sabbath morning — 200 years

---

Abraham Smith beats the drum — to call the people together for the~~r~~ meeting

---

attendance is compulsory.

---

men wore three corner'd hats — small clothes.— silver buckles — ruffles & wrists — swords — ladies — brocade — [~~*illegible*~~] hoop'd petticoats

**[42]**

**[43]**
On the Sabbath, their apparel was simple and appropriate,— neat, but not gaudy.

---

people enter the Church — a humble edifice built of logs and thatch.

---

the hour-glass stands beside the Bible, to give note of the time.

---

He then (Rev) glanced at the Causes which led to our forefathers coming here.
(skip next pages)

**[44]**

**[45]**

subject for poems

---

High Tide
every thing culminating — prosperity
— all flush — every thing
crowded on to the utmost
of prosperity — rose-color
— wealth — friends —
luck —

---

then
Low Tide

the reverse

**[46]**

**[47]**
May 1672 — the town entered into an agreement with Rev. John Pruden, to preach for them, under the Presbyterian system of doctrine.

---

Jamaica has been Presbyterian from the beginning — and proved her devotion so through a long contest in the early settlement.

---

This is surely the oldest Presbyterian Church on the American continent — 10 years older than the one in Maryland.

**[48]**

**[49]**

[*torn away*]

— what an advance since that day — there are now 5500 Presbyterian ministers.

— ~~18~~ 8000 churches 775,000 communicants

— more than double what now exist in Great Britain and provinces

**[50]**

[*torn away*]

coffee & cakes < [*illegible*]

Henry's — next door

---

**[51]**

14 ~~00~~ millions and a half of Church property

---

Congregation ^at present in Jamaica is one of the largest in rural

---

Whitfield here 1740 & 1764 preached here in Jamaica

---

last convert ^made by of Whitfield died in 1840, aged 95, having been a communicant[?] 75 years — here in Jamaica

**[52]**

**[53]**

— wound up by an appropriate close.

---

no gulf every[?] really divides one generation from ~~one~~ another — ~~they~~

- ~~we~~

— he took a cheerful view of the present, encouraging all to hope, through the present crisis of our nation.

**[54]**

**[55]**

---

~~Th~~Wednesday 8th was a meeting ~~of~~ gathering of Clergymen, elders, emigrants &c —

to-day from ~~Rev.~~ venerable Dr. Shelton who has been an elder here 40.

---

Rev. Mr. Crane } spoke
" " Everett }

with reminiscences &c

---

Representation from Philadelphia

Rev. Mr. Breed —

Rev. Dr. Krebs | Rev. Mr. Higbie

**[56]**

**[57]**

will be published

---

Rev. Dr. Krebs ~~deliv~~ preached Wednesday night —

---

Thursday, the Lord's supper will be administered —

---

— will be the conclusion

---

Tablets in church

{ from 1666 to 1840

---

[58]

[59]

Krebs — the Presbytery of New York

connection between the church & the family

---

Rev. ~~Dr.~~ Reeve Mr. Breed, of Philadelphia

---

Mr. Reeve of the Presbytery of L. I.

---

this church has sent out 25 or 30 ministers

---

[60]

[61]

$14 full suit.

---

3 ¾

---

[62]

Rosse's "Index of Dates."

(in Bohn's Scientific Library.

---

Hadyn's "Dictionary of Dates."

| | |
|---|---|
| | 18 |
| 9 | 14 |
| 5 | 72 |
| | 18 |
| | 252 |

shelf for undershirts &

drawers — 10 (18) 180

neck handkerchief ~~~ 1

hat 2

**[63]**

leaves Jamaica 10 m before 5 & half past 6

---

**[64, *back cover*]**

## *English runic*[17]
## [1860]

**[1, *front cover*]**

**[2]**

**[3]**

English ~~Pica~~ runic þ

Calamus { 60 ¼
2 line pica rustics
? 3 " " "

[great?] primer ornamented [*illegible*]

pica rustic ᵖ 6[2?]

2 line pica ornamented No. 7 p66

---

"Enfans d'Adam
? (2 line pica Saxon ornate shaded
p 82

[*illegible*] 2 line [trim?] pica modern text
p 85
☞ 2 line English scribe text shades
p 87

---

## Calamus

<u>canon</u> scribe text shad[*torn away*]
p. 87 Johnson's book
3 line sm pica rustic " p 68

**[4]**

Chants Boston [*illegible*]
Democratic — 2 line primer

---

or pa[ge?] 32 Johnson's book

---

2" Democratic — double Paragonm[?] composite
p 89 Johnson's book

---

Calamus 2 line gr[eat?] primer [r?]ust
— Rogers book Boston
(type foundry

---

canon ornamented
p 81 Johnson's book

---

Enfans d'Adam
2 line pica ornamented
Rogers book

---

Leaves of Grass.
double paragon scribe text
shaded — p 8[7?] Johnson's book

---

also same page four six line small pica
German text ornamented

---

☞ see two dashes on p [*illegible*] Johnsons book

**[5]**

George S. Phillips
Chelsea
Mass
January Searle

---

[6]

John W A Scott

cor of River & Cottage sts
Cambridgeport.

---

down Lowell st to Forest hill st — turn to the left, 3^d house.

[7]

Brookline

---

find Mr Lyman's place
— Col. Perkins' (dead)

---

Mr Billings
59 Camden

[8]

In the South, (S. C., Georgia &c) "the most beautiful wild flower, in the piney region is the wild pink — the most fragrant the jessamine."
blackberries and huckle
berries abound —
Wilmington, N C

[9]

Blacks.— You see not near as many black persons in Boston, as you would probably expect; they are not near as plenty as in New York or Philadelphia. Their status here, however, is at once seen to be different. I have seen one working at case in a printing office, (Boston Stereotype Foundry, Spring lane,) — and no dis-

[10]

Converse, Harding & Co. from 3 to 4 million

---

Beebe & Co 5 $_{\text{million}}$

---

Jordan, Marsh & Co

---

prices of real estate in the commercial quarters

---

in New Devonshire st. on the Blake estate, at auction
$10,70 a square foot

---

on State st. $30 a foot is a not uncom price

**[11]**
tinction made between him and the white compositors. Another I noticed, (and I never saw a blacker or woolier African,) an employee in the State House, apparently a clerk or under-official of some such kind.— At the eating-houses, a black, when he wants his dinner, comes in and takes

**[12]**

C. A. Leonard
21 Stuyvesant st

---

routinist

---

Mrs. Case
296 Bleecker
near Grove,
Mrs. Ferris

---

**[13]**
a vacant seat wherever he finds one — and nobody minds it. I notice that the mechanics and young men do not mind all this, either. As for me, I am too much a citizen of the world to have the least compunction about it. Then the blacks here are certainly of a superior

[14]

Mr. Shales

---

among the Algerines

---

now 84 years of age

---

66 years ago — the Eaton affair

---

[15]

order — ~~quite as good to have in contact with you as the average of "our own color."~~

there is a black

lawyer, ^named Anderson (a resident of Chelsea,) practising here in Boston, quite smart and just as big as the best of them.

---

and in Worcester, they are now put on the jury list, two of the names put on being black men, one of them a fugitive slave who has purchased his freedom

[16]

the Reservoir

Beacon Hill

the court quarter

---

walk with Mr. Redpath

---

the castle — the little courts

---

Ira Mudgett
85 Dover st
corner Washington
Boston Mass

**[17]**

Charles H Horton
32 Tyler st.
Lowell, Mass

---

C F Hovey
sumner st
fine store
like Stewart's

**[18]**

Federal street
the Chaning Building

---

**[19]**

**[20]**

Pavements

Washington streets has all kinds of pavements, Russ, cobble, iron, and a kind they call "kidney stone." The last would make a very good kind of pavement for a street ~~only~~ moderately traveled, but it wears off too quick elsewhere — Some of the "kidney stone," put down last fall, when now taken up

**[21]**

Broad st
Tilden
block & others — granite

---

Wholesale groceries & drugs

---

in Custom House st
the old Custom houses

---

the old buildings on Long wharf
storage, & ship Chandelry

---

also India Wharf

---

☞ noblest of all
State St. Block — east
of the Custom house

rough granite
☞ the above probably one of the noblest pieces of com. arch. in the world

**[22]**

In Commercial St. the rush, about 4 oclock P.M — the carts, drays, trucks, express wagons, crowding — goods, boards, ~~wa~~ vehicles of all sorts

**[23]**

The Old Elm.— This tree has been standing here for an unknown period. It is believed to have existed before the settlement of Boston, being fully grown in 1722, exhibited marks of old age in 1792, and was nearly destroyed by a storm in 1832 — Protected by an iron enclosure in 1854 J.V.C. Smith Mayor

**[24]**

Washington st fine [trees?]

Leopold Furman hot air furnace

---

Wentworth & Bright Carpets

---

John Collamore China &c
also the adj building on the corner

---

iron front building of Parker, Towle & Sons

[25]

Corner of Wash

also

iron front building

Am Tract Society

toward foot of Washn St

---

Oliver Brewster's

cor State st gray granite

---

Codman Buildings

gray granite

---

Wash st

Warren & Co

Chickering, vry good pianos

[26]

In Wash st you will not seldom see a spike team of a horse on the lead and two oxen at the wheels, ~~dra~~ hauling a big ^str[*illegible*] box of a wagon

---

Franklin (died seventy years ago

(I suppose Franklin is about the fairest and best Representative man of Massachusetts — remembering also Webster, Emerson and may be one or two others

[27]

Standing on the porch of — — Market on Commercial st. the most magnificent blocks of buildings opposite, both side of City Wharf st., ~~espee~~ of which Quincy Market ~~block~~ Buildings are a specimen, noble architecture ~~the~~ fronted with rough gray ~~bloe~~ pieces of stone.

---

and in Clinton st. and down ~~east~~ north of it in Commercial st very noble

[28]

~~Highest point on Myr~~

elevation of Washington Park, ~~10~~ 110 feet above high water

---

Reservoir on Prospect Hill — 220 feet.

---

ground at City Hall

70 feet

---

Highest level in Brooklyn at ~~B~~ corner of Hicks and Pierrepont 80 feet

---

Ridgewood Reservoir

107 feet

---

[29]

Geo. S. Phillips

office N.Y. Illustrated News, N.Y. City

---

R. M. Hunt

architect of

south building on

south bay — grey stone

(carte blanche to finish interior and exterior

---

[30]

Saml D. Tillman

7 Spruce st

N. York

[31]

**[32]**

fine buildings

---

Franklin street, (all built within the last two years) — previously dwellings) — granite fronts — quite a variety — some quite ornamental —
New Devonshire st.— / we are now in the im. neighborhood of Edward Everetts residence, and of the late Rufus Choate — Fine [*illegible*] brown freestone front block — dry goods

**[33]**

— Yankee manufactures — Lowell & elsewhere

---

some of the stores on the same large scale as the best modern ~~sto~~ wholesale houses in New York, with all the adjuncts of steam-power, great rooms under the walks, lit by

---

Kilby st
dry goods

**[34]**

the crowd at Charleston Bridge, when, (at 6) the drawbridge is raised (at sunset) — the sights, Bunker Hill monument — the river, the declining sun — the crowd rushing quick when the bridge is put right

**[35]**

---

burin — ^or "graver" i.e. the tool, or "graver" a sort of composite of gouge, chisel, knife, &c used by the engravers — used by wood engravers — also

---

Wm Miller
rear of 204
Washington
up stairs

---

Mrs Cheney
No 90 Livingston

**[36]**
fine stores on Wash st.
(Jones, Ball & Co
Rich Ornamental goods & Jewelry
(Williams & Everitts,
Pictures & Rich engravings)
Geo. W Warren & Co
dry goods

**[37]**
Mechanics Hall — a fine new building, of brown free-stone, in Bedford street, very handsome building

**[38]**

Beacon st.

---

Boylston st

---

~~48~~ 50 acres

---

50

---

132 Northampton

**[39]**

---

on Commercial st

---

~~east~~ opposite and north of the Faneuil Hall Market — several more noble granite blocks

[40]

the gilt-capped cupola of the State Houses

---

the old Hancock house with its fan-spreading window trimmings

[41]

[42]

Wash
the old Marlboro Hotel
& the Adams House

---

^churches the old South

---

Burnhams (book
window store

---

Mechanics
Hall fine new
brown free stone

Bedford st)

[43]

the main cattle-yards ~~markets~~ ^and slaughter-houses are at Brighton & Cambridge — ~~but~~ the beef on the hoof coming ^thither from all parts of the Northern States, and from Canada — prices, ^by the quarter, range from 5 to 12 cents a pound.

---

Mr Snow's story of Wm Evans and his contracts with the city

[44]

C. L. Heydc, Burlington
a real Yankee farm
scene, July hay-cutting,
the hay-cocks, the
loading, one horse

grazing, a part of
the field not yet
mowed, &c

---

meadow \ M. J. Heade
fine clouds Providence R.I.

**[45]**

Silas S Soule
Lawrence,
Kansas

**[46]**
Fine building

---

Washington Building
in Washington st. opposite
Franklin st (
material coffee-and-milk color

---

Seeing the Yankee

---

(Washington St.
seamless goods of felt, from the factory at ~~Mat~~ Mattewan, &
boots, shoes, slippers, coats, ^vests, gaiters gloves, caps,

**[47]**

Milk street

---

all varieties — great many clothiers

---

the gt. manf. towns are Lowell & Lawrence

---

Congress st
Clothing, dry goods
variety — all kinds

---

☞ the lobsters
the ma[?]
the stands

**[48]**

Simeon Carter

Stoneham
Map

**[49]**

**[50]**

Summer & Franklin streets indicate the best architecture and for stores, &c

---

April 12th Thursday, the grass begins to look~~s~~ green, on the Common — the buds on the elms are russet,— the young fellows are playing foot ball.— Foot ball! a noble and manly game — there they are in their shirt-

**[51]**

sleeves, running ∧crowding, tumbling, ~~crow~~ together, quite an inspiriting sight

[*torn away*]

**[52]**

Pearl st[?] [*illegible*]
P[*illegible*] &c

---

cor Franklin & Devonshire

---

Franklin

---

[*torn away*]

**[53]**

[*illegible*] whistling
and whistling call of
the robin, clear
and [~~firm~~?] short
¶as he repeats it
over and over — and answered by
As he flits from
bough to bough
while I walk
my walk at
early candle-
light —

---

with intervals, or
quick succession

**[54]**

cor [*illegible*]
& Milk st

---

fine [*illegible*]

---

Pearl St. [*illegible*]
of High street —
grani

---

also the block corner [*illegible*] Purchase and Pearl st opposite the old store (now Roman Catholic Church)

**[55, *back cover, inside*]**

**[56, *back cover, outside*]**

## *81 Clerman*[18]
## [ca. 1860–61]

**[1, *binding*]**

**[2]**

**[3, *hand-written trial title ("Physique") pasted in twice, and a note, not in Whitman's hand, that this is a "Note Book / Walt Whitman"*]**

**[4]**

**[5]**

[*illegible*]
81 Clerman

1 Mr[?] M Lenan

81 Claremont Av

---

Doremus tailor
96 Court st

---

Charles Hine
174 10th av.
between near 21st st & 22d st

---

Mrs. Price
33d St. bet. 7th & 8th av.
white marble stoop

---

Sloan
corner — Houston & Thompson
basement

**[6]**

**[7]**

Swinton

54th St. Bet. Broadway & 8th av. north side — stone cottage off the st. bet 2 white marble houses.

turn [*illegible*] of
When[?] all the ~~unknown~~ future
the ~~future~~ unknown is
waiting for you

---

Quatuor

---

Quatruna

---

Quadriune

---

Quatruna

---

**[8]**

Ada Clare

86 42d st.

**[9]**

Swinton

54th right hand side going from 7th to 8th av.
cottage — next to marble block

---

Wilkins
corner ^N.E. Amity & Wooster
English basement

---

Ada Clare 86 42d st

---

Hinton
48 Beekman street

---

**[10]**

Swinton
739 Sixth av.

---

ring the 3d bell

---

William Giggee
Company E
1st Reg't N.Y. } Col. Allen
Volunteers
Camp Hamilton
Fort Monroe
Va.

**[11]**

~~Where~~ I stand and look
~~in~~ in the the dark under a
cloud,
But I see ^in the distance where the
sun shines, ~~through~~ I see the
~~in~~ thin haze, on
the ^tall white steeples of
the city, ~~in~~
I see the glistening of
the waters in the
distance.

Quaterniune

[12]

[13]

What is this world literally
and diffusely?—
Proletaire

[14]

This forthcoming one of Lincoln's
is the 19th Presidentiad

Ald. John Leech
— old Brooklynite

**[15, *this page, apparently a spelling lesson, does not appear to be in Whitman's hand*]**

*Arthur Henry.*
*A r t h u r*
*A r t h u r*
*A r t h u r*
*A A A A*
*A A A A*
*A A IA r r r*
*r*
*A r r t h*
*Arthur*

**[16]**

**[17]**

Subject — looking peering in the faces of people, continually passing —

---

red olive color (Mullen) woman in Central America

---

Paumanok's barefoot
sea-boy

**[18]**

**[19]**

A.B. Newcomb
37 Park Row
Room 17

**[20–22, *pencil sketches of human figures, likely not in Whitman's hand*]**

**[23]**

a Poem.
Phantoms — (a dream of the Sea.)
— bring up in a phantasmagoria all the drowned wrecks — the wrecks of the ships — — spread the sails — sail them on the sea again — silent, in the mist — the rafts from wrecks — crowd the sea all over with them thick — (get a talk with some of the pilots or sailors —

**[24–25, *blank*]**

**[26]**

Ben Prince
264 Jay st
9 or 3 o'c

---

name of pieces
cluster

Kosmic gales
Winds of Kosmos
Breezes of Kosmos
[*illegible*] Winds from Kosmos
— blow winds of Kosmos
first ☝ line of piece

**[27]**

The omnibus receipts of London are $3,000,000 a year. For the week ending Oct 10. last they were $60,000

---

Pyle's Dietetic Saleratus
345 Washington st. N.Y.

---

Kanawha
Saltworks
Virginia

---

Wm. H. Jones
Dover, New Jersey

---

Breeze's Express
cor Washington & Courtland

---

**[28]**

**[29]**

the grappler with his
grappling-irons — I
see him ahold of

the long handles —
working them deep in
the water, carefully
feeling

**[30, *not in Whitman's hand*]**

*Henry Beck Jr*
*At Manhattan Gas Works*
*18th St & 10th ave*

**[31, *not in Whitman's hand*]**

*M[?] Jerry [Jenny?] Danforth*
*No 2 Washington Place, "Sivori Hotel*
*Room 11*
*[illegible] — 12 — at home always till 1 P.M.*

**[32]**

**[33]**

Nov. 26, '60 — Lippard

Gardette's account to me, (in Pfaff's) of George Lippards life,— was handsome, Byronic, — commenced[?] at 18 — wrote sensation novels — drank — drank — drank — died mysteriously either of suicide or mania a potu at 25 or 6 — a perfect wreck — was ragged, drunk, beggarly —

**[34]**

**[35]**

Aholibanah. (Hebrew.)
"the tabernacle is exalted — "
(or raised)

---

old specs
Sandy's story of the
stage[?] driver

**[36]**

**[37]**

∧The other in adv. poets write with reference to the Costume of the body,— or, at most, with reference to the body, costumed. But I write my poems with reference to the ~~bod~~ perfect body, divine, ~~eternal~~ irrespective of costumes — in it I have eternal faith beyond all the [*illegible*] of critics

**[38–40, *blank, includes an indiscernible sketch by an unknown artist*]**

**[41]**

(Shanlys book

Arabian

I see ~~the~~ tombs, built
with masonry, with a stone pillar at the head — I
see the sex indicated,
by the carved turban
~~at the head,~~ or by
the ~~carved~~ veil,

**[42, *sketch of fruit and flower, artist unknown*]**

**[43]**

[To Picture-Makers:

Make a Picture of America
as an <u>Immortal Mother,</u>
surrounded by all her children
young and old — no one re-
jected — all fully accepted —
no one preferred to another.
Make her seated — she
is beautiful beyond the
beauty of virginity — she
~~is neither young nor~~ has the inimitable beauty
of the mother of many

**[44]**

children — she is nether youthful nor aged — around her are none of the emblems of the ~~feudal~~ classic goddess — nor any feudal emblems — she is serene and strong as the ~~beauty of the~~ heavens. [*illegible*]

Make her picture, painters! And you, her statue, sculptors! Try ~~to achieve it~~, age after age, till you achieve it! For as ^to many sons and daughters the perfect mother ~~of many sons — b~~ is the one where all meet, and binds them all together, as long as she lives, so ~~one~~
The Mother of These States binds them all together as long as she lives.

**[45]**

Make a "Picture" of the Indian girl looking at the turtle by an aboriginal American creek

---

Write a cluster of pieces on the sentiment, elevation, acceptation of <u>Old Age</u>.

**[46]**

**[47]**

Leaf

---

on a silver coin
? gold

---

Through what hands pass'd

[*Pasted-in newspaper clipping about rapid reversals of fortune*]

---

| a picture — or direction to make

**[48]**

**[49]**

Brochure

---

Two characters as of a Dialogue between A. L — n and
W [W?] — — n
—
— as in ? a dream

---

---

? or better
Lessons for a President elect

---

Dialogue between W W. and "President elect"

**[50–51, *blank*]**

**[52]**

Two ∧antique records there are~~;~~— two ∧religions — platforms
On the first one, stands the Greek sage, the classic mas
terpiece of virtue — — ~~philosophy~~ ~~conscience, justice~~
~~reasinging, eternal conse~~ · · · · — Eternal
conscience is there ∧ — doubt is there — — philosophy,
questioning, reasoning, is there.
On the second stands ∧the Jew, the Christ, the Consolator
~~the Jew, the Christ~~ . . . . There is love,
there is drenchéd purity . . . there, subtle, is the unseen Soul, before
which all the ~~grea~~ goods and greatnesses

**[53]**

of the world, become insignificant:
But now ~~I give~~ a ~~modern & second~~ third religion
I give . . . . ~~standing~~ I include the two antique
~~Greek sage~~ . . . I include the divine
Jew ∧and the Greek sage
~~More still I include~~ . . . . ∧More still — that which
is not conscience, but against it —

that which is not the Soul, ^I include
^These, and whatever exists, I include — I surround
all, and dare not ^make ~~a~~ single exclusion.

**[54–55, *blank*]**

**[56]**

Why now I shall know whether there is
any thing in you, Libertad,
I shall see ~~whether~~ how much you
can stand
^Perhaps I shall see the crash — is all then
lost?

---

~~O! Old England~~
~~The Queen of~~
T

**[57]**

What then? Have ~~you~~ those thrones
there stood so long?
Does the Queen of England represent
a thousand years? And the
Queen of Spain a thousand
years?
And you

**[58]**

Welcome the storm — welcome the
trial — let the waves
Why now I shall see what the
old ship is made of
Any body can sail ~~in in~~ with ~~before~~
a fair wind, ~~before~~ ~~above~~ or a
smooth sea

**[59]**

Come now we will see what
    stuff you are made of
    Ship of Libertad
~~W~~ Let others tremble and turn pale
    — let them          ?
I want to see what          ? before
    I die,
I welcome this menace — I welcome
    thee with joy

**[60]**

    Ship of Libertad
Blow mad winds!
Rage, boil, vex, yawn wide, yeas~~ty~~ ?
    waves
Crash away —
Tug at the planks — make them groan —
    fall around, black clouds — clouds of
    death

**[61]**

Ship of the World — Ship of Humanity
    — Ship of the ages
? (Ship that circlest the world
Ship of the hope of the world — Ship
    of Promise

**[62]**

**[63]**

the vine-hills of Germany
(viz: "in Germany the name of the ~~spe~~ vineyard is vein-berg i.e. vine-hill")

---

but in California they plant the vine preferably on flat tracts

**[64, *a penciled profile portrait of a man with mustache and hat, almost certainly not Whitman's handiwork*]**

**[65]**

Poem on a
Prostitute's Funeral

adv. or on L of G

The ~~world noisy~~ topics of the world, ~~with all that~~ — the world itself with all ^of its affairs, divide away, and disappear in comparison with those things that come directly home to, or rise ~~u~~ up out of, your own body and Soul.

These are the things made the themes of L of G.

**[66]**

**[67]**

Thursday, April 18. 61.

I have this hour, this day r e s o l v'd to inaugurate for (my se lf) a (p ure) (per fect) sweet, cleanblooded (ro bust) body by ignoring all drinks (but) water and pure milk — and all fat meats late suppers — — a great body — a purged, cleansed, spiritualised invigorated body —

**[68–69, *more penciled profiles (not Whitman's) of a bearded, Socratic bust, and a wild-eyed bearded drunk, respectively*]**

**[70]**

(?) Poem

The Hills of Brooklyn.

Here roamed the
~~H~~ newly ? landed
Hollander
Here stood Washington

———

The last war

**[71]**

**[72, *another penciled profile, of a bearded man with an aquiline nose*]**

**[73]**

**[74, *a pencil-sketched banner for the NY* Saturday Press, *unlikely to be Whitman's. The main headline reads* "The Bohemian"; *a misspelled subheading reads* "Tate[?] Saturdy Press"]**

**[75]**

**[76, *penciled profile of a bearded man with a pipe*]**

**[77]**

Jos Sprage

Died Dec 12, 1854 in his 72d year

---

born in Massachusetts,

---

Come here before the war of 1812 — quite a lad

---

was in business in New York during the war

---

was a Jeffersonian Democrat

---

married at Bedford, L.I.

---

**[78–79, *blank*]**

**[80, *pencil profile of a man with a Van Dyke beard and small, caricature-like body, holding a gavel or mallet*]**

**[81]**

Of My Poem

All the others were singing for the
distinctions, and what was to be preferred.
~~All~~ ^Therefore I thought I would sing

a ~~few~~ songs of inherent
qualities, ∧in a man, indifferent whether
they are right or wrong.

**[82]**

**[83]**

a cluster of poems for children — (fables)

— the earth in space as a story of the divine ship sailing the divine sea

---

Story of Leonidas

---

This, children, is the
story of Leonidas, of
the race of Hercules,
Twenty-two hundred years
before These States.

**[84]**

**[85, *pencil drawing of an Irish harp*]**

**[86]**

**[87, *pencil drawing of Whitman, not a self portrait*]**

**[88]**

**[89, *pencil profile of a clean-shaved man in a tall hat*]**

**[90, *pencil profile of a bearded man in a tall hat, possibly a caricature of a "Bohemian" Whitman*]**

**[91, *pencil profile of what appears to be a caricature of Whitman*]**

**[92]**

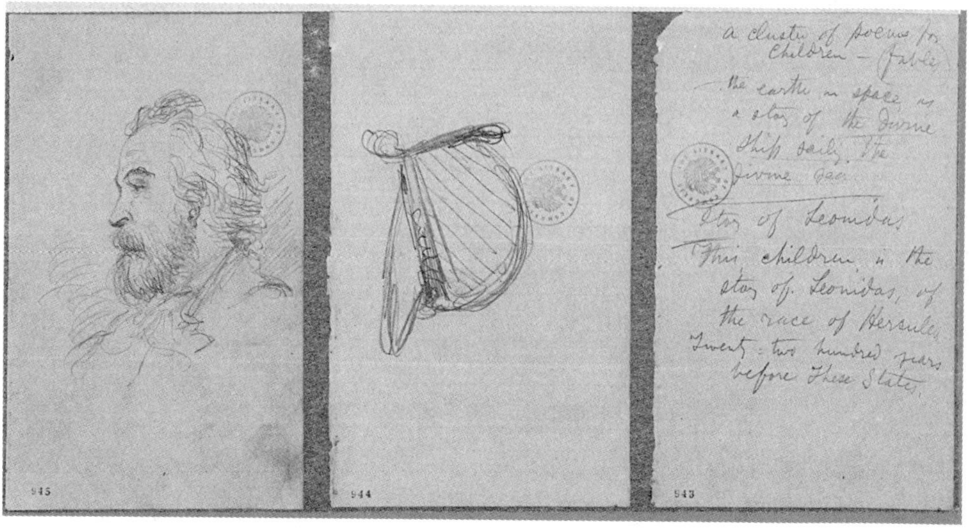


Leaves from *81 Clerman* notebook (ca. 1860–61).

Leaves from *81 Clerman* notebook (ca. 1860–61).

**[93, *another portrait of a bearded man, possibly Whitman*]**

**[94–95, *blank*]**

**[96, *pencil sketch of a hatted skeleton with its heart pieced by a rapier, floating before a sunset*]**

**[97]**

The Cid} two centuries before Chaucer, primitive, heroic, warlike, stirring full of loyalty & devotion

---

Is like the Nibelungen, which in its present form is about the same date)
Consists of 3000 lines.
Could not have been composed later than the year 1200

Subject — the warlike adventures, character, of a Spanish nobleman, Roderigo Diaz (Ruy Diaz) born in the northwestern part of Spain, about 1040. Died in 1099, at valencia, which city he had rescued from the Moors.

The title Cid,, is believed to have come from five Moorish chiefs (or princes,) whom he conquered, acknowledging him as their Seid or king — and the additional title, Campeador, (Champion), is the popular ~~expression,~~ affix

for his efforts in freeing the Country from the Moors — the name comes from a very early date, "El Cid Campeador" — the Lord Champion, or King Champion

**[98]**

**[99]**

— he seems to have passed nearly the whole of his life in warlike efforts, in the service of his Country

— So the Cid is the great fellow in poetical Spanish history and reminiscence — (as Homer's Achilles, or perhaps as the English Alfred — ? or Roman Æneas.) —

There are numerous "Lives of the Cid," as well as lots of "Ballads," (160 or more,) — besides the old epic itself

He was the great defender of his nation against the Moorish invaders.
The Poem of the Cid is mixt with much fable, very much

[100]

[101]

It is a contemporary and vivacious song, and chronicle, of ~~the~~ those chivalrous, ~~and~~ warlike, ~~primitive~~ and romantic times of early Spanish ~~history,~~ life — full of quaint pictures, hints, opinions, and suggestions — — the very language, just extricating itself from its mother's womb, the Latin — full of the strong, ~~ro~~ free, individuality of its times — the metre, and rhyme rude and irregular — —

— A few pages at the begining are lost

The author of the "Poem of the Cid," is unknown

("Castilian" and "Spanish" seem convertible terms)

[102]

[103]

The contest between the Christian Spaniards, and the Moors, continued for Seven Centuries — briefly stated the "poem of the Cid," and the other old ballads and poetical Spanish Chronicles, celebrate their countrymens prowess and sufferings, in this war.

(Castile,— so called from its many castles)

---

It is from this period of tempests 11–1200 and wars, ^of the Spanish race that we hear the first notes of their wild national poetry, mingled with dauntless war-shouts, and flaunting with banners and curses, and the smiting of steel weapons

[104]

[105]

Hannah Brush, (my grandmother Whitman,) and her

---

asonante (a Spanish metrical style, not ~~exactly~~ rhyme, yet giving ^ ~~almost~~ somewhat the same effect as rhyme, by ~~a~~ carefully terminating~~, of~~ the lines with by words whose vowels harmonize,— ~~the~~ Castilian poetry is alone in this peculiarity — (Longfellow has perhaps ~~con~~[?] imitated it, and come as near to it as possible in English, in his "Hiawatha")

**[106]**

**[107]**

[*torn away*]

"Old Spanish Ballads"

(Ticknor's Hist. Spanish Literature)

over 1000, authors unknown — the true antique national poetry — all written previous to the middle of the 16th century

**[108]**

**[109]**

Mr. Rowland, fruit

300 Barclay st

---

Melissa Rowland

---

175 Morgan st

Jersey City

between Prospect & Grove

**[110–111, *blank*]**

**[112]**

Oct 14 '60|

Thomas P. Nichols

69 Carlton avenue

---

**[113]**

**[114]**

I want a Latin motto which conveys the following

~~Four in One~~

sense —

of the words

"Four in One"

Quatuor in Uno

or, better,

Quatuor juncta in Uno

au courant

Quarto

Quatuor

**[115]**

292

---

Quadratura

---

John Schoonmaker
133 Clermont av
Brooklyn

---

Wm Metzler
Tuskilwa
Bureau Co
Illinois.

**[116]**

**[?]**

Poem on the Incompleted

---

The Incomplete.

Always unfinished — always ~~nev~~ [in]completed,
The best yet left — the road but fairly started,
The ~~house~~ ~~learning house~~ [*illegible*] learning practice so far only practice
The seed but sown — the test the fruit.

---

That is best which wears the longest

## excerpt from *Words*[19]
## [ca. 1856–60]

**[1]**

[*Clipping: "It is estimated that there are 587 languages and general dialects in Europe, 937 in Asia, 226 in Africa, and 1,263 in America, in all nearly 3,000."*]

[*Clipping: editorial estimating the number of words "good writers" use, which it pegs at 100,000.*]

The Virtues

| | |
|---|---|
| Knowledge | Courage |
| Health | Charity |
| Activity | Cleanliness |

Domus, a house — hence domestic

[*Clipping: editorial on the etymology of "telegram" and other -gram derivates.*]

Webster's Dictionary Prefaces

---

On Enlglish Language, from
70 to 80,000 words

---

Or rather, (same authority, about
100,000 words

**[2]**

Ethnic — heathen
pot sherds — broken pieces pot

? laissez aller
euphuism — (of the time of Elizabeth)
[*illegible*] something
[*illegible*] wellbuilt thing[?]
[*illegible*] an aristo-
[*illegible*] anti-
[*illegible*] laying
their heads together
to oppr[*illegible*] and
rule [*illegible*]
tete-a-tete
[*illegible*] between two?)
[*illegible*]
estafette — (Express)

---

pessimist (a universal complainer
(the reverse of optimist

**[3]**

[*Clipping: a quote from Aubrey on the "Days before Books."*]

**[4]**

Grammar.

Drawing language into line by rigid grammatical rules, is the theory of the martinet applied to the ~~most ethereal~~ processes of the spirit, and to the luxuriant growth of all that makes art.— It is for small school-masters, not for great souls.— Not only the Dictionary of the English Language, but the Grammar of it, has yet to be written.—

**[5]**

[6]

All through, a common
gender ending in ist

| | | | |
|---|---|---|---|
| as — | lovist<br>hatist | } | both masc & fem |
| — | hater m<br>hatress f | } | &c |

[7]

[8]

Murray's Grammar

The fault ~~principally~~ that he fails to understand ~~to where~~ ^those points where the language [*illegible,* is?] strongest, and where [*illegible*] developements should [*illegible*] most encouraged, namely, in being elliptic and idiomatic.— Murray would make of the young men merely a correct and careful set of writers under laws.— He would deprive writing of its life — there would be nothing voluntary and insouciant left.—

[9]

[10]

as, punctuation marks, were not extant in old writings or inscriptions — they were commenced about (1520) three hundred years ago.

[11]

[12]

Mácrocosm (as ensemble) — (from Greek) The great
whole world, in opposition
to the part that comes in
minute experience.—
— more large indefinite

Mícrocosm — the world
of man — (? the little
world concentred in man)
Man as an epitome of
all — (more definite)

---

Hél - lé - nés

---

riffacciamento — rumble
[sort of mosaic work
mixture
mess —]

**[13]**

[*Clipping: about the spread of the "Anglo-Saxon race" and the English language, which "is gaining upon the languages of the earth."*]

imbroglio, a mixed up ~~mess of~~ troubles

---

Did he ~~dit~~ do it a purpose?

---

That's so, easy enough.—

---

That's a sick ticket

---

Well I was looking for a man — about your size

---

"go back" — "go back on him"

---

He works on his own ~~k~~ hook

---

a good American word
centurion

---

Kosmos, noun masculine or feminine,

a person who scope of mind, or whose range in a particular science, includes all, the whole ∧known universe

**[14]**

**[15]**

There should could easily be be a dictionary made of words ∧fit to be used in in an English (American) opera,— or for vocal-lyric purposes, songs, ballads, recitatives, &c

**[16]**

[*illegible*]in
[*illegible*]d by some that the
[*illegible*]~~democracy~~ human
[*illegible*] down in the
[*illegible*]act of These

**[17]**

"Words" — the New
York Bowery boy
"Sa-a-y!"

---

Whåt- å-t ?

**[18]**

**[19]**

"hold up your head up."
"Bully for you"
a "nasty" man.
"that's rough."
log — rolling

**[20]**

**[21]**

all right
swim out
cave in
~~dry up~~ dry up
switch off
— git and git
he is } on that
I am }

"So long"
— (a delicious American — New York —
idiomatic phrase at parting
equivalent to "good bye"
"adieu" &c

may-be (mebbee)
bub honey-fugling.
sis

---

~~Guau~~ — Guacho [wá-ko]
give him away

**[22]**

**[23]**

(Words)

Empiricism — as an acquaintance with a number of isolated facts, yet not of the subtle relation and bearing of them, the meaning — their part in the ensemble — ~~their~~ the instinct of what they prove.—

---

☞ Modern sense of the term

---

simply the direct facts, by rote, without grasping the spirit, the real meaning of them.

**[24]**

**[25]**

Sachem passim
wardance (every where
powwow, here and there,
Moundbuilders, used as a word
Mohekan of reference.)
prairie,

---

"on the stump"
(from the western practice at times, of political speakers mounting a tree-stump, ~~for their~~ and so holding forth

---

barracoon — collection of slaves in Africa, or any where
("I see the slave barracoon")

---

collaborateurs
? co-laborers
? co-laboraters

**[26]**

**[27]**

Is it not self-proved that the ^African (? & Asiatic) hieroglyphs are more ancient than the phonetic sounds of the Phenician letters.— Yes, it seems clearly so to me

**[28]**

**[29]**

Alphabetic letters introduced
— into Europe 1500 B. C.
viz: Phenician letters, by
Cadmus, into Greece.
— facts veiled in the vapory tradition of

**[30]**

**[31]**

desideratum — Sound-Marks.

One of the first desiderata [*illegible*] a font of type, in a Dictiona[ry] [*illegible*]th in printed composition [an]y-how, is a set of arbitra[ry] [so] und-marks attached to letters each mark belonging to that specific sound.— How clear this would make language! especially to a child, an illiter[ate r] eader aloud, or a foreigner —

leg is la tive

---

O "Voltaire, Montesquieu, Jean-Jacques Rousseau, Buffon, and Diderot,— all the genius of the French tongue is to be found in the style of those five writers."

Arsene Houssaye.
1850

**[32]**

**[33]**

Feuilleton
Feuilletonist
regime

Attache
at – a – shá
one attached to any person, establishment or what not.

vis-a-viz, face to face opposite, person seated opposite

---

viser v n to take aim
visee — noun ví za — aim, end, object
— to aim at
vidette

---

genre ja (zhän-r) peculiar to that person, period or place — not universal

---

accroupie (Venus accroupie)
Ma femme ("She is mine — ma femme"
parvenu
forte — (strong —

---

(I prefer dilletant
dilletante singular and
dilletanti pl "dilletants"

finale col-pŏr-teŭr (peddler)

largesse [ arriere
- behind ]

petit

**[34]**

**[35]**
Martinet
~~chaff — "The omnibus man~~
chaffs another"
"load" "sold" — sold him — got a
gag load on them
dodge — ("that was only a dodge")
such words as) Hurry-graphs, (the name of a book of sketches)

---

(?) chapparral

---

peon

---

doctrinaire (
lay-brother — theorist.

(doctorate)
soi (self)
soi disant self-styled
would-be

seance (see ánz) n.f.

pl seances) sitting — a meeting seaten [?]

(the spiritualists held a seance)

**[36]**

**[37]**

pantaloons — "pants" — trowsers ~~what root?~~

— breeches —

---

Do not these words illustrate a law of language, ~~viz~~namely, that with the introduction of any new thing, (as the pantaloons) the word, from the same land or source, is introduced with them?

---

Family names

Surnames —

Roman style of names — Greek

American aborigines

Japan — India — Peninsulas

Sumatra Borneo

---

Russian — American aborigin

# *Fragments*

## *dithyrambic*[1]
[1846–54]

**[1]**

dithyrambic

| | |
|---|---|
| trochee | dactyle |
| iambic | spondee |

anaepest.

Hexameter

Pentameter

---

pyrrhic, a poetic foot of two short syllables.

an ancient quick military danse)

---

Spondee

Two long syllables, in poetry.

---

Hexameter,— in ancient poetry, a verse of six feet the first four of which may be either dactyls or spondees,— the fifth must regularly be a dactyl — the sixth always a spondee,

So thus hav ing spok en the casque nod ding
Hec tor de part ed.

**[2]**

**[3]**

Iambus

Iambics,

(Anciently — Certain songs, or satires, supposed to have given birth to ancient comedy.)

Iambus — a poetic "foot" consisting of two syllables, the first short, the last long, as in "de-light"

"He scorns — the force — that dares — his fu — ry stay."

Trochee

(from a Greek word, signifying "to run.")

A poetic foot consisting of two syllables, the first long, the second short.

(I suppose such as this)

Would you — gaze up — on the — wa ters,
Of the — lordly — Missis — sippi?

---

Dactyl

(from the Greek word for "finger," the joint nearest the hand being long, the other two joints short.)

A poetic foot of three syllables, the first long — the others short

(I suppose such as)

"Thun der ing — up ward and — down ward the — sur ges roll'd."

**[4]**

## *is rougher than it was*[2]

[1848–87, probably 1848]

is rougher than it ~~h~~[w]as on Michigan or Huron: (on St. Clair it was smooth as glass;) and our boat rolls a little.— Whether it be from this cause, I don't know, but I feel rather unwell.— The day is bright and dry, with a stiff head wind.— We shall doubtless be in Buffalo this evening.— I anticipate a great deal of pleasure in viewing the Falls of Niagara.— — (By Wednesday night I expect to be home.)

The water of Lake Erie looks[ed] like Michigan, the morning we started out of Chicago — that bright, lively, blue color, so beautiful and rare.—

We arrived in Buffalo on Monday evening, spent that night and a portion of the next day in examining the place.— In the morning of the next day, got in the cars and went out to Niagara.— Great God! what a sight! — We went under the Falls, saw the whirlpool, and all the other things, including the suspension bridge.—

On Tuesday evening we started for Albany; and travelled all night.— From the time daylight afforded us a view of the country, found it very rich and well cultivated.— Every few miles there were large towns and villages.—

On Wednesday evening arrived in Albany.— Spent the evening in loitering about; there was a political meeting (Hunker,) at the Capitol, but we passed it by.—

Next morning started down the Hudson in the Alida.— Never before did I look upon such grand and varied scenery.— Arrived about 5 o'clock in Brooklyn. Found all well.—

## *wooding at night*[3]
## [1848–87, probably 1848]

**[1]**

wooding at night — the 20 deck hands at work briskly as bees — in going up the river the flat-boat loaded with wood was attached to the side of our steamer and taken along with us, until the wood was transferred —

Spectacle of the men lying around in groups in the forward part of the lower deck at night — some asleep some conversing — glare of the fire upon them — Some emigrants on their way "up country" — young fellow and his stout young German wife.— Gruffness of the mate to the boat hands — (Life, lot, appearance, characteristics, pay, recklessness, premature deaths, etc etc of the western boat-hands.)

Expressions of the mate.— "Step-along, ~~my~~ bullies!" Come, bullies, hop, now! hop now!"

Mixture of passengers.— A couple of those respectable old gentlemen who are sent to "great" Conventions.— Our two were on the

**[2]**

way to Philadelphia?— At the place where we took one of them up (describe his appearance, his silver mounted cane etc,) he had about two-score hands to shake, and as many "good-byes" to utter.—

"Now, ^Uncle Daniel, you must nominate Clay," said one.—

"Taylor, Uncle Dan" sang out another

(Had there been time, we should no doubt have had an argument; but western steamboats, like wind and tide, wait for no man, on certain occasions; and this was one of them.— (Describe this old gentleman's manner on the boat his kid gloves.)

The other convention man, seemed to be generally known too.— he was called "Doctor"; wore a white cravat; was deaf, tall, apparently rheumatic, and slept most of the passage — except about meal [*illegible*]—

**[3]**

Cookery of the boats bad — raw strong coffee — too much grease — haste of the people to get to the table — would rush in and seize their chairs, ready to spring into their places the moment the bell rang.—

Long monotonous stretch of the Mississippi — Planter's dwellings surrounded with their hamlets of negro huts — groves of negro men women and children in the fields, hoeing the young cotton

Our competition, or race, with the "Grand Turk" — continued from day to day.— Deceptiveness of the steamboat officers as to time of starting, etc.— Gallantry toward the females — Painful effect of the excessive flatness of the country.—

**[4]**

## *I know well enough*[4]
[pre-1854]

I know well enough that
man grows up becoming
not ~~an animal~~ a physical being
merely, but markedly
the mental being of the
earth — the esthetic and

spiritual being ~~of the~~
~~earth~~, — the benevolent
and
But the main thing is, in
the same connection,
that he is to be the
seer of nature — he
only can celebrate
things, ~~and~~ animals, and
landscapes — His mentality
is a quality to be used
toward things, as his
vision is used
If he depart from animals and things he is lost.—
In other words, man is not only an
animal like the others, but
he alone has the quality of
understanding and telling how
divine a thing an animal is —
~~Li~~ what life, matter, passion,
volition, are
He alone carries ~~the~~ all the substances of the
world, by this quality, ^in himself and illustrates them.

## *The genuine miracles of Christ*[5]
## [ca. 1850–55]

The genuine miracles of Christ were such miracles as can always be produced.— They come from something ~~which ne~~ whose perfume neither originated with tha[t?] fragrant lily of souls, nor was exhausted by him.— ~~They are not more wonderful,~~ Except that their ~~law~~ spirit encloses all the ot[hers — ?] they are not more ~~wonderful~~ marvellous than any of those mysteries we call the laws of ~~the Un~~ nature; and all alike are just the same this hour in the Atlantic states and the valleys of the west, as tens of centuries ago in ∧~~medi~~[a?] Palestine or ∧in Egypt ~~(Shinar)~~ Forever and forever ∧~~the~~ one of them, ~~and~~ and that Jesus ~~knew,~~ saw, is the immortal testifier of Love the semen ~~whence~~ ~~comes~~ ~~comes~~ ~~is born~~ of the ~~entire~~ Universe~~.~~, ~~∧the one~~ ~~showing~~ ~~It shows~~ ~~itself in~~ ∧and cause of this ~~that~~ vast elemental sympathy, which, ~~of all we yet know,~~ only the human soul is capable of generating and emitting in steady and limitless floods, best visible ~~shown~~ to the world through a superbly transparent and perfect nature, a sweet and clean body in which ~~was~~ is no guile, or any thing selfish or [~~unseemly?~~] occult or mean.— Every hour, every atom, every where is chock with ~~beautiful~~ miracles, but I consider the ∧sympathetic power of ~~the affections of the~~ [~~human?~~] men's and women's hearts to be ∧the nighest of all ∧we yet know ~~we can behold with mortal eyes~~ to the ~~primal source and~~ ∧unfathomable depth of all [~~we?~~] we do not ∧yet know. No god nor demigod of the antique — no power of Kronos, or Zeus his son or Hercules his grandson, begins with such a power as this.— Of the being who embodies it in ~~boundless~~ finished perfection, — ~~and~~ of whom there have been one or two examples in as many thousand years, as if to encourage the earth and show it how, — and of whose presence to say it is divine I do not wonder, — things more incredible than ~~the~~ any myths of Jah, or Brahma, or Osiris, descend from the tips of his fingers, from the smell of his body, from the vapor of his lungs, whether they act to day ∧or fifty generations gone,— whether in Asia, or ~~in~~ New York or San Francisco, or London.— For a soul

## *med Cophósis*[6]
## [ca. 1852–54]

**[1]**

med Cophósis, deafness, dumbness, or dulness of any sense.
med Cōpos, a morbid lassitude
<u>Sensorium</u>, the seat of sensation, doubtless the brain
Liaison (lē-a-zohn), a binding or fastening together

Because women do not appear in history and philosophy with any thing like the same prominence as men — that is no reason for thinking them less than men:— The great names that we know are but the accidental scraps.— Mention to me the twenty ~~grea~~ most majestic characters that have existed upon the earth, and have their names recorded.— It is very well.— But for that twenty, there are millions upon millions just as great, whose names are unrecorded.— It was in them to do ~~grander~~ actions as grand — to say as beautiful thoughts — to set ~~the~~ examples for their race.— But ∧in each one the book was not opened.— It lay in its place ready

The greatest and truest knowledge can never be taught or passed over from him or her who has it, to him or her who has it not.— It is in the soul.— It is not susceptible of proof or ~~demon~~ explanation.— It applies to all things and encloses them.— ~~All that there is in what~~ ~~The enti~~ What men think enviable, if it ~~were~~ ∧could be collected together for ten thousand years, would not be of the least account, compared with this wisdom.— It is the ~~sight of the~~ consciousness of the reality and excellence of every thing.— It is happiness.— ~~Every~~ Each man ∧and ~~every~~ each woman is eligible to it, without education just ~~the~~ as readily as with Whoever reads these words, let him or her set out upon the search this day, ~~and never rest till~~

My Lesson

Have you learned ~~the~~ my lesson complete:
It is well — it is ∧but the gate to a larger lesson — and
∧~~And~~ that to another ∧~~still~~
And ~~every one~~ each successive one ~~opens~~ to another still

399
~~70~~
~~329~~
70

<u>Poem "Praise of things"</u>

**[2]**

* <u>down</u>

spór-a-des, scattered islands, stars, &c

Novel?— Work of some sort ∧Play?— instead of sporadic characters — introduce them in large masses, on a far grander scale — armies — twenty-three full-formed perfect athletes — [*~~illegible~~*]orbs — take characters

through the orbs — "spiritualism"
nobody appears upon the stage singly — but all in huge aggregates
nobody speaks alone — whatever is said, is said by an immense number

---

Shade — An ^twenty-five old men old man with rapid gestures — eyes black and flashing like lightning — long white beard — attended by an immense train — no warriors or warlike weapons or helmets — all emblematic of peace — shadowy — rapidly ~~approaches and pauses~~ sweeping by —

if in a play — let the descriptions ~~not~~ that are usually put in brief, in brackets, in italic, be also in poetry, carefully finished as the dialogue

The answerer

Plot for a Poem or other work — A manly unpretensive philosopher — without any of the old insignia, such as age, books ~~eth~~etc.— a fine-formed person, of beautiful countenance, &c — sits every day at the door of his house — To him for advice come all sorts of people.— Some come to puzzle him — some come from curiosity — some from ironical contempt — his answers — his opinions

¶ 2 A man appears in public every day — Every time he appears with a companion — one day it is a beautiful youth — another time with a voluptuous woman — another time with a poor pale emaciated sick person, whom he has brought out for a little air — another

☞ good subject Poem — Variety of characters, each one of whom comes forth every day — things appearing, transfers and promotions every day.

There was a child went forth every day — and the first thing that he ~~saw~~ looked at with fixed love, that thing he became for the day.—

* Bring in whole races, or castes, or generations, to express themselves — personify the general objects of the creation and give them voice — every thing on the most august scale — a leaf of grass, with its equal voice.—
☞ — voice of the generations of slaves — of those who have suffered — voice of Lovers.— of Night — Day — Space — the stars — the countless ages of the Past — the countless ages of the future —

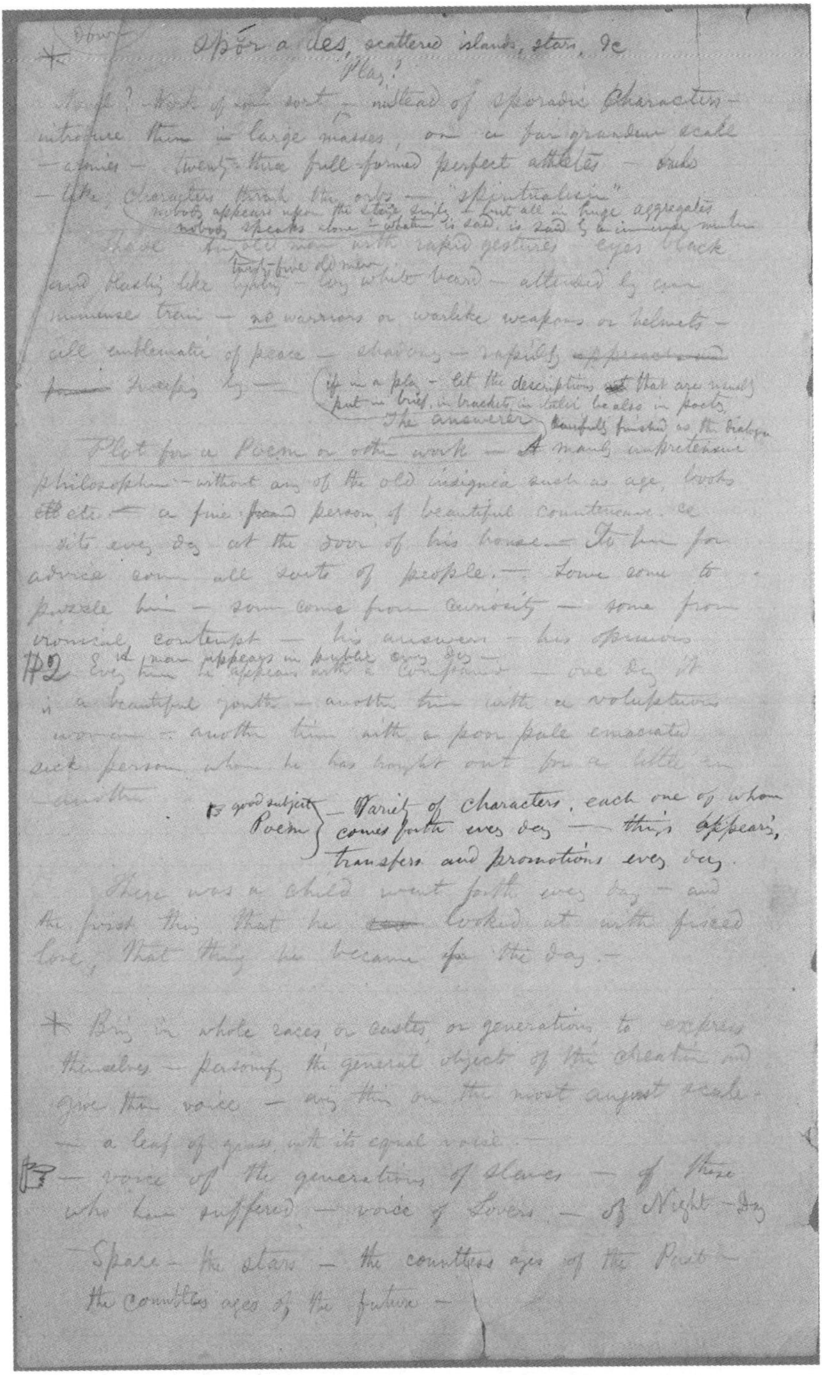

Leaf from *med Cophósis* fragment (ca. 1852–54).

[3]

(a spiritual novel?

Man's Muscular capability. Phren. Jour. vol 7, page 96

A tradition — that to eat the meat of serpents is restorative and helps longevity

In writing, the same taste and law as in personal demeanor — that is never to strain, or exhibit the least apparent desire to make stick out the pride, grandeur and boundless richness — but to be those, and let the spirit of them vitalize whatever is said

In writing, give no second hand articles — no quotations — no authorities — give the real thing — ready money —

---

A poem in which all things and qualities and processes express themselves — the nebula — the fixed stars — the earth — the grass, waters, vegetable, sauroid, and all processes — man — animals.

---

Can a man be wise without he get wisdom from the books?

Can he be religious and have nothing to do with churches or prayers?

Can he have a great style, without being dressed in fine clothes and without any name or fame?

In writing, every thing is to be brought in in its human relations — this invariably.— It is not needful that this should be made ŧpalpable to all ages — but it must be, and it must act supreme in all the plot or course of writing.—

---

A large stone cavity, exactly cut out — in this is placed a man — he has plenty to eat — he has whatever he asks for — money unbounded is around him — but there he lives — he walks around carrying with him that portable impenetrable stone coffin.—

---

"String team" — the horses, — three, four, or five — in single file, without curb or bit, that draw the cars, or other vehicles — the peculiar manner of calling to 'em and directing them — "Black Jack's" illustrations of the way of guiding them —

[4]

You are one of The common statesman thinks of men as people to be governed — thinks a government a great thing in itself — takes much care about checks and balances — offices — &c.—

You are The common philosopher maps out his system, fortifies it by powerful argument — proves how it is true — how much better than all ~~that~~ the rest of its rivals — &c.

Do not fancy [*illegible*] that I have come to descend among you, gentlemen — I encompass you all

A rule or two invariable in personal and literary demeanor.— Never to complain of any attacks or harsh criticisms upon myself, or my writings — never to defend either by a single word or argument — never to deprecate any one's enmity or opposition — nor vindicate myself.— Not to suppose or recognize ~~th~~ as a possible occurrence, that it can be necessary for me to prove I am right ~~and~~ or ~~great~~ clean.—

---

It is only the common ambition that is satisfied with the eminence that comes from wealth or office.— Far above these is the eminence of personal qualities — a grand presence — wit — conversational power — that charm, we don't know what it is, which goes with the mere face and body ^magnetism of some men and women, and makes every body love them, wherever they go.— Even the movement of one's limbs, and the gestures of the hands are ~~great~~ can fascinate.— ~~But all~~ That which comes from the mere possession of riches, is ~~little.— It is~~ rather a blur upon the highest ~~action; it is~~ forms of humanity

A Crayons in brief

an illus~~tration.~~— ^ Socrates, sauntering through the market place, attracted by the princely youth of Athens — cross-questioning — his big paunch — his bare feet — his subtle tongue —

## *Summer duck*[7]
## [ca. 1852–55]

**[1]**

"Summer Duck" or "Wood Duck" ∧"wood drake" very gay, including in its colors white, red, yellow, green, blue, &c crowns violet — length 20 inches — common in the United States — often by ~~creeks~~ streams and ponds — rises and slowly circuits — selects hollow trees to breed in — keep in parties — generally move in pairs at least

King Bird "Tyrant Flycatcher" length 8½ inches — loud shrill voice — attacks hawks and crows as if for amusement — when tired it retreats to some stake or limb, with a triumphant twitter.—

Peewee — ∧one of the earliest comers in spring — builds nest often under the eaves of a deserted house or barn — pleasing note —

"Redstart" — beautiful small bird arrives here latter part of April, returns south late in September — common in woods and along roadside and meadow — feeds on insects — active — has a lively twitter.—

☞ All the above are met on Long Island

young squaw
Papoose — old squaw

One personal deed, — one ~~great~~ effusion of some grand strength and will of man — may go far beyond law, custom, and all other conventionalisms — and seize upon the heart of the whole race, utterly defiant of authority — or argument against ~~them~~ it.—

Do you suppose the world is finished, at any ∧certain time — like a contract for paving a street?— Do you suppose because the American government has been formed, and public schools established, we have nothing more to do but take our ease, and make money, and ~~let this grow~~ sleep out the rest of the time?

Fear ~~delectation!~~ ~~delicatesse~~ grace! Fear ~~grace! —~~ delicatesse!—~~al~~ del-i-ca-teśs—These precede the (what is it in fruit when just ripe) terrible ripeness of nature — the decay of the ruggedness of ~~a~~ men — ~~the~~ and of ~~a~~ nations.—

[2]

Go on! go on! we ha'n't got time

Ens — a being, existence, essence, that recondite part of a substance from which all its qualities flow, (old term in metaphysics)

— — — Look out there's

"Take heed to yourselves — there's a mad man ~~stalking~~ loose through in the ship, with a knife in his hands," — such was the warning sung out at night more than once below in the Old Jersey prison ship, ∧1780 moored at the Wallabout, in the revolution.— Utter derangement was a frequent symptom of the aggravated sicknesses that prevailed there.— The prisoners were allowed no light at night.—

No physicians were ~~allowed~~ provided.—

Sophocles, Eschylus, and Euripides flourished about the time of the birth of Socrates 468 B.C. ∧and years afterward.— Great as their remains are, they were transcended by other works that have not come down to us.— Those other works, often gained the first prizes.—

In Eschylus the figures are shadowy, vast, and majestic — dreaming, moving with haughty grandeurs, strength and will

In Sophokles, the dialogue and feelings are more like reality and the interest approaches home,— great poetical beauty.—

In Euripides, love and compassion — scientific refinement,— something like skepticism.— This writer was a hearer of Socrates.—

Phallic festivals.— wild mirthful processions in honor of the god Dionysus (Bacchus) — in Athens, and other parts of Greece — unbounded license — mocking jibes and irony — epithets and biting insults

<u>To the Poor —</u>

I have my place among you
Is it nothing that I have preferred to be poor, rather than
to be rich?
The road to riches is easily open to me,
But I do not choose it.
I choose to stay with you.—

**[3]**

(bring in a few
of ancient, and modern times — the worst I can find and the most
[comely?] and their ope ~~effects —~~ practical operations.)

Does any one tell me that it is the part of a man to obey such enactments as these?

I tell you the world is demented with this very obedience —

When a man, untrammeling himself from blind obedience to ~~pries~~ the craft of priests and politicians, branches out with his own sovereign will and strength — knowing that ~~himself~~ the unspeakable ∧greatness of himself, or of the meanest of his fellow creatures — expands far beyond all the laws and governments of the earth — then he begins really to be a man.— Then he is great.—

(From the baldness of birth to the baldness of burials and shrouds

Something behind or afterward.— Leave the impression that no matter what is said, there is something greater to say — something behind still more marvellous and beautiful —

**[4]**

He does better with spare
out, hunger, starvation, opposing enemies, contentious

Riches.— It is only the mean and vulgar appetite that craves money ~~and property~~ ∧as the first and foremost of its wants

---

I have appeared among you to say that ~~all~~ what you do is
right, and ~~that~~ what you affirm is
right;
But that [~~it is~~?] they are only the alphabet[?] of right.—
And that you shall use them as beginnings and
first attempts.—

I have not appeared ~~to take any~~ with violent
hands to pull up by the roots any thing
that has grown,

Whatever has grown, has grown well.—
Do you ~~suppose~~ fancy there ~~was any flaw~~ ∧is some waters in the semen of the ~~first~~ perpetual copulation?
Do you ~~believe~~ of suppose the ~~universe~~ [~~*illegible*~~]celestial laws ~~of~~ might be reformed and rectified?

[*illegible*] Virtue and about Vice?
[*illegible*] what

## *After all*[8]
[ca. 1853–54]

After all ~~that can be~~ is said and done in the way of argument, ~~the innumerable it~~ the whole ~~amount to~~ ~~means but a is a makes~~ raises but a bubble of the sea-ooze ~~in comparison with~~ against that unspeakable Something in my own soul which makes me know without being able to tell ∧how it is ~~or prove~~ ∧how ~~that is I know.~~— ~~If~~ Though ~~I were opposed by~~ ~~what I felt~~ the ~~science~~ linguists and lore of the whole earth deny what I say, it amounts but to this: So it seems to them.— I simply answer, So it seems to me.— The greatest of thoughts and truths, are ~~not~~ never ~~to [*illegible*] be~~ put in ~~language~~ ~~writing or~~ print..— They are not susceptible of proof like a sum in simple multiplication

I ~~can~~ even see myself ~~struggling~~ sweating in the fog with the linguists and learned ~~old~~ men.— I look back upon that time in my own days.— I have no ~~gibes nor mocks~~ mockings or laughter;— I have only to be silent and patiently ~~to~~ wait.—

## *What we call Literature*[9]
[ca. 1853–55]

What we call Literature is but [a?] the ~~blind~~ moist and wobbling cub, ~~new~~ just born and its eyes not open yet in many days.— ~~I am~~ ∧You are a living man, and think; in that alone is a more heightless and fathomless wonder than all the productions of letters and arts in all the ~~years~~ ^nations and periods of this earth.—

## *Picture of the most flowing grandeur of a man*[10]

[pre-1855]

**[1]**

Picture of the most flowing grandeur of a man

---

When a man joined to his great power, and wealth and strength, has the ^knowledge of the perfect equanimity and

---

A man of gigantic, stature, supple, healthy, accomplished, powerful, ^and resistless~~,~~ is a great man — But when ~~such an one~~ a man with all that is not trapped into any partiality ~~or sh~~ — when he strikes the ~~eternal~~ balance between the eternal average of the developed and the undeveloped — when he ~~is~~goes on the square with those who have not yet climbed as high as he — tender to children and old people and women — indulging most the stupid the sinful and the vulgar — because them the world is most down upon —

**[2]**

4

steamboats and vaccination, gunpow[der?] and spinning-jennies; but are our people half as peaceable and happy as ^were the Peruvians and Mexicans, ere the Spanish navigators introduced ~~among~~ to them the blessings of ~~civilization~~ artificial science and ^of the true faith?—
It is out of this mass of folly, wickedness, and injustice, and its influence, that ~~an individual~~ a man is required to lift himself, as the very first step toward his being a perfect. ~~man~~ He must have a very high faculty of independence.— The mere authority of law, custom, or precedent, must be nothing, absolutely nothing at all, with him.— High,

## *Poem — a perfect school*[11]
[pre-1855]

a TG 2 get — [*illegible*] description of [*illegible*]

Poem — a perfect school, gymnastic, moral, mental and sentimental, — in which magnificent men are formed — old persons come just as much as youth — gymnastics, physiology, music, swimming bath — conversation,— declamation —

— large saloons adorned with pictures and sculpture — great ideas not taught in sermons but imbibed as health is imbibed — ←

— love — love of woman — all manly exercises — riding, rowing — the greatest persons come — the president comes and the governors come — political economy

— the American idea in all its amplitude and comprehensiveness —

— grounds, gardens, flowers, grains — cabinets — old history taught —

1833
1776
67

## *Priests!*[12]
[pre-1855]

**[1]**

^Priests! Until you can explain a paving stone, ^~~to every ones my perfect satisfaction O~~
~~Priests~~, do not try to explain God:

Until your creeds can do as much as apples and hen's eggs, [~~restrain~~?] ^[~~pull~~?] let down your eyebrows ^a little,

¶ Until your Bibles and prayer-books are able to
walk like me,
And until your brick and mortar can procreate
as I can,
I beg you, Sirs, do not presume to put them
above me.
X ~~take in~~

[2]

for droppings

Poem — embodying the sentiment of perfect happiness, in myself ~~th~~ body and soul being all right — regardless of whatever may happen.

## *In metaphysical points*[13]

[pre-1855]

~~Pure and Positive Truth~~ ^ ~~About Metaphysical points~~ ~~.— It seems to me,~~ ^ In metaphysical points, here is what I guess about pure and positive truths. I guess that after all reasoning and analogy and their most palpable demonstrations of any thing, we have the ^ ~~only~~ real satisfaction ~~comes~~ only when the soul tells and tests by its own arch-chemic power — ~~something as~~superior to the learnedest ~~and reasoning~~ proofs ~~and finest reasoning~~, as one glance of ~~the~~ ^ living sight, is more than quarto volumes of ~~the elaborate~~ description ^ ~~and~~ and of maps.— ~~filling a thousand quarto volumes.—~~ There is something in vast ~~learning~~ erudition melancholy and fruitless as an Arctic sea.— With most men it is a slow ~~large~~ dream, ~~and in a fog too~~ dreamed in a moving fog.— So complacent! So much body and muscle; fine legs to walk,— large supple hands — but the eyes are owl's eyes, and the heart is a mackerel's heart.— These words are for the great men, the ~~giants~~ ^ gigantic few that have ~~reached~~ plunged themselves ~~out into space~~ deep through density and confusion, and pushed back the jealous coverings of the earth, and ~~told us the~~ brought out the true and great things, and ^ the sweet ~~true~~ things, ~~that hang~~ and hung them like ^ ~~round ripe~~ oranges, ~~on the~~ rounder and riper than ~~ever before,~~ all the rest, ~~on the limbs of~~ among our ~~of~~ literature and science.— These words are for the ^ five or six grand poets, too; and the masters of artists:— ^ I waste no ink, nor my throat, on the ~~huge~~ ever-deploying armies of professors, authors, lawyers, teachers and what not; ~~let us waste no words ink or breath.~~ ~~type.~~— Of them we expect ~~of them to~~ that they be very learned, and nothing [~~of~~] more.—

What gentlemen! what then? Do you suppose it is for your geology and your chemistry and your mathematics

## *Nehemiah Whitman*[14]

## [mainly 1845–55, additions as late as 1861]

**[1]**

____ Whitman built the old [homestead?] in which was born

Nehemiah Whitman, [~~*illegible*~~] ~~rents~~ [~~*illegible*~~] [~~was born at?~~] [~~the?~~] descended from one of the earliest English emigrants to America, was born and died on the old [~~Hills?~~] homestead at West Hills — which was inherited by his son, His wife was ~~Phebe~~ Sarah White —

| | | |
|---|---|---|
| Jesse Whitman, born Jan. 29, 1749 | | Sarah White born about 1713<br>" " died " 180[1?] |
| " " | died Feb. 12, 1803 | see next page-bottom |
| Hannah Brush | born Oct. 6 1753 | Married, April 22, 1775 |
| " " | died Jan. 6, 1834 | |

The Whitman and Brush families were among the most ardent of the the "Rebels" of '76, in Suffolk county.— See "Reminiscences." — One of the latter, Maj. Brush, was often and angrily denounced by the British ^local proclamations, and by the loyalists of Long Island. He was confined for a time in the "Provost" in New York, under the charge of the infamous Cunningham

Jesse Whitman, jr born June 25, 1776

Died at Dix Hills, Sept. 8, 1845

Sarah Whitman, born Jan. 1, 1778.

died Feb. 2, 1852

Naomi Van Velsor died, February 1826

Major Cornelius Van Velsor ^born 1758. died August, 1837, aged 79

(He was son of Garret Van Velsor

| | |
|---|---|
| Garret Van Velsor, died 1812 | parents of |
| ~~Jenny Kossabon~~ Phebe Akeley | Major Van Velsor |

One of the sons of Nehemiah Whitman was a Lieutenant in Col. Josiah Smith's Regiment of the ^American Patriot Army ^of 1776 ~~under~~ ^~~chief~~ ~~com~~mand of Washington,

See 1st edition Reminiscences of Long Island, vol. 2, page 28 or vol 1, page 87

He was in the disastrous battle of Brooklyn ~~Col. Smiths~~ ^the reg. having been ordered to place themselves under Gen. Greene, some days before that battle~~, —~~by Brig. Gen. Woodhull, who ~~had charge general charge on L. I.—~~ was also President of the N. Y. Convention.—

The L.I. regiment were hemmed in the lines

over

**[2]**

We moved to Brooklyn, (Front st.) in May, 1823.

Moved to Cranberry st. (opposite the church,) in '24

" " Johnson st. May 1st 1825.— (Covert, the villain

" Across the way, (Van Dyke's) were there 4th July 1826

" Adams st, lived there spring of '27

" To Tillary cor. Washington, (Miller's) 1st May 1827

" To own house in Nov. and lived there till Nov. 1831

Lived in Henry st. (near Cranberry,) the winter before the first cholera summer.

Moved to Liberty st. Were there ~~the first~~ one of cholera summers.— (The old Hardenburghs up stairs) (I was there alone in the house a while.) The miserable scoundrel Gil. Reid, and the suffering he caused us all.— Graham the old devil, that owned the house.)

Moved from Liberty st. to Front st, (eastern part, and lived there in spring and early summer of 1833.— ^mother very sick. X (Mrs. Sibley.)

Family Moved in the country.— Lived at Norwich in 1834 I remained in Brooklyn

I remaining in Brooklyn {
From there to Hempstead — were there 1835–6.—
Moved from Hempstead to Babylon, Aug. 1836
" to Dix Hills in May, 1840
" from Dix Hills to Brooklyn Aug. 6, 1844.
}

Moved into house in Prince st. in Dec. 1844

I Built the place 106 Myrtle av. in winter of 1848–9, and moved in, lattcr part of April '49

I [~~Built?~~] Sold the Myrtle av. house in May, '52, and built in Cumberland street, where we moved Sept. 1st, '52.

Sold the two 3 story houses in Cumberland st. March 1853. Moved into the little 2 story house ∧Cumberland st April 21st, '53 (lived there just one year exactly.)

Built in Skillman st, and moved there May, 1854

Moved in Ryerson st, May 1855.— Lived in Classon ∧from May 1st '56, '7 '8 '9

Lived in Portland av. from May 1st '59 '60 '61

Sarah White, my great grandmother Whitman, lived to be 90 years old.— She was a large, strong woman, chewed tobacco, opium &c.— petted her slaves, and had always a crowd of little niggers about her.— She would sit with her feet up before the fire, just like a man — was every way decided and masculine in behavior

The tradition of my grandfather, Jesse Whitman, was that there were four brothers, Englishmen ∧his remote ancestors who came over here.— One settled on Long Island — West Hills was formerly inhabited and owned very largely by Whitmans.—

## *Silence*[15]

[top fragment, probably 1860s; bottom fragment, pre-1855]

Silence.— ∧Years ago In the Parsons affair, in New York, after ~~the~~ Mayor Westervelt had been worsted, a vast mass of ~~ten or~~ some ten to fifteen thousand, after hearing P., on Sunday afternoon, took a freak into their heads to ~~adjourn~~ visit in perfect silence the Mayor's house, as a rebuke.— They did so; ∧— only the tramping of their feet was heard — a prodigious army drawing up and standing around [~~there?~~] his door, and neighborhood, without a word or any insulting gesture ∧or look, for about half an hour, and then dispersed.—

---

[*paper glued*]

Silence.— (The ~~tr this to last ¶)~~ original god ∧of whom Osiris ∧was one type, in his highest capacity of goodness, was adored by the Egyptian priests in silence,— without words, without movements.—)

The greatest love is that which makes no professions
The greatest anguish is the misery that neither weeps nor complains.—
The greatest contempt utters not a ∧single word.

To the gainer of one or two signal victories the subtle-souled Greeks ~~made~~ ~~frequently~~ offered the compliment of a colossal statue, put ∧on a ~~proportionately~~ gigantic pedestal, in ~~th~~ some public porch.— To the ~~grand~~ veteran of ~~a dozen of the~~ ~~twenty~~ treble or quadruple ~~the~~ of mightiest successes they ~~∧invariably~~ built a statue strictly of his own size, and ~~placed~~ planted it on a level with the eye.—

After all there is in eloquence and rage,
I guess ~~that~~ there is more still in silence.—

## *Living Pictures*[16]

[front: pre-1855, possibly quite early; back: post-1860]

**[1]**

~~Life~~ Living Pictures

~~Evening~~, Nowhere, in the known world, can so many, and such beautiful living ~~Pictures be seen as in these United States!~~

America

Here ~~labour is~~ different from any other country in the world ∧all forms of practical labour is ~~manly~~, recognized as honorable.— The man who tends the President's horses, not one whit less a man than the President.— The healthy, fine-formed girl who ~~tends~~ waits upon the ~~great~~ wealthy lady, not less than the wealthy Lady.—
He, who carries bricks ∧& mortar to the mason, not less than the mason,
The mason who lays the bricks, not one tittle less than the builder, who ~~engages~~ employs, him,
The ∧architect & builder of the house, no less than

**[2]**

A cluster of poems, (in the same way as "Calamus Leaves") expressing the idea and sentiment of

Happiness,
Ecstatic life, (or moods)
Serene Calm
Infantum
Juvenatum
Maturity — a young man's moods.
[*~~illegible~~*] Middle-age
  Strong, well-fibered, bearded, athletic, full of love, full of pride & joy
☞ Old Age
Natural Happiness
Love, Friendship

## *Of this broad and majestic universe*[17]

[pre-1855, probably 1853–54]

**[1]**

Of ~~all that there is in the~~ this broad and majestic universe, ~~you can mention nothing either~~ ∧all in the visible world, ~~or~~ ∧and much in the greater world invisible, ~~that is not~~ ~~but what~~ is owned by the Poet.— He owns the solid ~~ground~~ and tills it and reaps from ~~every~~ field and harvests ~~fro the~~ cotton and grain, ~~dried grass~~—. ∧~~the timothy~~ and ~~the~~ clovers.— All the woods and all the orchards — the corn, ~~with its~~ ear and stalks and tassels — the buckwheat ~~with~~ ~~and~~ its ~~sweet~~ white ~~blossoms~~ tops ~~where~~ and the bees ∧that hum ∧there all day —

**[2]**

Will you have the walls [*cut away*] the world with the air and the fringed clouds

---

The Poet says God and me
What do you want from us
Ask, and may be we give it [you?]

---

The Soul addresses God as his equal — as one who knows its greatness — as a younger brother

## *Remember that the clock*[18]

## [pre-1855, probably 1853–54]

Remember that the clock and the hands of the clock, only tell the time — they are not themselves the aggregated years.— ~~Time~~ Which is greatest — time, which baffles us, or its indexes, made [~~by~~?] of wood and brass, ~~at~~ by ^a workman at ten dollars a week?— Time itself knows no index — it is merely ~~for~~ to stand us a little in help that ^we combine sets of springs and wheels [~~are~~?] and arbitrarily divide ^it by hours and quarters — and call ~~these miserable~~ this measuring ~~of~~ time.— ~~Contemptible enough~~ indeed ~~are they such~~ they all, ~~measuring, compared with that vast~~ But that stunning, swimming puzzle envelop~~ings~~ ~~God~~ the soul him itself and the Elder Brother of the soul and ~~which~~ had no beginning and can never cease

## *poet of Materialism*[19]

## [pre-1855, probably 1853–54]

[*illegible*] poet of Materialism — (put this section forward [*illegible*] [in Reality?] and demonstration [with?] the opening.)

[*illegible*] — that this earth is under a constant ~~and~~ [process?] of amelioration — as it always has been — that it, in some manner not perhaps demonstratable in astronomy, expands outward and outward in a larger and larger orbit — that our immortality is <u>located</u> here upon earth — that we <u>are immortal</u> — that the processes of the refinement and perfection of the earth are in steps, the least part of which involves trillions of years — that in due time the earth ^beautiful as it is now ~~and~~ will be as much ~~beyond~~ ^proportionately different from what it is now, as ~~wh~~ it now is proportionately different from what it was in its earlier gaseous or marine period, uncounted cycles before man and woman grew.— — That we ^also shall be here proportionately different from now, and beautiful [*illegible*]

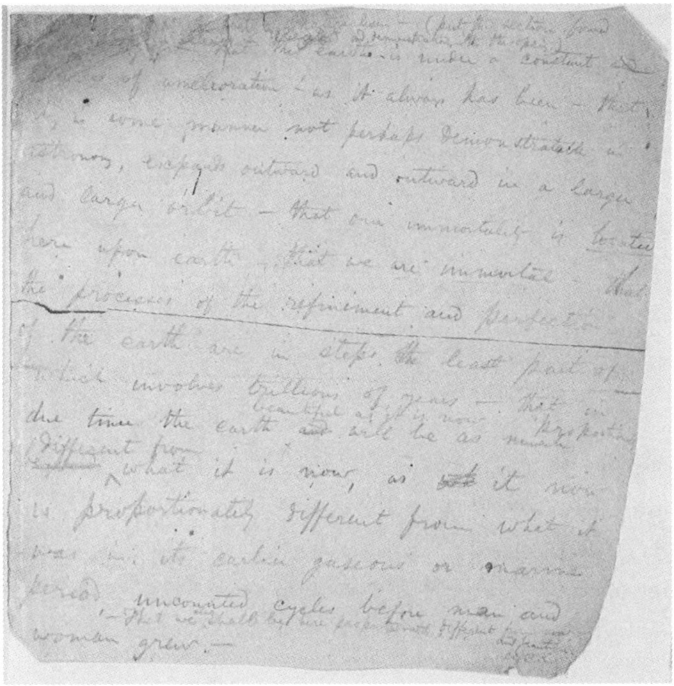
[illegible] — (put in section [illegible]
[illegible] demonstrated the theory)
that the earth is under a constant [illegible]
of amelioration — as it always has been — that
in some manner not perhaps demonstrable in
astronomy, expands outward and outward in a larger
and larger orbit — that our immortality is located
here upon earth — that we are immortal — that
the processes of the refinement and perfection
of the earth are in steps, the least part of
which involves trillions of years — that in
beautiful as it is now
due time the earth and will be as much proportionally
different from
what it is now, as it now
is proportionately different from what it
was in its earlier gaseous or marine
period, uncounted cycles before man and
— that we shall be here [illegible] different [illegible]
woman grew. —

Recto of *poet of Materialism* fragment (pre-1855, probably 1853–54). David M. Rubenstein Rare Book and Manuscript Library, Duke University.

Verso of *poet of Materialism* fragment, showing wallpaper pattern. David M. Rubenstein Rare Book and Manuscript Library, Duke University.

## *Loveblows*[20]

[pre-1855, probably 1854–55]

Loveblows
Loveblossoms
Loveapples
Loveleaves)
Loveclimbers
Loveverdure
~~A~~ Lovevines
Lovebranches                Loveroot.
~~Loveroot~~ ~~Seedling~~ Climber-blossom — -mine.—
~~Bloss~~ ~~Branched~~ Verdure, ~~blossom~~ branch, fruit and vine

The irregular tapping of rain off ~~the~~ my house eaves at night ~~when~~ after the storm has lulled.

Broadaxe
~~The iron leaf all~~ gray-blue spirit so hardened grown
~~The Handle that~~ [~~came?~~] ~~produced~~ ~~from~~ a ~~little seed sown~~
Head from the mother's bowels ~~come~~ drawn
Body ~~as~~ shapely ~~and~~ naked and wan
Fibre produced from a little seed sown

Loveroot,
juicy ~~reacher~~ climber-~~blossomer~~-mine
Verdure, crotch, ~~branch,~~ ~~crotch~~ ~~fruit~~ bulb and vine
Silk ______
Juicy climber mine
Bulb, silkthread, crotch and f

## *Rules for Composition*[21]
[ca. 1850–54]

Rules for Composition

A perfectly transparent plate-glassy style, artless, with no ornaments, or attempts at ornaments, for their own sake — ∧they only ~~coming in where~~ ∧~~answering~~ ∧looking well when like the beauties of the person or character, by nature and intuition, ∧and never lugged ∧in ~~in~~ ∧~~in by the colla~~[r] to show off, which ~~founders~~ nullifies the best of them, no matter ~~under~~ when and where, ~~or under~~ of ~~the most favorable cases.~~

[*paper glued*]

Take no illustrations whatever from the ancients or classics, nor from the mythology nor Egypt, Greece, or Rome — nor from the royal and aristocratic institutions and forms of Europe.— Make no mention or allusion to them whatever, except as they relate to the New, present things — to our country — to American character or interests.— Of specific mention of them, even for these purposes, as little as possible.—

Too much attempt at ornament is the blur upon nearly all literary styles.

Clearness, simplicity, no twistified or foggy sentences, at all — the most translucid clearness without variation.—

[*paper glued*]

Common idioms and phrases — Yankeeisms and vulgarisms — cant expressions, when very pat only.—

~~Mention not God at all~~

## *you cannot define too clearly*[22]
[1850s, probably 1853–54]

you cannot define too clearly what it is you love in a poem or in a man or woman.

A work of ^a great poet is not remembered for its parts — but remembered as you remember the complete person ^and spirit of him or her you love.—

---

[*illegible erasure*]

When he becomes is vitalized with nationality and individuality from top to toe — when he seizes upon life with ~~simple and~~ masculine power — when he stands out in simple relief, as America does —

---

bully-poet

## *Sculpture*[23]
[1850s, probably 1853–54]

Sculpture

— then sculpture was necessary — it was an eminent part of religion it gave grand and beautiful forms to to the gods — it appealed to the mind, in perfect harmony, with ~~the people~~, the climate, belief, ~~times~~, governments, and aspirations.— It was the ~~true~~ ^needed expression of the people, the times, and their aspirations.—

It was a part of architecture — the temple ~~was not~~ stood unfinished without statues, and ^so they were built made with reference to the temple — they were not made abstractly by themselves.—

---

give a similar dash
at painting

# *Sweet flag*[24]

[1853–55]

**[1]**

Sweet flag
Sweet fern
illuminated face
clarified
unpolluted
flour-corn
aromatic
Calamus
sweet-green
bulb
and melons with
bulbs ~~swee~~ grateful

to the hand

I am a look
mystic
in a trance
exaltation

something wild and
untamed — [~~*illegible*~~]
— half savage

---

common[?] things
The ~~sweet trickling~~ trickling Sap
^that ~~trickles~~ ~~drops~~ flows
from the end of the
~~pole little~~
manly maple
tooth of delight
tooth — prong
— tine

---

spendt spend

---

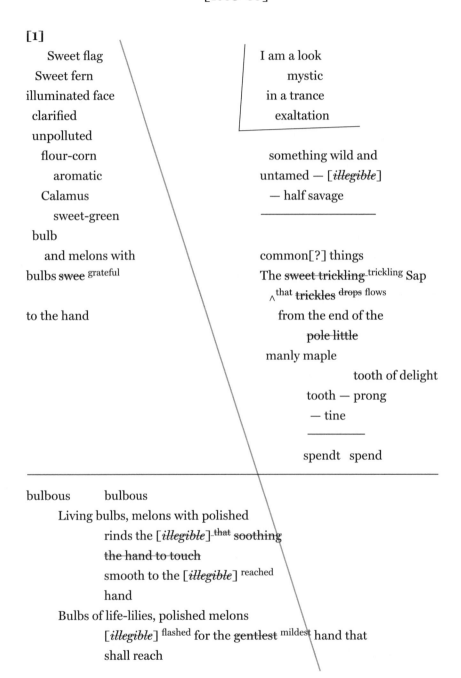

bulbous bulbous
Living bulbs, melons with polished
rinds the [~~*illegible*~~] ~~that~~ ~~soothing~~
~~the hand to touch~~
smooth to the [~~*illegible*~~] reached
hand
Bulbs of life-lilies, polished melons
[~~*illegible*~~] flashed for the ~~gentlest~~ mildest hand that
shall reach

**[2]**

To be at all — what is ~~greater~~ better than that?
I think if there were nothing more developed,
    the clam in its callous shell in
    the sand, were august enough.— |

I am not in any callous shell;
I am cased with supple conductors,
    all over;
They take every object by the hand, and
    lead it within me.—

They are thousands, each one with his entry
    to himself;
They are always watching with their little
    eyes, from my head to my feet.
One no more than a ~~pencil's~~ point, ∧~~lead,~~ lets in
    and out of me, ~~of me more bliss~~
    ~~than I thought the spheres~~
    ~~could carry.~~
    such bliss and magnitude, ¶ I think
    I could [~~then?~~] ~~dash~~ lift ~~put~~ the girder
    of ~~the earth~~ ∧~~a globe~~ the house away if it lay between
    me ∧then and whatever I wanted.—
My
The

## *Make no quotations*[25]

[pre-1855, probably post-1847]

Make no quotations, and no reference to any other writers.— ~~nor~~

Lumber the writing with nothing — let it ~~fly~~ go as lightly as a bird flies in the air — or a fish swims in the sea

Be careful to temper down too much ~~personality or~~ [*cut away*]

## *It seems to me*[26]
[pre-1855, probably 1854–55]

It seems to me — to avoid all poetical similes — to be faithful to the perfect likelihoods of nature — healthy, exact simple, disdaining ornament.

## *The most perfect wonders*[27]
[pre-1855, probably 1854–55]

The most perfect wonders of the earth are not [~~I~~?] rare and distant but present with every [~~*illegible*~~] person, — you as much as any!—

tr down Man! Woman! Youth! wherever you are, in the Northern, Southern, Eastern, or Western States — in Kanada — by the sea-coast, or far inland — ~~the~~

~~Th~~ What is more amazing than the ~~day~~ sun-rise, the day, the floods of light enveloping ~~the~~ fields, ~~t~~ waters, grass, trees, persons?— What is more beautiful than the night, the full moon, and the stars?— The prairies, the lakes, [~~t~~?] rivers, forests,— ~~all~~ are

Not distant caverns, volcanoes, cataracts, curious islands, birds, foreign cities, architecture, costumes, markets, ceremonies, shows, are any more wonderful than ^what is common to you, near you now, and continually with you.—

## *Light and air!*[28]
[1854–55]

~~The nightly magic of~~ Light and air!
Nothing ugly ~~is~~ ^can be disgorged — ~~brought~~ ^¶ Nothing corrupt or dead set before them,
But it ~~shall~~ [~~*illegible*~~] surely becomes translated or enclothed
Into supple youth or ~~dr~~ a dress of ~~surpassing~~ living richness
spring gushing out from under the roots of an old tree
barn-yard, pond, yellow-jagged bank with white pebblestones
timothy, sassafras, grasshopper, pismire, rail-fence

rye, oats, cucumbers, musk-melons, pumpkin-vine,
long string of running blackberry —

regular ∧sound of the cow crunching, crunching the grass —
the path ∧worn in the grass — katy-did, locust, tree-toad,
robin — wren —

## *The Analogy holds*[29]

[pre-1855]

The analogy holds in this way — that the soul ~~or Spirit~~ of the Universe is the ~~Father~~ Male and genital Lord master, and the [~~animating and?~~] impregnating and animating spirit.— ~~The Female All~~ ∧~~Universal~~ Physical matter is ~~the~~ Female ∧and Mother, and waits barren and bloomless, the jets of life from the masculine vigor, the undermost first cause of all ~~vigor and motion~~ that is not what Death is.—

## *The only way*[30]

[pre-1860, probably pre-1855]

The only way in which any thing can really be owned, is by the infusion or inspiration of it in the soul.— ~~The ignorant~~ ∧Can I dully suppose that ~~they may~~ I may attain to certain possessions,— as houses or stocks or lands or goods; and ~~that such property will be theirs,~~ when ~~they~~ I have paid ∧the money and ~~got~~ taken the receipts and warranty deeds, — then such property will be ~~theirs~~ ∧mine to enter upon and enjoy.— Yes, may-be as ~~those~~ people stone blind from their birth, ~~enter~~ enjoy the exhibitions of pictures and sculpture.—

## *My poems, when complete*[31]

[ca. 1855–60]

My Poems, when complete, should be A Unity, in the same sense that the earth is, or that the human body, (senses, soul, head, trunk, feet, blood, viscera man-root, eyes, hair,) or that a perfect musical composition is —

[*Glued-in newspaper clipping, titled "The Unity of the Bible," in which Whitman underlines the following passage, emphasizing it with a manicule: "one idea, worked out through all the changes of measure and of key, now almost hidden, now breaking out in rich natural melody, whispered in the treble, murmured in the base, dimly suggested in the prelude"*]

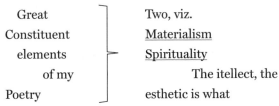

Great Constituent elements of my Poetry } Two, viz.
Materialism
Spirituality
The itellect, the esthetic is what is to be the medium of these and to be beautiful, govern, & make serviceable these

## *in the west*[32]

[ca. 1855–56]

in the West
a vision ? (Poem of ? vision — of future

— Depicting the West a hundred years from now — ~~th~~two hundred years — five hundred years —
(This ought to be a splendid part of the the Poem — (? Poem of Ohio?) — it ought to lay in the colors and draw the ~~lines fo~~ outlines with a ~~fr~~ large, free, and bold, hand

## *This is the Earths word —*[33]
[1855–56?]

[*illegible*] — This is the Earths word —
the pervading sentiment or lesson is to be that the only good of learning the theory ~~and~~ of the fluency ~~largeness exa~~ and generosity and unpartiality, largeness and exactitude of the earth is to use all those toward ^the theory of character — human character

---

## *most poets finish*[34]
[1856]

most poets finish single specimens of characters — I ~~sh~~ will never finish single specimens; I will shower them by exhaustless laws, as nature does, indicating not only themselves but successive productions out of themselves, later and fresher continually

---

Perfect Sanity
Divine Instinct
Breadth of Vision
Healthy rudeness of body
Withdrawnness
Gayety
Sun-tan & Air-sweetness

Hungary

[*Glued-in newspaper clipping, referring to Mihály Vörösmarty. The text just below Whitman hand-copies from this clipping, except for the date, which he adds.*]

Orphans of Vorosmarty, the greatest Hungarian poet, June 1856
(just dcad) 1856

---

Heinrich Heine (just dead 1856) "Pictures of Travel." (1856), portrait
— leaning, sleeping head —
— poems, (as translated) seem to be fanciful and vivacious, rather ironical and melancholy with a dash of the poetical craziness[?]

## *Produce great persons*[35]
## [1856]

Produce great persons and the producers of great persons .... all the rest surely follows.— What has ^[~~*illegible*~~] been but indicated in other continents, in America must receive its ~~natural~~ definite and numberless growth. the time is arrived and the[?] land got ready and ~~the each century helps~~ every present age is to pass the sinewy lesson [~~*illegible*~~] and add to it.—

Produce great persons .... (all) the rest surely follows.— The time is arrived and the land got ready for the free growth of that which (the) other continents have has been indicated

---

Etymology — origin and derivations
— distributes words into parts of speech, tenses, genders, &c

---

Syntax — constructing words in a sentence —

---

Prosody — accent versification, laws of harmony —
Give ~~us~~ me something savage and luxuriant,
Give me large, full voiced, men

---

Preterit — past — noting the past tense of a verb, as "I wrote."

## *Feb. 25th '57 Dined with Hector Tyndale*[36]
[February 25th, 1857]

Feb. 25th '57 Dined with Hector Tyndale

Asked H. T. where he thought I needed particular attention to be directed for my improvement — where I could especially be bettered in my poems —

He said — "In massiveness, breadth, large, sweeping effects, without regard to details,— as in the "Cathedral at York" (he said) "I came away with great impressions of its largeness, solidity, and spaciousness without troubling myself with its parts"

Asked F. Le B. same question viz: What I most lacked — He said — "In euphony — your poems seem to me to be full of the raw material of poems, but crude, and wanting finish and rhythms."

Of others the answer has been —

"You have too much procreation"

---

Put in my poems

American things, idioms, materials, persons, groups, minerals, vegetables, animals, &c

☞

## *The Great Construction of the New Bible*[37]
[June, 1857]

The Great Construction of the New Bible

Not to be diverted from the principal object — the main life work — the Three Hundred & Sixty five — (it ought to be ready in 1859.— (June '57)

## *A main part of The greatness*[38]
## [ca. 1857?]

∧A main part of The greatness of a humanity is that it ~~is at no~~ ∧never at any time ~~nor~~ or under any circumstances, ∧arrives at its finality — never ~~so that it can~~ is able to say, Now ∧as I stand, I am fixed ~~as I am~~ ~~stand~~ forever.— If any one has the feeling to say, I am fixed — and retains that feeling — then ∧a longer or shorter farewell to the greatness of that humanity.—

— Every day something more — something ~~it was less~~[?] unsuspected the previous day.— Always changing, advancing, ∧retreating enlarging, condensing, widening, being wafted to spirituality — Always ∧new materialism and things.—

(O I see now that I have
the make of materialism and
things,
And that intellect is ∧to me but as
hands, or eyesight, or ∧as a vessel,

## *(Of the great poet)*[39]
## [1855]

**[1]**

(Of the great poet) (Finally) For preface.
It is not that he gives his country great poems; it is that he gives his country the spirit which makes the greatest poems [*illegible*] and the greatest material for poems.—

(He could say)
I know well enough the perpetual myself in my poems — but it is because the universe is in myself,— it shall all pass through me as a procession.— I say nothing of myself, which I do not equally say of all others, men and women

? (or) (Finally) (It is not that he gives you his country)

He does not give you the usual poems and metaphysics.— He gives you ~~the~~ materials for you to form for yourself the poems, ~~and~~ metaphysics, ∧politics, behaviour, ~~and~~ histories ~~and~~ romances, ~~and~~ essays and every thing else.—

[that?] literature [*illegible*] ∧can embody

**[2]**

**[3]**

~~Here is~~

~~He is as~~ One having attained ~~to~~ those insights and contents which the ~~study of the~~ universe gives to ~~those~~ men capable of comprehending it, ~~is not~~ would publish the same, and persuade ~~all~~ other men and women to the same.— The conditions are simple, spiritual, physical, close at hand. . . .∧they are long and arduous and require faith, they ~~depen are~~ [~~*illegible*~~] ~~rest~~ exist altogether with the taught, and not with the teaching or teacher.—

---

What is wanted is not ~~questionings~~ inquiries and reviews and — We want satisfiers, joiners, ~~compacters~~, lovers.— ~~This~~ These heated, torn, distracted ages are to be compacted and made whole.—

**[4]**

**[5]**

It is not enough of these states that they are to hold sway over physical objects, over ~~those~~ armies, navies, wealth, ~~population~~ and ~~all~~ manufactures and ∧all substantial objects.— ~~They~~ They must be eminent leaders ~~and~~ of the mind and imagination.— Here must arise the great poets and orators ~~of the~~ that all new centuries continually wait for.—

**[6]**

## *Other poets*[40]

[ca. late 1850s]

‸(?) Other poets ~~Others~~ have [~~*illegible*~~] formed for themselves an ideal apart from ~~a the~~ positive life, and disdainful of it — but ~~as~~ for me, I ~~will offer~~ ask nothing better or more divine than real life, here, now, yourself, your work, ~~the~~ house-building, boating, or in any factory; and I say ~~you~~ of every ~~man~~ male and every female, ~~must~~ may ~~make~~ shape ~~his or her own~~ [~~*illegible*~~] ~~you~~ he or she can bring out of it all divine ? growths ? fruits ?

## *All through writings*[41]

[ca. late 1850s]

All through writings preserve the equilibrium of the truth that the material world, and all its laws, are as grand and superb as the spiritual world and all its laws.— Most writers have disdained the physical world, and [~~*illegible*~~]~~—~~they have not over-estimated the other, or soul, but have under-estimated the corporeal —

How shall my eye separate the ~~pleas~~ beauty of the ~~flower~~ blossoming buckwheat field from the stalks and heads of tangible matter?— How shall I know what the life is except as I see it in the flesh?— I will not praise one without the other or any more than the other — the least one of the

---

Let the idea of <u>Equality</u> stick out — my best —

---

Do not argue at all, or compose proofs to demonstrate things — State nothing which ‸it will not [~~*illegible*~~] do to state as apparent to all eyes.—

## *a new doctrine*[42]

[ca. 1855–56]

a new doctrine — leading feature — There is in the soul an instinctive test of the sense and actuality of any thing — of any statement of fact or morals.— Let this decide.— Does it not decide?

---

— Thus the soul of each man, woman, nation, age, or what not realizes only what is proportionate to itself.

---

For a new school (or theory)
Let the test of any thing proposed in metaphysics be this instinct of the soul — this self-settling power.—

---

First however prepare the body it must be healthy, mature, clean.

---

Other writers poets look on a laborer as a laborer, a poet as a poet, a President as a President, a merchant as a merchant — and so on.— He looks on the President as a man, on the laborer as a man — or the poet and all the rest, as men.—

## *Make the Works*[43]

[1856]

Make the Works —

Do not go into criticism or
arguments at all
Make full-blooded, rich, flush,
natural Works —
Insert natural things, indestruc-
tibles, idioms, characteristics,
rivers, states, persons, &c
Be full of strong sensual germs.—

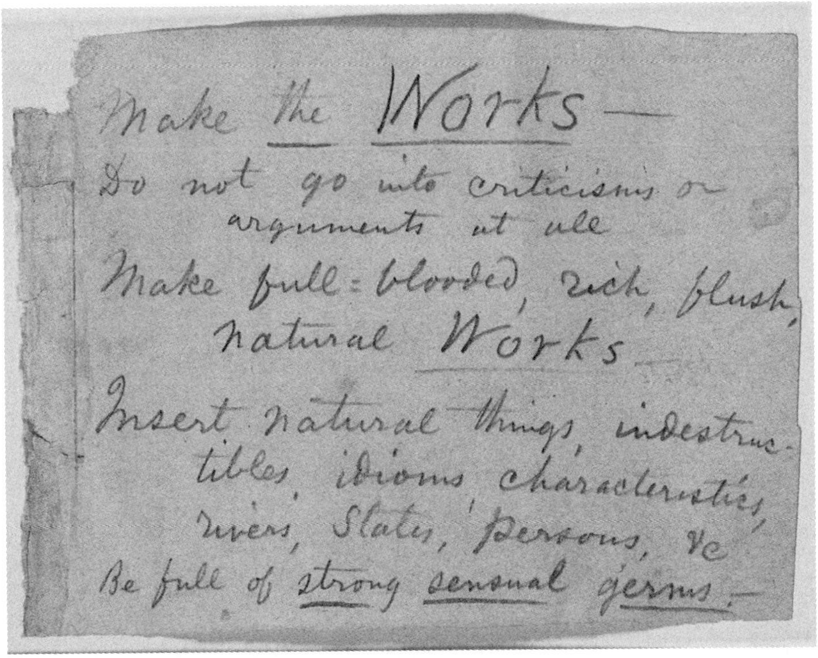
Make the Works—
Do not go into criticisms or arguments at all
Make full-blooded, rich, flush, natural Works
Insert natural things, indestructibles, idioms, characteristics, rivers, States, persons, &c
Be full of strong sensual germs.—

*Make the Works* fragment (probably 1856).

## *Drops of my Blood*[44]

[pre-1860]

Drops of ^my Blood.

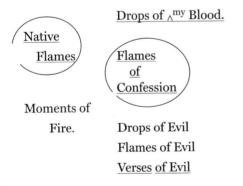

Native Flames

Flames of Confession

Moments of Fire.

Drops of Evil

Flames of Evil

Verses of Evil

## *my two theses*[45]
[ca. 1856]

— my two theses
— animal & spiritual
— became gradually
fused in Leaves of Grass

---

runs through all ~~my~~ the poems &
gives color to the
whole

## *Boldness*[46]
[1854–61]

Boldness — Nonchalant ease & indifference
To encourage me or any one continually to strike out alone — So it seems good to me — This is my way, my pleasure, my choice, my costume, friendship, amour, or what not.—

## *Broadaxe*[47]
[1855–56]

Broadaxe — First as coming in the rough ore out of the earth.— Then as being smelted and made into usable shape for working — then into some of the earlier weapons of the axe kind — battleaxe — headsman's axe — carpenter's broadaxe — (process of making, tempering and finishing the axe.) — inquire fully

| | | |
|---|---|---|
| uses of the Broadaxe<br>in cutting away masts when the ship is on her beaments<br><br>in heaving the great timbers for the oldfashioned houses and barns<br><br>passage describing the putting up of a goodstyled logcabin in the western woods — the whole process — joining the logs — the company — the fun — the axe.<br><br>The sylvan woodsman or woodboy<br><br>The cutting down of an unusually large and majestic tree — live oak or other — for some kelson to a frigate or first-class steamship.— (what wood is the kelson generally?) | in shipbuilding<br><br>in cutting a passage through the ice<br><br>the butcher in his slaughterhouse<br><br>full picture<br>The antique warrior always with his great axe — the brawny swinging arm — the clatter and crash on the helmeted head — the death howl and ~~the~~ [*illegible*] ~~fully~~ [*illegible*] quick tumbling body and rush of friend and foe thither — the summons to surrender — the battering of castle-gates and city-gates — | all through the framing of a house — all through — the hewing of timbers — the knocking of beams in their places — laying them regular —<br>The framers wielding the axe — their attitudes standing, bending — astride the beams driving in pins — as the frame is being raised — they on the posts or braces — holding on — their limbs — the hooked around the plate, the other arm wielding<br>the axe.— |
| Procession of<br>portraits of the different users of the axe —<br>the raftsman, the lumberman, the antique warrior, the headsman, the butcher,<br>the framer of houses,<br>the squatter of the west<br>— the pioneer — | building wharves and piers<br><br>full picture of the pioneer<br><br>The Roman lictors preceding the consuls<br><br>The sacrificial priest — ~~both Grecian~~ Grecian, Roman and Jewish.<br><br>What in Scandinavia? | episodic in the cutting down of the tree — about what the wood is for — for a [*illegible*] saloon, for a ceiling, or floor, for a coffin, for a workbox, a sailor's chest, a musical instrument, for firewood — for rich casings ~~of~~ or frames |
| founding of cities<br>Make it the American emblem preferent to the eagle. | | In a terrible fire the use of the axe to cut down ~~the~~ connecting woodwork to stop the fire — the excitement — the firemen — the glare — the hoarse shouts — the flames — the red faces and dense shadows |

## *Poem of Language*[48]

[1855–56]

Poem of Language

How curious —

---

The immense variety of languages —

— The points where they differ are not near as ~~numerous~~ remarkable as where they resemble — all resemble

---

The simple sounds —

---

music

## *Whole Poem*[49]

[1855–56]

Whole Poem

— Poem of Insects?

---

Get from Mr. Arkhurst the names of all insects —

---

interweave a train of thought suitable — also trains of words

---

## *Mocking all the textbooks*[50]

[front: pre-1865, probably pre-1860; back: pre-1855, probably 1854–55]

**[1]**

[*cut away*] ~~Behind Eluding~~ Mocking all the textbooks and professors' expositions and proofs and diagrams and practical show, stand or lie millions of the [~~*illegible*~~] all the most beautiful and common facts.— [*cut away*]

**[2]**

[*cut away*] is wider than the west.—

---

~~The orbed opening of whose mouth~~ —

---

Nature is rude at first — but once begun never tires
Most works of art [tire?] [*cut away*]

## *As of Forms* [51]
## [1856–60]

<u>As of Forms.—</u>

Their genesis, all genesis,
They lost, all lost — for
they include all.—

The earth and every thing in it,
The wave, the snake, the babe, the
landscape, the human head,
Things, faces, reminiscences, presences,
conditions, thoughts — ~~Such~~ tally
~~in the soul to~~ ^and make definite a divine in-
distinct, spiritual delight
in the Soul.—

Of the arts, as music, poems, ar-
chitecture, outlines, and the rest,
they are in their way to provoke
this delight out of the soul,
They are to seek it where it waits —
for I see that it always pa-
tiently waits.—
Have you sought ~~after~~ ~~for~~ the inkling?

Have you wandered ~~far~~ after ~~your~~
~~inkling of~~ the meanings of the
earth? You need not wander;
Behold those forms.—

### *Others may praise what they like*[52]
[front: pre-1865; back: probably 1860]

**[1]**

<u>Others may praise what
they like.</u>

Others may praise what they
like,
But I, from the banks of the
running Missouri, praise
nothing, in art or aught
else
Till it has breathed ~~of~~ the
atmosphere of this river~~,~~—
or ~~of~~ the prairies of Illinois
& Indiana,
And fully exudes it again.

**[2]**

[*cut away*] are already getting to be pretty numerous and outspoken.—

Walt Whitman.

Sometimes I think it would be better still to make a compact and finished Vol. of the <u>whole issue</u> of "Leaves of Grass," including the former ones with the new ones, for they are all of a uniform pattern.— This would afford a splendid living American Vol. that would go like the devil through the West, and among the young men everywhere.—

## *Poem of Materials*[53]
## [ca. 1860]

**[1]**

THE Poem) (? One grand, Eclipsing poem

Poem of Materials

? several poems

Many poems on this model —

the bringing together of the materials — words, figures, suggestions —

— things — (words, as solid as timbers stone, iron, brick, glass, planks, &c)

— (all with reference to main central idea ideas —

---

~~br~~ with powerful indications —

---

yet loose, fluid-like, ^leaving each reader eligible to form the resultant-poem for herself or himself.—

---

leading Chicago poem

**[2]**

recommendation to the ^~~American~~ young men of all The States ~~without preference~~ of North and South, East and West, of ~~one over another~~, that he has ^~~like a prudent~~ wise kept his position so free and ^spacious ~~open~~ ~~ample~~, ~~and~~ standing this day day before ~~you~~ us no ~~not at all as~~ the ~~exclusive~~ particular representative ~~candidate~~ of any one party ~~one set up persons —~~ no tied and ticketed ~~special~~ democrat, whig, abolitionist, ^~~not a~~ republican ^~~representative of the tariff, nor~~ ~~nativist~~ ~~of free-trade, nor of the owners of slaves, nor of~~ the ~~abolitionist, s~~ — no bawling — nor spokesman ^~~especially~~ of ~~the know nothings, nor of the Irish~~ natives against foreigners,

# *Notes*

## ABBREVIATIONS

With the exception of *Autobiographical Data*, all notebooks have been transcribed from digital images of the original manuscripts.

| | |
|---|---|
| Barrett | Papers of Walt Whitman, Clifton Waller Barrett Library of American Literature, Albert H. Small Special Collections Library, University of Virginia. |
| Beinecke | The Yale Collection of American Literature, Beinecke Rare Book and Manuscript Library, Yale University. |
| Berg | The New York Public Library's Henry W. and Albert A. Berg Collection of English and American Literature. |
| *D&N* | Walt Whitman, *Daybooks and Notebooks*, 3 vols., ed. William White (New York: New York University Press, 1978). White's transcriptions maintain Whitman's struck-through words but, for space, largely ignore indents and stanzification. |
| Feinberg | The Charles E. Feinberg Collection of the Papers of Walt Whitman, 1839–1919, Library of Congress, Washington, DC. |
| Harned | The Thomas Biggs Harned Collection of the Papers of Walt Whitman, 1842–1937, Library of Congress, Washington, DC. |
| IC | Integrated Catalog of Walt Whitman's Literary Manuscripts, housed at the *Walt Whitman Archive* online (https://whitmanarchive.org/manuscripts/finding_aids/integrated.html). |
| *LoG* | Walt Whitman, *Leaves of Grass*. Published in six American editions: 1855, 1856, 1860–61, 1867, 1871–72, and 1881–82. |
| Lion | The New York Public Library's Oscar Lion Collection of Walt Whitman. |
| Miller | Matt Miller, *Collage of Myself: Walt Whitman and the Making of* Leaves of Grass (Lincoln: University of Nebraska Press, 2010). |

*NUPM* Walt Whitman, *Notebooks and Unpublished Prose Manuscripts*, 6 vols., ed. Edward F. Grier (New York: New York University Press, 1984). Grier's transcriptions are unhelpfully "finalized," meaning he relegates all of Whitman's struck-through words and lines to footnotes.

Rutgers Special Collections and University Archives, Rutgers University Libraries.

Stovall Floyd Stovall, "Dating Whitman's Early Notebooks," *Studies in Bibliography* 24 (1971), 197–204.

Trent Trent Collection of Whitmaniana, David M. Rubenstein Rare Book and Manuscript Library, Duke University, Durham, NC.

*UPP* *The Uncollected Poetry and Prose of Walt Whitman*, 2 vols., ed. Emory Holloway (Garden City, NY: Doubleday, Page & Co. 1921).

*Workshop* *Walt Whitman's Workshop*, ed. Clifton J. Furness (Cambridge, MA: Harvard University Press, 1928).

*WWA* The *Walt Whitman Archive* online (https://whitmanarchive.org/).

*WWQR* *Walt Whitman Quarterly Review* (https://ir.uiowa.edu/wwqr/).

## NOTEBOOKS

1. *Poem incarnating the mind.* Harned, box 2, notebook LC 85, https://www.loc.gov/item/mss454430063/ (digital image); *WWA*, Notebooks (digital image and transcription); IC loc.00346 (digital image); *NUPM* 1: 102–12 (pages reordered by Grier). Quite a bit of the material in this notebook is draft language for poems in *LoG* 1855, as well as for "A Song of the Rolling Earth" and "Miracles" in *LoG* 1856.

2. *a schoolmaster.* Harned, notebook LC 82; *WWA*, Notebooks (loc.04588); *NUPM* 1: 97–99. The primary plot laid out in this notebook corresponds to Whitman's novel *Life and Adventures of Jack Engle: An Auto-Biography*, which he serialized anonymously in the New York *Sunday Dispatch* (March 14–April 18, 1852). *Jack Engle* was unknown to scholars until its rediscovery in 2016. See Zachary Turpin, "Introduction to Walt Whitman's 'Life and Adventures of Jack Engle,'" *WWQR* 34 (2017): 225–61; reprinted in *Life and Adventures of Jack Engle: An Auto-Biography* (Iowa City: University of Iowa Press, 2017), vii–xxii. The two pasted-in newspaper clippings are from the 1852 *New York Tribune*, dated March 5 and 12, respectively. A slight misquotation of Robert Blair's poem "The Grave" (1743) appears on msp. 19. The following line ("O, earth") may be a quote as well, but no source is known. No back cover is extant for this notebook.

3. *No doubt the efflux.* Feinberg, Notes and Notebooks, box 38, n.d., Thoughts, Ideas, and Trial Lines (3 vols.); *WWA*, Notebooks (loc.00025); *D&N* 3: 764–70 (White's transcription is still quite serviceable). Lines in this notebook anticipate

the drift of many of Whitman's poetic clusters in *LoG* 1855, including those he would eventually title "Song of Myself," "The Sleepers," "Faces," and "Great Are the Myths." More directly, the first few paragraphs of this notebook appear, slightly modified, in *LoG* 1856 as "Poem of the Road" (later "Song of the Open Road").

4. *Talbot Wilson*. Harned, box 8, notebook LC 80 (https://www.loc.gov/item/mss454430217/); *WWA*, Notebooks (loc.00141); *NUPM* 1: 53–82. Grier lists the notebook as "albot Wilson" and provides extensive notes on the notebook's provenance and dating. His transcription was made from photostats after the notebook had been lost. On the eventual recovery of this notebook and three others, see Alice L. Birney, "Missing Whitman Notebooks Returned to Library of Congress," *WWQR* 12 (1995): 217–29. Although dating this item has been difficult, the notion that it is Whitman's earliest notebook is no longer generally accepted. For discussions of its dating, see Stovall; Andrew C. Higgins, "Wage Slavery and the Composition of *Leaves of Grass*: The 'Talbot Wilson' Notebook," *WWQR* 2, no. 2 (Fall 2002): 53–77; and Miller, 2–8. Its contents contribute a good deal to *LoG* 1855, as Grier explains throughout. The editors of the *WWA* note that this notebook "features an early (if not the earliest) example of Whitman using his characteristic long poetic lines, as well as the 'generic or cosmic or transcendental "I"' that appears in *Leaves of Grass*."

5. *you know how*. Harned, box 8, notebook LC 86 (https://www.loc.gov/item/mss454430218/); *WWA*, Notebooks (loc.00142); *NUPM* 1: 124–27 ("You Know How the One"). Some lines in this notebook have parallels in the first "Leaves of Grass" cluster in *LoG* 1855 (later "Song of Myself"). This notebook is missing its back cover.

6. *Autobiographical Data*. Harned, box 6, notebook LC 87; *WWA*, Notebooks (loc.05935); *NUPM* 1: 209–21. The original manuscript disappeared during World War II and is still missing today, so Grier bases his transcription on partial photostats of this notebook, combined with renditions of the remaining passages from *UPP* and *Workshop*. Without a known arrangement of the pages, Grier establishes a rather arbitrary order for them, which we follow, though we restore torn stubs and partially illegible portions that Grier omits. For discussions of the notebook's dating, see *UPP* 86; *NUPM* 1: 209; and Higgins, "Wage Slavery and the Composition of *Leaves of Grass*." Lines in this notebook seem to anticipate Whitman's finished but likely never published prose pamphlet. "The Eighteenth Presidency!" (ca. 1856).

7. *women*. Harned, box 7, notebook LC 84; *WWA*, Notebooks (loc.05589); *NUPM* 1: 138–55 ("Memorials"), transcription from photostats. For discussions of the notebook's dating, see Stovall and *NUPM* 1: 138. Its contents can be linked to poetry in *LoG* 1855, 1856, and 1860–61, including two recognizable lines from "Debris" (1860–61).

8. *In his presence*. Feinberg, Notes and Notebooks; *WWA*, Notebooks

(loc.00483); *D&N* 3: 760–64. Lines from this notebook contribute to "The Sleepers" (originally titled "Leaves of Grass" in *LoG* 1855, "Night Poem" in *LoG* 1856, and "Sleep-Chasings" in *LoG* 1860–1861).

9. *The regular old followers*. Harned, box 2, notebook LC 83; *WWA*, Notebooks (loc.00024); *NUPM* 1: 113–17 (noting connections to the sections in *LoG* 1855 that would ultimately be titled "Song of Myself" and "Song of the Answerer").

10. *I know a rich capitalist*. Lion; *WWA*, Notebooks (nyp.00129); *NUPM* 1: 128–35. Identifiable passages from "Song of Myself" (*LoG* 1855, originally titled only "Leaves of Grass") and "Song of the Open Road" (1856) appear in this notebook, as do possible lines from what would eventually be titled "A Song for Occupations" (1855), "Great Are the Myths" (1855), and "Our Old Feuillage" (1860–61).

11. *9th av*. Feinberg, Notes and Notebooks, box 38, Thoughts, Ideas, and Trial Lines (https://www.loc.gov/item/mss1863001156/); *WWA*, Notebooks (loc.00354). Whitman writes in this notebook from both ends, a situation that is complicated by some leaves having fallen out over the years and replaced in haphazard fashion. We have followed *WWA*, which in turn honors the earliest account of this notebook's order, Fredson Bowers, *Whitman's Manuscripts: "Leaves of Grass" (1860) A Parallel Text* (Chicago: University of Chicago Press, 1955), xxxiii–li, 40–56. Like Bowers, *WWA* transcribes the notebook straight through, without reordering. White reorders in his transcription in *D&N* 3: 777–803. A significant portion of the notebook contains draft language for "Proto-Leaf" (1860–61), a poem later retitled "Starting from Paumanok." Smaller passages may be related to the poems "Song of Myself" (1855, originally titled only "Leaves of Grass"), "Miracles" (1856), and "Song at Sunset" (1860–61).

12. *The scope of government*. Feinberg, Notes and Notebooks, box 37 (loc.00157); *NUPM* 1: 283–92 (we largely follow Grier's transcription arrangement). Passages in this notebook relate to lines in "Faith Poem" (1856, later "Assurances") and "This Compost" (1856), as well as possibly to the prose tract "The Eighteenth Presidency!" (ca. 1856).

13. *George Walker*. Feinberg, Notes and Notebooks, box 37, 1855–56, Crossing Brooklyn Ferry trial lines; IC loc.00143. See *NUPM* 1: 226–43 for a transcription and dating notes, as well as Harold Blodgett, *Walt Whitman: An 1855–1856 Notebook toward the Second Edition of "Leaves of Grass"* (Carbondale: Southern Illinois University Press, 1959). Whitman wrote in this notebook from both ends, inverting the notebook when he switched from one end to the other. Regardless of continuity, we present the pages in sequential order, flipping them when necessary. This notebook contains lines that find their way into much of *LoG* 1855 and 1856, including poems that would ultimately be titled "Song of the Broad-Axe," "Crossing Brooklyn Ferry," "I Sing the Body Electric," "Starting from Paumanok," "A Song for Occupations," "By Blue Ontario's Shore," "Salut au Monde!," "To One Shortly to Die," and "A Woman Waits for Me."

14. *Dick Hunt*. Feinberg, Notes and Notebooks, box 38, 1857, Trial Lines and Descriptions (https://www.loc.gov/item/mss1863001148/); IC loc.00028; *NUPM* 1: 246–80. Grier notes connections to many poems in *LoG* 1855 and 1856, including those Whitman would eventually title "Song of the Broad-Axe," "To a Common Prostitute," "You Felons on Trial in Courts," "Starting from Paumanok," "Trickle Drops," "I Was Looking for a Long While," "Poem of Joys," "Facing West from California's Shores," "To the States," "A Song of the Rolling Earth," "On the Beach a Night Alone," "Full of Life Now," and "With Antecedents." For more on Whitman's games of twenty questions in this notebook, see C. Carroll Hollis, "Whitman's Word-Game," *Walt Whitman Newsletter* 4 (1958): 74–76.

15. *Calamus-Leaves* ~~*Live Oak, with Moss*~~. Barrett; *WWA*, Manuscripts (https://whitmanarchive.org/manuscripts/liveoak.html). A great deal has been written about this manuscript, which is less a notebook than a fair copy of a poem. Given its rarity in print, we have provided it in recognition of its being one of the most important manuscript documents of Whitman's life. For more discussion of "Live Oak, with Moss," as it is now known, see Fredson Bowers, "Whitman's Manuscripts for the Original 'Calamus' Poems," *Studies in Bibliography* 6 (1953): 257–65; Alan Helms, "Whitman's 'Live Oak with Moss'," in *The Continuing Presence of Walt Whitman: The Life after the Life*, ed. Robert K. Martin (Iowa City: University of Iowa Press, 1992), 185–205; Hershel Parker, "The Real 'Live Oak, with Moss': Straight Talk about Whitman's 'Gay Manifesto'," *Nineteenth-Century Literature* 51 (1996): 145–60; and *Walt Whitman's Songs of Male Intimacy and Love: "Live Oak, with Moss" and "Calamus,"* ed. Betsy Erkkila (Iowa City: University of Iowa Press, 2011).

16. *W. Whitman Portland av.* Harned, boxes 2–3, New York City notebook (https://www.loc.gov/item/mss454430071/); IC loc.00348; *NUPM* 1: 453–58. Whitman's notes detailing the Jamaica Presbyterian bicentennial yielded his article "Important Ecclesiastical Gathering at Jamaica, L.I.," Brooklyn *City News*, January 9, 1862.

17. *English runic*. Harned, box 2, [1860] Boston notebook; IC loc.04605; *NUPM* 1: 419–21. Whitman used this notebook during his March–May 1860 trip to Boston, where he was working with the publishers Thayer and Eldridge to print *LoG* 1860–61, hence, his references in the first few pages to the typography and printing of the third edition.

18. *81 Clerman*. Harned, box 2, Notebooks 1860–61 (https://www.loc.gov/item/mss454430069/); IC loc.00029; *NUPM* 1: 431–42. Passages in this notebook are drafts for poems both pre- and postwar, including "By Blue Ontario's Shore" (1856), "Out of the Cradle Endlessly Rocking" (1859), "Chanting the Square Deific" (Drum Taps 1865–66), and "The City Dead-House" (1867). The page containing the "Poem on the Incompleted" is no longer extant; it is represented in Grier 1: 438 as being the notebook's final page, but to indicate our uncertainty we designate it with a [?] rather than a manuscript page number. See *Workshop* 48 for the earliest representation of this now lost page.

19. Excerpt from *Words*. Feinberg, Notes and Notebooks, box 37, mss18630 (https://www.loc.gov/item/mss1863001147/). White's transcription in *D&N* 3: 664–73 reproduces the text of Whitman's clippings, which we largely avoid here in the interest of space. In full, this notebook stretches to nearly three hundred pages of notes and clippings, which, along with a similar notebook from this period, *The Primer of Words*, Whitman seems have intended to make into a book-length etymological treatise. For more on a similar treatise Whitman may have partially ghostwritten around 1859, see C. Carroll Hollis, "Walt Whitman and William Swinton: A Co-operative Friendship," *American Literature* 30 (1959): 425–49; and James Perrin Warren, "Whitman as Ghostwriter: The Case of *Rambles among Words*," *WWQR* 2 (1984), 22–30.

## FRAGMENTS

1. *dithyrambic*. Rutgers; *WWA*, Manuscripts (rut.00022); *NUPM* 1: 355.

2. *is rougher than it was*. Trent, MS f 129; *WWA*, Manuscripts (duk.00786). Whitman used these notes as the basis for his article "New Orleans in 1848," *New Orleans Picayune* (January 25, 1887), later reprinted in *November Boughs* (1888). The back of this page contains notes and dates regarding Whitman's family. Also included is a clipping of a brief newspaper obituary for Whitman's father. This material is omitted in the interest of space.

3. *wooding at night*. Trent, MS q 111. As with *is rougher than it was*, this fragment helped form the basis of Whitman's "New Orleans in 1848," *New Orleans Picayune* (January 25, 1887); later reprinted in *November Boughs* (1888).

4. *I know well enough*. Trent, MS f 53; *NUPM* 1: 362.

5. *The genuine miracles of Christ*. Feinberg, Literary File, box 36; *WWA*, Manuscripts (loc.01019).

6. *med Cophósis*. Feinberg, Notes and Notebooks, box 39 (https://www.loc.gov/item/mss1863001198/); *WWA*, Notebooks (loc.00005). White transcribes this notebook remnant in *D&N* 3: 773–77. For discussion of its likely dating, see Miller, 11–16. White notes connections in these pages to Whitman's "Who Learns My Lesson Complete?," "By Blue Ontario's Shore," "Song of the Answerer," and "There Was a Child Went Forth," and *WWA* editors also suggest thematic and philosophical connections to "Song of Myself" (the first "Leaves of Grass" cluster in *LoG* 1855).

7. *Summer duck*. Feinberg, Notes and Notebooks, box 39; *WWA*, Notebooks (loc.00158); *D&N* 3: 770–73. Though White and others have classified it as a notebook, we recategorize it as a fragment, given its length and apparent relationship to the "med Cophósis" fragment (both of which appear to have originated as part of a larger notebook). An up-to-date discussion of its dating may be found in Miller, 26–29, complete with a visual comparison alongside the "med Cophósis"

fragment (30–31). White points out that lines at the beginning and end of this notebook connect to "Song of Myself" (1855).

8. *After all*. Trent, MS 3; *WWA*, Manuscripts (duk.00797); *NUPM* 1: 183.

9. *What we call Literature*. Trent, MS q 32; *WWA*, Manuscripts (duk.00295); *NUPM* 4: 1558.

10. *Picture of the most flowing grandeur of a man*. Trent, MS q 32; IC duk.00293; *NUPM* 1: 178. The back of this page contains an overstruck passage, seemingly unrelated, comparing United States citizens to "Peruvians and Mexicans" and praising the "faculty of independence" in the midst of social customs and conventions.

11. *Poem—a perfect school*. Walt Whitman Ephemera Collection, University of Tulsa, box 1, folder 2; *WWA*, Manuscripts (tul.00011). On the back of this page are draft lines used in the third poem in the first edition of *Leaves of Grass* ("To Think of Time"). This material is omitted in the interest of space.

12. *Priests!* Feinberg, Literary File Series, box 28; *WWA*, Manuscripts (loc.00013).

13. *In metaphysical points*. Trent, MS 67; *WWA*, Manuscripts (duk.00159); *NUPM* 1: 172. Though this fragment's opening words are "~~Pure and Positive Truth~~," this fragment is named after the first words to appear (inserted) in the uppermost left-hand corner, connected by a transposition mark to the text below.

14. *Nehemiah Whitman*. Berg; *WWA*, Manuscripts (nyp.00556). Grier's transcription is in *NUPM* 1: 8. In addition to various notes about Whitman's family and Brooklyn residences, on the back of this page Whitman references "Covert," a character in both Whitman's short story "Revenge and Requital" (1845) and his novel *Life and Adventures of Jack Engle* (1852).

15. *Silence*. Beinecke, box 3, folder 140; *WWA*, Manuscripts (yal.00441); *NUPM* 1: 474. On the back of this page is a brief, crossed-out prose note on slavery. This material is omitted in the interest of space.

16. *Living Pictures*. Barrett, MSS 3829; *WWA*, Manuscripts (uva.00516).

17. *Of this broad and majestic universe*. Lion; *WWA*, Manuscripts (nyp.00549).

18. *Remember that the clock*. Trent, MS q 32; *WWA*, Manuscripts (duk.00298).

19. *poet of Materialism*. Trent, MS q 44; *WWA*, Manuscripts (duk.00104). These comments are written on a scrap of wallpaper, likely Whitman's own. The wallpaper's pattern and coloring are evident on the reverse of this fragment.

20. *Loveblows*. Lion; *WWA*, Manuscripts (nyp.00122).

21. *Rules for Composition*. Trent, MS q 136; *WWA*, Manuscripts (duk.00130); *NUPM* 1: 101.

22. *you cannot define too clearly*. Trent, MS 68; *WWA*, Manuscripts (duk.00164); *NUPM* 4: 1593.

23. *Sculpture*. Trent, MS 48; *WWA*, Manuscripts (duk.00148); *NUPM* 6: 2033.

24. *Sweet flag*. Trent, MS 2; *WWA*, Manuscripts (duk.00883).

25. *Make no quotations*. Trent, MS f 33; *WWA*, Manuscripts (duk.00305); *NUPM* 1: 159.

26. *It seems to me*. Trent, MS f 33; *WWA*, Manuscripts (duk.00302); *NUPM* 1: 157.

27. *The most perfect wonders*. Berg; *WWA*, Manuscripts (nyp.00057); *NUPM* 1: 186.

28. *Light and air!* Trent, MS q 4; IC duk.00260.

29. *The analogy holds*. Harned, Recovered Cardboard Butterfly and Notebooks Series; IC loc.05176; *NUPM* 1: 176.

30. *The only way*. Rutgers; WWA, Manuscripts (rut.00023); *NUPM* 1: 118.

31. *My Poems, when complete*. Trent, MS 126. There is no digital image of this available at the *WWA*; however, we have consulted an image made temporarily available on the Duke University Libraries exhibit webpage, *I Sing the Body Electric: Walt Whitman and the Body* (https://exhibits2.library.duke.edu/exhibits/show/whitman/poetry-and-the-body).

32. *in the west*. Feinberg, Notes and Notebooks, box 40; Literary, n.d., Poem of the Vision of the West folder; *WWA*, Manuscripts (loc.00168); *NUPM:* 4: 1323.

33. *This is the Earths word*. Trent, MS q 193; *WWA*, Manuscripts (duk.00019).

34. *most poets finish*. The Walt Whitman Collection, Rare Books and Manuscripts Department, Boston Public Library, Whitman Mss.3; IC bpl.00004.

35. *Produce great persons*. Trent, MS 51; IC duk.00166. Notes on various British writers, including the Romantic poets and Dickens, occupy the other side of this page. These appear to be written over a faint and not entirely legible draft of lines from "Poem of The Singers, and of the Words of Poems" (1856), a poem eventually assimilated into "Song of the Answerer" in 1881. In addition, according to an editorial note in the IC: "Whitman pasted at least two newspaper clippings on the manuscript, one on each side. However, markings on both sides of the leaf indicate that Whitman potentially pasted a third, unidentified, newspaper clipping on this manuscript. One of these, which had covered Whitman's paragraphs but has since been detached, is included in the file; another is still pasted to the manuscript."

36. *Feb. 25th '57 Dined with Hector Tyndale*. Trent, MS 124. Digital images of this fragment are currently available only through the *WWA*'s private image warehouse.

37. *The Great Construction of the New Bible*. Trent, II-7C 198; *WWA*, private image warehouse. Grier's transcription is in *NUPM* 1: 353.

38. *A main part of the greatness*. Trent, III-6A; IC duk.00152; *NUPM* 1: 365.

39. *(Of the great poet)*. Trent, MS q 69; *WWA*, Manuscripts (duk.00128).

40. *Other poets*. Trent, MS 115; *WWA*, private image warehouse; *NUPM* 1: 358.

41. *All through writings*. Walt Whitman Collection, Annenberg Rare Book and Manuscript Library, University of Pennsylvania; *WWA*, private image warehouse; *NUPM* 1: 360.

42. *a new doctrine.* Barrett, box 1, folder 61; *WWA*, private image warehouse; *NUPM* 1: 331.

43. *Make the Works.* Trent, MS q 204; *WWA*, private image warehouse; *NUPM* 1: 325.

44. *Drops of my Blood.* Trent, MS f 29; IC duk.00276. This fragment is displayed on a backing sheet along with three other fragments of lesser interest. "Drops of my Blood" is taped to its backing, so that the reverse side is accessible; the reverse side contains two partially legible and overstruck lines in which Whitman exhorts young men "to extract the unformed poe[*torn away, illegible*]." In the interest of space, only the side with what appears to be title ideas for a poem, likely "Trickle Drops," has been included.

45. *my two theses.* Barrett, box 1, folder 49; IC uva.00009; *NUPM* 1: 383.

46. *Boldness.* Trent, MS q 204; *WWA*, private image warehouse; *NUPM* 1: 321.

47. *Broadaxe.* Trent, II-5A 12; IC duk.00033; *NUPM* 1: 299.

48. *Poem of Language.* Trent, MS f 30; IC duk.00251; *NUPM* 1: 1325. This fragment is mounted on a backing sheet, together with "Whole Poem," a note demonstrating Whitman's research-based creative method for a "Poem of Insects." An image of the reverse side is unavailable. A transcription of "Whole Poem" follows in this volume.

49. *Whole Poem.* Trent, MS f 30; IC duk.00251; *NUPM* 1: 1349. This fragment is mounted on a backing sheet, together with "Poem of Language."

50. *Mocking all the textbooks.* Berg; *WWA*, Manuscripts (nyp.00024).

51. *As of Forms.* Barrett, box 1, folder 5; *WWA*, Manuscripts (uva.00124).

52. *Others may praise what they like.* Beinecke, box 3; *WWA*, Manuscripts (yal.00079).

53. *Poem of Materials.* Trent, MS 12mo 15; IC duk.00042; *NUPM* 1: 335.

## *The Iowa Whitman Series*

*The Afterlives of Specimens: Science, Mourning, and Whitman's Civil War*, by Lindsay Tuggle

*Conserving Walt Whitman's Fame: Selections from Horace Traubel's Conservator," 1890–1919*, edited by Gary Schmidgall

*Democratic Vistas: The Original Edition in Facsimile*, by Walt Whitman, edited by Ed Folsom

*Every Hour, Every Atom: A Collection of Walt Whitman's Early Notebooks and Fragments*, edited by Zachary Turpin and Matt Miller

*Intimate with Walt: Selections from Whitman's Conversations with Horace Traubel, 1888–1892*, edited by Gary Schmidgall

*Leaves of Grass, 1860: The 150th Anniversary Edition*, by Walt Whitman, edited by Jason Stacy

*Life and Adventures of Jack Engle*, by Walt Whitman, introduction by Zachary Turpin

*A Place for Humility: Whitman, Dickinson, and the Natural World*, by Christine Gerhardt

*The Pragmatic Whitman: Reimagining American Democracy*, by Stephen John Mack

*Song of Myself: With a Complete Commentary*, by Walt Whitman, introduction and commentary by Ed Folsom and Christopher Merrill

*Supplement to "Walt Whitman: A Descriptive Bibliography,"* by Joel Myerson

*"This Mighty Convulsion": Whitman and Melville Write the Civil War*, edited by Christopher Sten and Tyler Hoffman

*Transatlantic Connections: Whitman U.S., Whitman U.K.*, by M. Wynn Thomas

*Visiting Walt: Poems Inspired by the Life and Work of Walt Whitman*, edited by Sheila Coghill and Thom Tammaro

*Walt Whitman: The Correspondence, Volume VII*, edited by Ted Genoways

*Walt Whitman, Where the Future Becomes Present*, edited by David Haven Blake and Michael Robertson

*Walt Whitman and the Class Struggle*, by Andrew Lawson

*Walt Whitman and the Earth: A Study in Ecopoetics*, by M. Jimmie Killingsworth

*Walt Whitman's Reconstruction: Poetry and Publishing between Memory and History*, by Martin T. Buinicki

*Walt Whitman's Selected Journalism*, edited by Douglas A. Noverr and Jason Stacy

*Walt Whitman's Songs of Male Intimacy and Love: "Live Oak, with Moss" and "Calamus,"* edited by Betsy Erkkila

*Whitman among the Bohemians*, edited by Joanna Levin and Edward Whitley

*Whitman and Dickinson: A Colloquy*, edited by Éric Athenot and Cristanne Miller

*Whitman East and West: New Contexts for Reading Walt Whitman*, edited by Ed Folsom

*Whitman Noir: Black America and the Good Gray Poet*, edited by Ivy G. Wilson

*Whitman's Drift: Imagining Literary Distribution*, by Matt Cohen